LIVING WITH WILDLIFE

❧

How to Enjoy, Cope with, and Protect
North America's Wild Creatures
Around Your Home and Theirs

THE CALIFORNIA CENTER FOR WILDLIFE

with Diana Landau and Shelley Stump

SIERRA CLUB BOOKS

San Francisco

The Sierra Club, founded in 1892 by John Muir, has devoted itself to the study and protection of the earth's scenic and ecological resources—mountains, wetlands, woodlands, wild shores and rivers, deserts and plains. The publishing program of the Sierra Club offers books to the public as a nonprofit educational service in the hope that they may enlarge the public's understanding of the Club's basic concerns. The point of view expressed in each book, however, does not necessarily reflect that of the Club. The Sierra Club has some sixty chapters coast to coast, in Canada, Hawaii, and Alaska. For information about how you may participate in its programs to preserve wilderness and the quality of life, please address inquiries to Sierra Club, 85 Second Street, San Francisco, CA 94105.

www.sierraclub.org/books

For further information about the California Center for Wildlife and its programs, contact:
California Center for Wildlife
76 Albert Park Lane
P.O. Box 150957
San Rafael, CA 94915-0959
Phone: (415) 456-7283 (SAVE)

Neither the California Center for Wildlife nor Sierra Club assume any liability for any injuries or property damage that may result from contact with wild animals as described or implied in this book. We have emphasized repeatedly that all wild animals are dangerous, especially if approached, and wherever possible have recommended methods of resolving problems of wildlife-human interaction that do not necessitate approaching or handling the animals.

Library of Congress Cataloging-in-Publication Data
Living with wildlife : how to enjoy, cope with, and protect North America's wild creatures around your home and theirs / the California Center for Wildlife with Diana Landau and Shelley Stump.
        p.   cm.
Includes index.
ISBN 0-87156-547-1
1. Wildlife conservation—North America. 2. Wildlife rehabilitation—North America. 3. Wildlife pests—North America. 4. Urban fauna—North America. 5. Human-animal relationships.
I. Landau, Diana, 1950– . II. Stump, Shelley, 1949– . III. California Center for Wildlife.
QL84.L58   1994
639.9'097—dc20   93-33982

Living with Wildlife was prepared for publication at Walking Stick Press, San Francisco
Linda Herman, Design Director
Diana Landau, Editorial Director
Barbara Fuller, Copyeditor

Illustrations by Peg Magovern
Cover and book design by Linda Herman

What is man without the beasts?
If all the beasts were gone,
men would die from great loneliness of spirit.
For whatever happens to the beasts, soon happens to man,
All things are connected.

Chief Seattle (Duwamish tribe)

Contents

Acknowledgments

Several leaders in the wildlife rehabilitation field graciously contributed their time and knowledge in providing background research for this book. The California Center for Wildlife (CCW) wishes to thank Jay Holcomb, Executive Director, International Bird Rescue Center, Berkeley, California; Ed Clark, Executive Director, The Wildlife Center, Weyers Cave, Virginia; Guy Hodge, Director, Humane Society of the United States, Washington, D.C.; and Mark A. Pocras, DVM, Assistant Professor of Wildlife Medicine, Tufts University Wildlife Clinic, North Grafton, Massachussetts.

CCW and the authors are also grateful to Connie Parsons, the Center's former Executive Director, and current Executive Director, Coral Cotten, for their initiation and support of this publication, as well as for their personal commitment to the work of the Center and to wildlife rehabilitation education.

Sierra Club Books publisher Jon Beckmann was instrumental in guiding the project from concept to reality, aided by staff editor David Spinner and freelance copyeditor Barbara Fuller. Designer Linda Herman of Walking Stick Press gave the book its clear and attractive form, and illustrator Peg Magovern enhanced it with her drawings of wildlife and humane control techniques.

Readers Jay Holcomb and Professor James Mackey of San Francisco State University checked the manuscript for errors and helped us resolve some problems with the taxonomic identification and organization of animals. We have tried to make the book reasonably accurate and up-to-date in this regard; however, zoological taxonomy is a complex and ever-changing field. Since this is intended as a general handbook and not a scholarly reference, we hope that any remaining errors will not impede its usefulness.

We thank Wendy Johnson of Green Gulch Farm and the San Francisco Zen Center for permission to reprint portions of her invocation "Plants and Animals in the Garden."

Introduction

- You head up to the attic one day to investigate some strange noises that have been disturbing your sleep and find that a family of raccoons has taken up residence.
- Your prized climbing rose is suffering from heavy nightly "pruning" by deer.
- Your child runs into the house carrying a fledgling bird found out on the lawn after it apparently fell from its nest.
- Upon returning from a day hike on a camping trip in bear country, you discover that your food supplies have been raided and scattered all over the campsite.

These are scenarios of just a few of the chance encounters with wild animals we are likely to experience in our lifetimes. Although we live in a "developed" nation and are accustomed to thinking that our environment is chiefly made, inhabited, and controlled by humans (along with our domestic creatures), wild animals are still a very real presence in the lives of many North Americans—especially those who live in rural areas or in suburbs adjacent to undeveloped land or who enjoy traveling and camping in wilderness parks.

Our reactions to such meetings with animals reveal a wide range of emotions: annoyance, indignation, fear, compassion, excitement, or wonder. They are inspired by the nature of the contact: for example, whether the creature's behavior is a threat to property we own or inhabit or even to our safety. A good place to start evaluating our reactions is with the idea of "ownership": we tend to think in the short term, and it's easy to forget that scant hundreds of years ago, the place where we live "belonged" only to its native animals and plants (and perhaps to a group of aboriginal humans).

But wherever on the spectrum our feelings fall, they are usually powerful. An encounter with wildlife stirs something deep within us; most psychologists would say it is the wildness in the human species that is usually so well shielded by civilization, the part of our animal nature we thought we had left behind. Whatever the deeper reasons, there is no doubt that a firsthand, close-up encounter with a wild creature—whether in the wilderness or in your own backyard—is a memorable experience for an adult, sometimes a life-shaping one for a child.

A survey carried out at Tufts University Wildlife Clinic in North Grafton, Massachusetts, supports this idea. Over a six- to eight-week period, the clinic questioned people who brought injured wildlife in for care. The results were a bit surprising: those running the survey had previously assumed that most people who would take time to care for a wild creature were already wildlife enthusiasts. Not so. Most had little prior experience of the natural world but, having come into direct, intimate contact with an animal, found that they were strongly affected and could not turn away.

Both the California Center for Wildlife (CCW, or the Center), which created this book, and the Tufts Clinic represent a fairly recent phenomenon in the history of human interaction with wildlife: organizations (and individuals) dedicated to the rehabilitation of injured wildlife and to public education about wildlife. Such efforts—along with the high level of public interest in wildlife films, books, photography, and observation—are the product of our changing relationship with wild animals.

In past eras, humans have viewed wildlife chiefly as game for food and sport or as dangerous predators or pests—excepting most aboriginal peoples, who have always maintained a spiritual or "familial" connection with their fellow creatures. Today, however, the threat of diminishing species and the awareness of the interdependence of life-forms are part of contemporary consciousness. To be sure, not everyone shares these attitudes, or a sense of urgency about translating them into public policy. But the fact remains that most of us feel differently about animals than our ancestors did. We have marveled, since childhood, at their beauty and diversity in visits to zoos and through the magic of film and video; we have learned about their habits and behavior through books and magazines, television, bird-watching groups, and so on; we recognize the need for their preservation on the public level; and we are inclined to rescue the injured songbird we find on our lawn.

But almost inevitably, certain encounters with wildlife will bring our general sympathy into conflict with our self-interest. When raccoons rattle the garbage cans and deer munch the shrubbery, it's all too easy to revert to the mind-set of wildlife as pests—or at least to feel torn about what to do. Resolving such conflicts in ways that protect human interests as well as the animals involved is, in large part, the purpose of this book.

How This Book Came About

The California Center for Wildlife is a nonprofit wildlife rehabilitation and education organization whose mission is to preserve the natural abundance and diversity of wildlife. Located in San Rafael, California, the organization originated in the early 1950s as the Marin Junior League, a natural history education organization, and eventually became the Louise A. Boyd Natural History Museum. In the early 1970s, as it shifted from a natural history museum to one of the first hands-on wildlife rehabilitation organizations in the United States, it took the name the Marin Wildlife Center. In 1990, in recognition of its growth and statewide influence, it became the California Center for Wildlife. The organization celebrated its fortieth anniversary in 1993.

Currently the CCW treats more than 4,000 animals a year, representing more than 150 native and migratory species. Half of those treated are successfully released back to the wild—a high success rate in wildlife rehabilitation. The Center employs a (mostly part-time) staff of 9, and more than 200 volunteers contribute many thousands of hours to caring for the animals and working in education programs. To comply with state requirements, the Center keeps records on each animal brought in—date and location found, diagnosis, result of care, and so on—information that forms the basis for nascent research programs in animal treatment procedures and other areas.

The Center's many years of experience in wild-animal care are the basis for its educational programs. These include a telephone hotline, which handles more than 12,000 calls annually from people who need help dealing with injured creatures or resolving wildlife nuisance problems. The other primary educational program is on-site tours, self- and docent guided. Visitors can view the permanent resident animals, which include—as of this writing—a golden eagle, owls, squirrels, pelicans, egrets, and other animals brought to the Center. All these animals have been nursed back to health but are permanently disabled in ways (such as a wing injury) that preclude release back to the wild. Other educational efforts include quarterly membership newsletters, in-house naturalist lecture programs, and guided local hiking tours.

Clearly, the CCW has become the repository for a great deal of practical information, some of which could be used by individuals in their occasional encounters with wildlife. Many of the situations reported to the Center occur with great frequency in any area where humans and wildlife meet; this is in part because many of the species we commonly come into contact with live all around North America: raccoons, many kinds of rodents, deer, skunks, and migrating birds.

Through sharing information with other wildlife rehabilitation groups around the country, the Center is ever expanding its database and knowledge of humane animal control practices. The CCW realized that this information could reach many more people than have direct contact with the Center if it were published in an accessible, clearly organized form. The interest of Sierra Club Books was the catalyst that led to synthesizing the material gathered and undertaking the additional research needed to make *Living with Wildlife* useful to readers all over the country.

What This Book Covers, and Why

In keeping with the California Center for Wildlife's educational mission, this book was created to provide the public with natural history and humane animal control information about common wildlife found in North America. Recognizing the intimate and life-sustaining connection among humans, wild creatures, and natural habitat is a critical step toward preserving the earth for future generations.

Experience has shown that the greatest hope for sustaining the diversity and abundance of our native wildlife lies in getting people involved on a personal level. That is why wildlife education based on firsthand interaction with animals is so effective. Though people and wildlife cannot coexist everywhere, there are many areas where they can and do. For any of us, our homes are one such place: chiefly oriented to the safety and comfort of humans, they can nevertheless accommodate the needs of many wild creatures. Conversely, places officially designated as wild can be hospitable to people and are prime locations for rewarding encounters with wildlife.

The primary focus of this book, then, is on describing those wild creatures with which humans are most likely to come into contact— chiefly in residential settings and secondarily in the course of wilderness or camping trips. The animal is described in a general way, along with its range and habitat, its notable behavior, and its enemies and defenses. Usually some information is provided about how to safely observe the creature at home or in the wild. Then, in most cases, we describe various situations in which the animal might present a problem and suggest a range of methods for dealing with that problem in the most humane fashion possible.

This last category of information is the practical core of the book, but the natural history that accompanies it is important, too. By better understanding the creature's needs and habits, readers will be better equipped to cope with the situation, as well as to appreciate that animal's unique qualities and help protect it.

Personal interaction is our main focus; however, the larger fate of wildlife in North America lies less in the hands of individuals and more in those of our social, economic, and governing institutions. The greatest threats—those of habitat loss and degradation through encroachment and pollution—will require large-scale and cooperative efforts to deal with. Educating individuals is key to addressing these issues, so we have devoted the first chapter of this book to summarizing some of the problems facing wildlife in North America today, what is being done about them, and what private citizens can do on the public level to help.

Chapter 2 shifts the focus from larger wildlife issues to those that arise in our personal lives. It talks about our homes as habitat for wild creatures as well as people and about how wildlife is affected by all the normal activities we pursue at home: building, landscaping, gardening, disposing of trash, enjoying our pets, and so on. It also describes how the choices we make as consumers affect wildlife and habitat.

Chapter 3 addresses the other main mission of the CCW: rescuing and caring for injured wildlife. We describe the appropriate actions for individuals to take when they find injured or orphaned wild animals; survey the brief history of wildlife rehabilitation; and suggest how readers can get involved in this fascinating and rewarding field.

Further Reading and Resources

All the available information that is useful for people in learning to live with wildlife cannot possibly be reproduced in one book, though we have included as much specific information as this book's scope permits. At the end of the book is an appendix of other resources— including state and federal wildlife agencies, many wildlife rehabilitation organizations, sources for specific humane control techniques, and habitat literature. Readers are encouraged to thus continue their self-education about living with wildlife.

CHAPTER 1

Americans and Wildlife:
An Evolving Relationship

Our current way of looking at wildlife and wildlife habitat is the result of a long evolutionary process. The idea that the interests of wild creatures and those of humans are fundamentally linked makes sense to us, knowing what we do now of ecological relationships, but that hasn't always been the case. In the cyclical way of things, our present-day views are coming full circle in their similarity to those held by the earliest humans living in North America.

We begin with an overview of how these attitudes have evolved, of the main challenges facing wildlife in America today, and of what individuals can do on the public level to help preserve wildlife populations and diversity. This sets the stage for our later chapters on personal interaction with wildlife: The better we understand how history has shaped our reactions to wild animals, the more likely we will be to make decisions that benefit both us and the creatures we come in contact with. The more we know about the reasons for safeguarding wildlife habitat, the more we realize that human health and happiness are among those reasons.

Wildlife and the First Americans

The history of wildlife conservation in this country is really one of six distinct eras of changing attitudes. The time before Europeans colonized the North American continent (pre-1600) can be seen as an era of balance and interconnectedness. For thousands of years, indigenous peoples lived in tribal societies from coast to coast.

Fishing provides most of the bald eagle's food, so these raptors need extensive, unpolluted waterside habitat.

Some tribes were agricultural, others nomadic hunters. The agricultural tribes planted corn, squash, beans, and other crops for annual harvest. With each planting and harvest they gave thanks for and celebrated the gift of life provided to them by the plants. These peoples also used the gifts provided by animals for food, tools, and clothing. The nomadic hunting peoples relied mainly on wild animals to provide their survival needs. The plains peoples followed and hunted great herds of buffalo; they also relied on other creatures such as deer, elk, and rabbits for food, shelter, clothing, and tools. They, too, gave thanks for the bounty provided by nature and appreciated that the animals and plants, by giving up their own lives, ensured that people might live.

For indigenous peoples, understanding the connectedness of all living things and revering nature were not separate from daily activities; they were a part of every moment. This relationship to animal and plant life survives today, for the most part, in traditional native cultures, despite the impact of European colonization.

Conquering the Wild

The explorers and settlers from the Old World brought with them a different set of attitudes toward the natural world and its inhabitants, based on the belief that nature needed to be subdued.

The first European settlement period (about 1600 to 1850) was characterized by a sense of abundance—of wildlife and all natural resources. The immense continent contained a seemingly inexhaustible supply of water, trees, plants, and animals, which the settlers believed they were entitled to take as they needed or wished. The need to conserve those resources for the future did not even occur to them.

The next era (about 1850 to 1900) brought the massive exploitation of natural resources. As a result of rapid population growth, industrialization, and urbanization in the East, and of westward migration and homesteading, huge chunks of native wildlife populations and habitat were destroyed. Many "game" species were nearly exterminated by hunting for market (meat and fur) or for sport (the slaughter of bison from trains). Many other species were threatend by loss of their habitat to agriculture and urban growth, and of the prey animals they relied on for food. In their haste to conquer and draw wealth from this new land, these early Americans seriously damaged the extraordinary natural legacy of North America, wiping out some species and reducing others to tiny proportions of their original abundance.

The Tide Turns

Luckily, early in the twentieth century, some farsighted citizens and legislators (many of them hunters) recognized the calamity that was befalling wildlife and other natural resources. Thus began the era of protection and preservation (1900 to 1930), as pressure was brought to bear on state and federal governments to regulate or ban hunting and to preserve habitats. The first "wildlife conservation" efforts started during this period, with land set aside and preserved in a natural state for wildlife and people.

Eventually those who took an interest in wildlife populations realized that simply "leaving wildlife alone" wasn't enough to ensure its survival. The advent of game wardens and restocking of species were inadequate responses to continued human demands on available land and water. As the failures of past approaches were recognized, so was the need for game management—the application of scientific knowledge and techniques to maintain, limit, or increase wildlife populations and their habitats.

This game management era (1930 to 1965) brought the passage of significant legislation to protect public lands and wildlife. One such law, the 1937 Federal Aid to Wildlife Restoration Act (commonly referred to as the Pittman-Robertson Act), created an excise tax on sporting arms, handguns, archery equipment, and ammunition at the manufacturer/importer level. The monies raised from that tax were—and continue to be—distributed to state wildlife agencies for acquisition of habitat, wildlife research programs, and training. Also during this period, many citizen-formed conservation organizations were created to assist in preserving and protecting wildlife and habitat. The efforts of both private groups and state wildlife agencies at this time were oriented toward game animals, that is, those hunted or trapped for meat, fur, or trophy.

Not coincidentally, the need for conservation became widely recognized during the Great Depression. The drought and dust-bowl years of the mid-1930s directly demonstrated the results of long-term habitat destruction and wasted wildlife. Much topsoil was lost because of ill-advised agricultural practices, and much common wildlife, like deer and wild turkeys, virtually disappeared. During World War II, conservation efforts necessarily did not receive much financial support. In the postwar years, however, conservation efforts funded by the Pittman-Robertson tax led to the significant rebuilding of wildlife populations.

Our current time (1965 to the present) can be characterized as the era of environmental awareness. Public concern for wildlife and habitat protection and preservation has broadened to include other environmental concerns such as pollution, pesticide use, and welfare of all wild animals (not just game) and plants. For the first time, many people have begun to understand and acknowledge that all living creatures have an intrinsic worth apart from any value humans may place on them, that we and they are connected in the web of life, and that we must act responsively as caretakers of the natural world.

Wildlife Conservation Today:
Success Stories and Current Challenges

Monies generated under the 1937 Pittman-Robertson Act are still the main source for wildlife protection funding in the United States (along with similar migratory bird and fish restoration taxes). Most of the funds are used to acquire and maintain wildlife management areas, with smaller amounts going to scientific research and education.

Since 1937, 4 million acres have been purchased, and nearly 40 million acres are managed for wildlife under agreements with landowners. In addition to buying land outright, state wildlife agencies negotiate leases with private landowners and work out cooperative agreements with other public lands agencies such as the U.S. Forest Service, the Bureau of Land Management, and the National Park Service. Such agreements provide access to public lands necessary for the survival of winter migrating species—such as pronghorn, elk, deer, and bighorn sheep—and have helped provide essential wetlands for migrating waterfowl.

In addition, the U.S. Fish and Wildlife Service was mandated to create a national wildlife refuge system for migratory waterfowl, which currently includes over 450 refuges in all 50 states and Puerto Rico. Located chiefly on major north-south flyways, they provide critical habitat where birds feed and rest during their spring and fall migrations, and they protect wetlands used by many other species. Certain refuges are sanctuaries for endangered species, such as whooping cranes and red wolves, or for species such as bighorn sheep that require specialized habitat. The U.S. Fish and Wildlife Service also has undertaken a combined effort with Canada, called the North American Waterfowl Management Plan, to attempt to reverse the decline in duck and geese species.

Due to conservation efforts, wood ducks have made an extraordinary recovery from near extinction to become the most common duck in North America.

Wildlife Management and Research

Because of the loss of natural habitat caused by human development, wildlife agencies must physically manage the remaining lands to provide the most suitable habitat for animals. Habitat management techniques include the

creation and protection of water holes for wildlife in the desert Southwest, planting of trees and shrubs in plains areas to create wildlife
"cover," limited clearing of heavily forested areas to provide varied food
and shelter for wildlife, control of livestock grazing on western grasslands, controlled burning of brush and tall grass, planting of small
patches of wildlife food (native plant species), and cutting of shallow
ditches in areas with high water tables to create marshy habitats suitable for many species.

The research funded by Pittman-Robertson and other protection
statutes has yielded effective techniques for managing wildlife and
information about wildlife's impact on human concerns. For example,
it has been learned that most big game animals do not directly compete
with livestock for food and seldom transmit contagious diseases to
cattle or sheep. Live-trapping, the use of tranquilizer darts for capture
and relocation, and the tracing of animals by radio have all become
standard practices after years of development and experimentation.
Data gathered from this research have enabled managers to keep
wildlife species in balance with their environment and each other.

Management has also led to successful restoration of many species.
For example, from a total of only 100,000 in 1920, the North American
elk population now approaches 500,000. From being scarce outside a
few southern states in 1930, wild turkeys now number over 2 million
and are found in nearly all the lower 48 states. From feared extinction
resulting in a hunting ban in 1920, the wood duck is now the most
common waterfowl in the eastern United States. From a population of
fewer than 500,000 in 1920, white-tailed deer have rebounded to over
14 million strong. More than 750,000 pronghorn antelope now graze
the wild grasslands of the West, from fewer than 25,000 in 1920.

Private Groups

Besides government agencies, many private conservation organizations raise funds for wildlife and habitat protection. Organizations such
as The Nature Conservancy, the Trust for Public Lands, and local land
trust organizations purchase land in its natural state to protect habitat
and wildlife from development. Other organizations, such as the California Center for Wildlife, the Nature Center in Howell, Michigan, and
the Wildlife Center in Weyers Cave, Virginia, operate clinics to rehabili-

tate injured or sick wildlife and release the animals back to the wild, as well as providing nature education for the public. Defenders of Wildlife and the National Wildlife Federation, among others, focus on strengthening legal protection for wildlife and wildlands.

Endangered Species

Despite notable success stories, many species still have become extinct or remain endangered. Since the late 1970s, few new laws or policies have been adopted to further wildlife conservation in this country. In fact, laws such as the Endangered Species Act have been deliberately undermined by lack of enforcement, attempts to limit them through rewriting, and redefinition of agency rules to gut the legislation's original intent. Inevitably such reactionary efforts will have some negative consequences for wildlife.

Since Europeans began to colonize North America, more than 500 species or subspecies of native animals and plants have vanished. The federal Endangered Species Act, adopted in 1966, with follow-up legislation in 1973, was and is a model for safeguarding imperiled wildlife. Many states have adopted similar legislation and maintain state lists of endangered and threatened species.

However, the federal law mandates a lengthy administrative process to have a species declared endangered and to begin developing a species recovery plan. As of this writing, the federal endangered species list contains 574 domestic species, of which only 308 have had the legally required recovery plans developed for them.

Besides those already declared endangered, 3,700 candidate species currently await possible listing. Listing is frequently delayed because of the backlog of requests that need to be addressed. This backlog is in part due to lack of support from responsible wildlife officials. At least part of the solution lies in continued and vociferous public pressure that demands good-faith efforts be made to enforce the letter and spirit of the laws.

Habitat Lost to Human Development

Loss of habitat is the single biggest reason for the continuing decline in wildlife populations. For example, since 1950 Florida has lost to human development half of its wetlands, a quarter of its forest, and

Many species of wildlife depend on wetland habitat.

most of its tropical hardwood hammocks, scrub, and coastal habitat.

Such habitat loss is occurring all over North America. Where people "develop" land and introduce housing, utilities, roads, shopping centers, and garbage dumps, the quality of once-wild habitat—the food, water, shelter, and amount of space or territory required for wildlife to reproduce and raise their young—is degraded, fragmented, and sometimes completely lost.

Wetland Preservation

Wetlands—areas around lakes, bays, and oceans, where the water meets the land—are among the most important and sensitive natural wildlife habitats. Marshes, swamps, bogs, and sloughs renew and rejuvenate life. All life-forms, from the smallest microscopic plants to the largest predators, require water and wetlands for survival. Food chains vital to many species—including humans—start in wetlands. Many species depend upon wetlands for breeding, feeding, and resting; in fact, more wildlife live in this kind of habitat than in any other. Furthermore, the water held in wetlands maintains soil moisture in croplands and restores groundwater supplies used by far-off towns and cities.

Because they usually occur near seacoasts and rivers, many natural wetlands are also favored living areas for humans. For example, the coastal regions of Florida and the San Francisco Bay Area both featured immense expanses of wetlands prior to extensive human development—which usually means adding landfill and covering over areas that people view as undesirable swamps and sloughs. So we have seen significant destruction of wetland habitats in this country, from a total of more than 127 million acres of wetlands in 1900 to only about 80 million acres currently. Consequently we are witnessing the decline or destruction of many wetland-dependent species.

Wide-scale efforts to preserve our remaining wetlands are imperative. Current laws require their protection, but in recent years, efforts have been made at the federal level to "redefine" wetlands, which would open large areas of currently protected habitat to development.

Wildlife Corridors

Studies have found that when development breaks up large land areas in which wildlife ordinarily live and migrate, some species are deprived of the space they need to survive. Many animals, from large predators to the smallest songbird populations, have large home-range requirements—that is, acreage needed to support a gene pool large enough to maintain healthy reproduction of the species.

When animals can range over a large area, population growth and diversity are encouraged. But many refuges, national parks and forests, and other public lands managed for wildlife are isolated from each other, keeping the animals from moving between these lands. The consequences of decades of development around conservation areas, and the isolation of wildlife populations by gigantic systems of roads, power lines, pipelines, and strip developments are among the most urgent issues in wildlife conservation.

Scientists have concluded that species loss in isolated preserves is similar to what occurs on true islands. Over the past several decades, 42 types of mammals have disappeared from 14 North American parks, although those species were present when the parklands were established. For example, badgers and black bears no longer are found at Zion National Park; pronghorn, beavers, flying squirrels, and red foxes have disappeared from Bryce Canyon National Park; and river otters, spotted skunks, and gray foxes have vanished from Crater Lake National Park. Many wildlife reserves are so small that they cannot support even one individual of the species they were intended to protect.

These problems can be addressed by a shift in the focus of habitat conservation from protecting separate parcels of land to acquiring wildlife corridors, greenbelts, and riparian buffer zones that link existing refuges and allow wildlife to move among them with little human contact. These linkages can sometimes be as simple as road underpasses that allow animals to travel under a roadway instead of across it.

The larger issue of perserving biodiversity is the principle that should guide wildlife conservation and land-use practices now and in the future. Both wildlife agencies and the public should recognize the definition of biodiversity as "life, and all that sustains life." Then we must identify the remaining areas with the highest biodiversity, protect as many of them in the largest blocks possible, and make land-bridge and waterway connections between them to encourage animal movement and seed dispersal. (Resources for more detailed information on wildlife corridor efforts are listed in the Appendices.)

People camping in bear habitat can avoid unwanted confrontations by taking sensible precautions, such as storing food out of bears' reach.

As Montana biologist and writer Douglas H. Chadwick observes, [t]he conditions are right for conservation to evolve again, this time to go beyond endangered species and beyond game. Our challenge now is to conserve the very nature of nature, which is the power to connect, to sustain, to heal and to invent; to keep filling the world with an infinite variety of wonders.... That is what bio-diversity and landscape linkages are all about.

How to Get Involved in Wildlife Protection

Almost everything we humans do affects wildlife and its habitat, either directly or indirectly. We are not alone in enjoying life on earth, and the needs and rights of wild animals are worthy of consideration in our decision making. Humans need to consciously consider the effects of development on wildlife and habitat.

When people become involved, they can make a significant difference. If we each would start taking responsibility for wildlife conservation in our local areas, eventually the entire country would make wildlife protection a significant priority. If we would make our daily living choices with wildlife and habitat concerns in mind, the irreplaceable wild legacy that we steward would be saved for future generations.

Understand and Support Wildlife Management Techniques

The public often misunderstands wildlife management techniques, including controlled burning and wetlands protection, because of perceived threats to human habitat. Yet while these practices may cause minimal, temporary inconvenience to people, they provide immense benefits to wildlife.

Fire, for example, is a natural process of change, not simply destruction. Burning trees and other forest plant life actually converts stored plant energy into nutrient-rich ash that fertilizes the forests. And the openings created by fires aid the growth of low shrubs and grasses that support many wildlife species; without fires, such species as bluebirds and fox squirrels would not survive. Similarly, wildlife managers protect and actually create some wetlands to encourage the plant life and conditions that support songbirds, muskrats, and many other creatures.

Take the time to inform yourself and your neighbors about wildlife management techniques used in your area, and support the local efforts of wildlife management professionals.

Volunteer and Vote for Wildlife

Private conservation organizations welcome and rely on volunteer assistance and grassroots activity; many are active in influencing legal and political treatment of wildlife. Nonprofit wildlife rehabilitation and education organizations offer rewarding opportunities to practice hands-on animal care and to educate others—both children and adults—about the importance of protecting wildlife. Government programs in national, state, and local parks and wildlife refuges also can use volunteer help, especially during budgetary hard times.

If you cannot actively volunteer, conservation efforts need your financial and moral support. Take time to write letters to politicians, newspapers, and government agencies to encourage and support legislation and government action to protect species and wildlife habitat. Communicate to government officials your concern for wetlands protection and preservation. Also, whether you hunt or not, support the Duck Stamp Program (the 1934 Migratory Bird Conservation Act) by purchasing duck stamps at the post office; the money raised from their sale is used to buy wetlands for wildlife refuges.

Inform yourself about the environmental records of those running for elective office and vote for those with a proven commitment to wildlife. In many states, the Sierra Club and the League of Conservation Voters research and provide information about the environmental records of political candidates.

Contribute to Wildlife Organizations

There are many ways to financially support wildlife and habitat protection organizations. In some states, tax money can be earmarked for wildlife funds by a simple mark in a special box on your income tax return. Others have special license plate funds that designate certain monies for wildlife trust funds. Use those options wherever they exist.

Private organizations for wildlife rehabilitation or habitat conservation rely heavily on individual contributions for their continued existence and good works. They ordinarily receive little if any goverment funding, and only a small percentage of their operating budgets comes from charitable foundation support. Through membership in local wildlife rehabilitation or educational organizations, you actually contribute to the care and protection of wildlife in your area and to educating other residents. Many such organizations have "Adopt an Animal" programs, where your contribution goes directly to aid a certain species; in return, you receive information about those animals.

Wildlife needs wildlands to survive and thrive. You can support groups such as The Nature Conservancy, the Trust for Public Lands, and local land trust organizations through financial and land donations. Another approach is to identify tracts of land in your area that provide unprotected wildlife habitat and organize a support group to encourage local, state, or federal agencies to purchase the property.

Other national organizations, such as Defenders of Wildlife, the National Wildlife Federation, and the Sierra Club, need continued private financial support to successfully influence national and regional wildlife and habitat policies. A list of resources that provide more information about all these efforts, as well as wildlife rehabilitation and protection organizations, is included in Appendix B.

Report Wildlife Violators

If you think you see a wildlife law being broken, make a report to the nearest wildlife law enforcement agency (either your state department of wildlife or the U.S. Fish and Wildlife Service). Illegal activities may include improper hunting, and killing or harassing protected species. Get as much information as possible—license plate number, location, time of day, descriptions of persons and vehicles—but do not attempt to personally intervene. You can make your report anonymously if you choose. Sometimes rewards may be paid for information leading to the arrest of wildlife violators.

Only People Can Make the Difference

Laws are only as good as their enforcement by the governing administration. In our democratic society, any administration is subject to the will of the people. We must urge our government to choose the path of recognizing and valuing the wildlife and habitat of which we are not owners, but stewards.

CHAPTER 2

Sharing Space with Wildlife

This chapter deals with situations where people and wildlife interact on a more personal level—around the homes we own or occupy and along the roads and trails on which we travel. We can do many things, on a small scale, to counteract the impact of habitat loss, correct misunderstandings about animals, and generally make life less stressful for the wild creatures native to places we have taken over. For many people, helping wildlife in this personal, individual way is more satisfying than contributing to an organization or supporting legislation (though these things are at least as important). And besides the altruistic motive, the rewards of enjoying wildlife in your own environment, and of knowing how to conduct yourself in theirs, can be great indeed.

Humans are great consumers, so we'll also talk about how our buying habits directly and indirectly affect the welfare of wild animals, and about how to be wildlife-conscious consumers.

Attitudes and assumptions we may not even be aware of strongly guide the way we react to wildlife encountered close at hand, so it's worth examining some of the most commonly held views of wild creatures. Although our views have evolved greatly since the European settlement of North America, as we saw in the last chapter, some outdated ideas remain. For example, many wildlife agencies and conservation organizations still think in terms of game and nongame animals. Many agencies and individuals still use words like *nuisance* or *damage* to describe the nature of wildlife and human interaction.

Even if we do not hunt or practice livestock raising, we may be influenced by the perspective of those with such interests and the agencies that are oriented largely toward serving them—that is, that wild animals exist chiefly for human use, and as such can be tolerated or encouraged unless they interfere with our livelihood or recreation.

On the opposite end of the spectrum are those who see wildlife as pets, who care only about saving the "cute" creatures, or for whom wild animals are less themselves than symbols of something missing from our lives. This mind-set, which centers on how animals can fulfill our emotional needs, or how well we can relate to them (furry mammals are perceived as the most valuable), has been called the "Bambi syndrome." It fails to recognize the independent and nonhuman attributes of wild animals and can often cause more harm than good. If translated into public policy, it may cause some animals to suffer due to favoritism shown to others; on the individual level, it can lead to wild animals becoming stressed or socialized by human interference.

We need to strive toward a balanced view of wild animals, recognizing our responsibility to safeguard wild habitat and act humanely toward individual creatures, while understanding the animals' right to exist free from human depredation and interference in their lives. Here are some of the things we can do (and avoid doing) that demonstrate a true knowledge of and empathy with the needs of wild creatures. Taking such steps is in our own best interests as well.

Ground Rules for Good Wildlife Neighbors

Do Not Keep Wild Animals as Pets

Do not buy animals that have been captured in the wild, and do not capture any wild animal to make it a pet. Wild animals are severely stressed by the presence of humans; that stress can weaken them, make them sick, or even kill them. Exotic birds and reptiles are often acquired as pets by people unaware that they may have been illegally captured and imported, threatening wildlife populations in other parts of the world. Possessing game or migratory birds without a permit is illegal and can carry criminal penalties. Even when possession of the animals is legal, take pains to ensure that any such creatures purchased as pets are captive bred and not taken from the wild.

Wild animals kept as pets inevitably become "imprinted" on humans or socialized to human presence—that is, they lose their identity as wild creatures to varying extents and often lose or fail to learn appropriate survival behaviors. Imprinting occurs with baby animals that are raised by humans from an early age and thus never learn their animal identity or the survival skills particular to their species. Sooner or later, they are no longer "cute" babies and may even become dangerous; usually they are doomed to life in a cage or to be put to death if they cannot be placed with a suitable wildlife organization. They cannot survive if released back to the wild and may be dangerous around humans who encounter them there.

When older animals are made captive (sometimes because they have been injured and are being cared for), they may become "socialized" to humans, a less irrevocable process than imprinting. Such animals retain their basic species identity and survival skills but grow comfortable around humans (tamed but not really tame). Even if strongly socialized, they may have a chance to survive in the wild; however, they may be especially dangerous to humans, because they are used to interacting with them, and may put themselves in harm's way of humans who react with fear or hostility.

The bottom line is that all wild animals remain wild, even in captivity. (Captive-bred creatures may do so to a lesser extent but are still genetically programmed for a wild existence.) Their behavior is unpredictable and potentially dangerous to humans, and their lives away from their natural environment can never be as nature intended.

Children should not be allowed to "collect" living wildlife, such as frogs, snakes, or insects. Capturing these animals stresses them greatly and can result in death. A better alternative is to take your children on nature walks and to places where they can observe animals in the wild. Help them to understand and appreciate the separateness of wildlife and its right to exist in its own natural habitat. It's also a good idea to take your children to nature centers, where they can learn more about the natural world and what they can do to help protect wildlife and its habitat. Finally, encourage environmental and wildlife education in school curricula.

National parks display a sign that should also be observed
at home: Do Not Feed the Animals.

Don't Feed the Animals

Many people are tempted to feed wildlife, but this practice should be strictly avoided. Putting out food for wild animals creates dependency, as the animals quickly learn where easy food sources are. If you regularly feed wild animals, those that have come to depend on your food can be severely deprived and even die when you go on vacation or move away.

The best way to provide food for wildlife is to re-create its natural habitat. If you plant your yard or land in native species, animals can feed on these natural foods that will be there for them even when you are not.

This recommendation extends even to the use of bird feeders, a practice of long standing and tradition and the easiest way to entice birds into open, easily viewable areas. We don't expect all backyard birding enthusiasts to give up their feeders, but we strongly urge you to observe these guidelines:

1. Understand that you are assuming a long-range responsibility, and be consistent in making food available once you have begun (which may necessitate making arrangements when you are away from home).

2. Provide only good-quality natural bird foods; other foods, such as bread crumbs, contain little nutritional value for birds. Consult a

more specialized bird book about which kinds of seed or mixtures are best for the birds in your area.

3. Keep feeders clean to limit the possibility of birds passing diseases among each other. Do not allow seed to mold or mildew as this creates bacteria that can seep into wood feeders and create ongoing disease problems.

Feeding animals in the wild, such as bears or alligators, is illegal and dangerous, as any park ranger will tell you, and the food offered is usually contrary to the animal's nutritional needs. Wilderness parks provide copious literature and signage to discourage the practice, which not only is hazardous to humans but often results in the need to relocate or kill habituated animals.

Observing Wildlife at Home and Abroad

Nowhere is our changing relationship with wildlife better demonstrated than in the dramatic rise of interest in wildlife observation activities. Americans currently spend much free time observing wild animals—on trips, in local parks and refuges, and in their own yards. According to a 1980 survey by the U.S. Fish and Wildlife Service, 53 percent of the U.S. population over age 16 (93 million) participated that year in some form of "nonconsumptive" use of wildlife (activities that do not involve the removal or intended removal of animals from their natural habitats), compared with 17 million who hunted and 42 million who fished. Based on responses to this study, an estimated 79 million Americans took a special interest in observing, identifying, photographing, or feeding wild animals.

The study also found, significantly, that most of this wildlife-oriented activity occurred in residential settings. Forty-seven percent (80 million) participated in wildlife observation and other non-consumptive activities within a mile of their homes, compared to 17 percent who traveled farther for the primary purpose of wildlife interaction. A total of 46 percent (79 million) enjoyed wildlife while on a trip away from home, while 28 million took trips primarily for wildlife enjoyment.

Wildlife observation and appreciation contribute millions of dollars to travel, leisure, and other industries in the United States and elsewhere every year. Large sums are spent on birdseed and other home wildlife gear, as well as on camping, hiking, photography, and other equipment used in wildlife observation treks. A whole new approach to travel, known as "ecotourism," has emerged in response to people's desire to experience the world's great natural areas, where native flora and fauna (and human cultures) remain relatively undisturbed.

Many state wildlife agencies (Alaska, Colorado, Idaho, Montana, Oklahoma, Oregon, Tennessee, and Wyoming, among others), as well as the federal Bureau of Land Management, have begun "Watchable Wildlife" programs, which provide information about the location of wildlife refuges, good wildlife viewing areas, and local animal and plant species. Defenders of Wildlife is actively supporting and promoting Watchable Wildlife programs throughout the country. Check with your state agency to learn whether such a program exists in your state and/or whether you can help create one. (See Appendices A and C.)

Enjoying Wildlife Responsibly

Responsible wildlife observation—that which does not adversely affect the wildlife—requires thoughtful consideration for the animals being observed. Animals are most vulnerable when injured, mating, giving birth, or rearing their young. Surprising them can cause great stress, which can affect their survival ability. Animals that live on subsistence diets (those that do not have food stored away but must catch each meal as needed) can suffer much harm if scared away from a hardwon meal. They use considerable energy to hunt for food, and if they cannot eat their prey, their survival may be endangered. Keep in mind that a single disturbance can stress an animal in the wild; imagine how stressful it must be for animals in areas that are heavily visited by humans.

By all means, enjoy observing wildlife. Make it one of your vacation activities. Enjoy state parks and nature centers. Encourage school wildlife field trips for your children, and take children bird-watching, hiking in the woods, or wandering on the beach. Look for signs of wild animals, such as tracks; use animal identification guidebooks; make collections of wildlife pictures or leaves. Help your child build a birdhouse or plant a native tree.

But before participating in these activities, inform yourself about the animals that live in your area, or in the place you are visiting. (Such information is available from local wildlife education organizations, park rangers and offices, and state wildlife agencies.) Awareness is the best protection for wildlife as well as humans. When enjoying these adventures, remember to stay on well-traveled roads and trails, because animals become acclimated to human patterns and can adjust their own patterns to minimize human-caused stress. Also, where appropriate, stay in your car or canoe. Animals are much more comfortable with humans if they cannot see our shapes.

Respect wild animals by giving them lots of space. If they flee, do not chase them. Watch for distress signals, such as birds diving at dogs or people, which indicates that you are coming too close to a nesting site. If you observe these signs, leave the area immediately to avoid further stress on the parents and young.

Wildlife and Our Homes

The most promising place for many of us to encounter and enjoy wildlife is right in our own backyards. Most of us spend more time at home than anywhere else, and it is an environment with which we become intimately familiar over time. Most of us are at home early in the morning, in the evening, and at night—times when many wild creatures are most active.

Our chances of encountering wildlife around our home depend on many factors. For city folk, the experience may well be limited to song-birds that alight to investigate plants, bird feeders, or a water source on one's terrace or fire escape; or to observing birds—including the occasional raptor—with binoculars. Birds are the ubiquitous messengers of the wild: able to travel freely and inhabit heavily developed areas now inaccessible to land-bound animals.

The range (and size) of creatures we are likely to have contact with is more or less in proportion to the amount of open, undeveloped land that exists around our home or around the general neighborhood. A wealth of wildlife may frequent even a community of tract houses on tiny lots or of condos clustered on a hillside if there are sizable green-belts nearby. Of course, those who make their homes in true rural areas, on ranchlands, or adjacent to protected lands are most likely to have contact with wildlife. Depending in part on how they make their living, these people are also most likely to either welcome wild creatures or consider them a nuisance.

Other preexisting factors that determine the extent and diversity of wildlife near your home include climate. Many herptile species, such as snakes, lizards, and alligators, are strictly limited by climate zones as they cannot tolerate freezing temperatures; conversely, some northern mammal species, such as Arctic hares and lemmings, are not found in southern latitudes. Season of the year is an important determinant for the presence of migrating species. The amount and type of vegetative cover (mature trees, dense shrubbery, meadow grasses), the type of soil (loose, diggable soils; hard clay), and the presence of water are also key factors.

Priorities

Aside from the basic facts of geography, open space, and species distribution, our own actions can help determine how much wildlife we see around our homes and whether the interaction is pleasant or troublesome. In general, we encourage readers to make their home places attractive to wildlife, but before taking any actions toward this end, consider carefully their consequences and your personal priorities. Is it more important that birds feel at home in your yard, or that your cat have unrestricted outdoor access? Is your passion growing exotic and delicate plants that are also attractive to roving deer or rabbits? Can you trim the size of your yard and plant native species as wildlife food sources, or must you have enough pristine lawn for a croquet field or a putting pratice area? Is your yard safe for wild creatures, or does your home-based business require that you store toxic substances that might cause harm if eaten? Or do you accumulate woodpiles that animals may nest in at the risk of disturbance?

Many apparent conflicts over land use can be easily reconciled (for example, by fencing certain garden areas). For those who decide that making wildlife welcome is among your priorities, this chapter suggests some general ways to do so, and you will find other suggestions in the reference guide to individual species. The Appendix directs you to sources of more detailed information, such as books about making your garden especially attractive to birds or butterflies.

If you take steps to encourage wildlife to share your land, and then experience what some people consider damage or nuisance problems, use the techniques described in the reference guide to help control wildlife interaction with humans. These are humane, nonharmful methods for discouraging or removing wildlife, while at the same time recognizing the need and right of wildlife to share the remaining natural lands that exist.

Housing Choices

The first choice we make regarding our homes is where to live, and among the many factors that enter into that choice, we might include how the type of housing we choose affects the fate of wildlife generally.

Properly designed clustered housing units, apartments, and duplexes are the most effective housing choices in terms of saving land for wildlife. You can help slow down the rate of habitat loss by selecting a home in a town or existing development, rather than developing a new site. Spacious, 5-acre lots in rural areas may provide luxurious country living for humans but are wasteful of land resources unless the homeowner donates some of the land to land trusts or leaves much of it natural and encourages wildlife use.

Wildlife Habitat in Your Backyard

Backyard habitat programs and resource materials offer excellent guidance on effectively managing your land for the benefit of wildlife (several are listed in Appendix C). We mention briefly here some of the general principles recommended by backyard habitat experts. To what extent you can follow them depends on your resources and whether you own or rent your dwelling.

Landscaping

ADVANCE PLANNING: Whenever possible, consider at the planning stage the impact of landscaping on wildlife. The more you can anticipate and plan for wildlife needs and issues at the beginning, the easier and more effective will be any control techniques. For example, the kinds of trees and shrubs you choose for your yard can directly encourage or discourage the presence of many animals. Many state wildlife agencies and plant nurseries have lists of plants preferred or shunned by deer. These plants vary according to your geographic location and climate, so it's best to seek specifics from local sources.

When deciding on placement of trees, shrubs, and trellis-type structures near the home, consider the climbing possibilities they offer wildlife such as raccoons and squirrels. If you have taken steps to ensure that any holes on the outside of the house large enough for entry are secured, then locating large plants and structures close to the building should not be a problem. However, keeping such ready-made wildlife ladders farther away will most effectively inhibit the climbing critters.

If your neighborhood is known to have resident populations of gophers, moles, armadillos, or other burrowing species, consider laying wire mesh over landscaped earth before adding topsoil and planting lawns and gardens. This preventive planning can virtually eliminate problems with burrowing animals.

LAWNS AND ALTERNATIVES: One of the most effective steps you can take to encourage wildlife to share your surroundings is *not* to install a lawn. Or you could replace an existing lawn with areas of trees, shrubs, and ground cover. Most people choose a lawn out of habit, because lawns have been part of the landscape of middle-class America. However, they actually act as wildlife deserts because they provide little

An ideal backyard landscape for wildlife includes plantings of different heights and types to provide food, cover, nesting, and reproductive areas; and a water source.

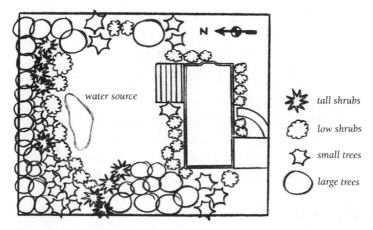

food or shelter for native animals. Moreover, they require large amounts of water and pernicious chemical fertilizers to be maintained in top condition. The first requirement may be a real problem in arid western regions; the second should be of concern everywhere. If you are replacing an existing lawn, a good rule of thumb is to cut its area at least in half.

When planning your landscaping, try to use native plant species. They are naturally adapted to thrive in your soil and climate, and they produce the best food sources for local wildlife. Also, native plants generally use less water and fertilizer and require less effort for controlling pests and disease.

WATER: Leave low spots on your property for water collection, rather than filling in and leveling the land. Make sure they are located where some amount of seasonal flooding cannot damage buildings. The low spots will encourage the formation of seasonal wetlands, so important to the life cycles of numerous plants and animals.

If no natural water source exists on your property, you can install a simple permanent water source for wildlife, such as a small pond, a birdbath, a recirculating waterfall, even a shallow dish or a dripping hose. Ponds can be stocked with fish and planted with appropriate species to produce fish and encourage wildlife.

WILDLIFE COVER: If your land is already wooded, leave at least one or two dead (snag) trees standing for each quarter acre. Dead trees provide habitat for many birds and animals. If a dead tree near your home is a safety hazard, cut the top off and leave the rest standing for birds, or support it with suspended wires. If no dead trees are available on your property, consider installing nest boxes designed for specific species of birds. (Resources for such designs are listed in Appendix C.)

Gardening

Gardening is a favored human pursuit with a high chance of interaction with wildlife. Again, depending on whether you want to share the bounty of your garden with the animals or keep them out, many safe techniques are available; specifics are given in the reference guide for each animal of concern.

Wildlife can be attracted by the varieties you plant and by gardens open to wildlife access. If you allow weeds and grasses to go to seed, they will often attract animals even more quickly than other plants and possibly spare some of your more valued flowers and vegetables. Providing water sources in or near gardens is also an enticement.

FENCING: Fences are the chief means of limiting wildlife contact with vegetable and ornamental gardens or fruit trees. Different animals call for different kinds of fences; for example, to limit access by deer, a fence must be tall, with a top section protruding outward to prevent jumping, and can be electrified. Lower fences restrict rabbits and burrowing animals but should have a portion buried below ground to block access from underneath.

Fencing or sheet metal can be wrapped around fruit tree trunks to impede certain animals from climbing to reach the fruit; its effectiveness is limited by the tree's jumping distance from other trees or structures. And some trees and other plantings can be covered with netting to prevent wildlife contact but permit continued growth. Another technique to discourage burrowers is laying wire mesh on the ground so that plants can grow through but animals can't get to the roots.

SCARE TECHNIQUES: Moving flags or pinwheels on lawns and gardens can deter some animals, such as woodchucks. Other scare repellents include loud noises, bright lights, and scarecrows.

PLANTING AND HARVESTING: Rotating crops and alternate planting of "undesirable" plants can help control wildlife damage. Another choice is to plant a separate "wildlife garden" to which animals are allowed access, while growing plants you want to protect in a fenced area. Animals are thus more likely to leave the protected garden unmolested.

Careful observation of wildlife and the harvest cycle of your garden is important in controlling wildlife impact. Harvesting ripe crops before the birds get to them can be a challenge, but garden netting used on a temporary basis can keep birds out of seedbeds and fully ripened crops and protect buds and flowers.

INSECT AND WEED CONTROL: Keep in mind that many animals are drawn to gardens not for the plants but to feed on insects that feed on the plants. So one of the best natural wildlife control methods is to control insect populations, in safe and nontoxic ways. (Sources for

Netting protects gardens and fruit trees from raiding birds and other animals.

information on safe pest management are listed in the Appendices.)

Many animals, especially birds, are drawn to gardens by nearby weeds and high grasses; if such animals cause problems, keep weeds and other wild growth near the gardens cleared and allow weeds and grasses to grow high in other areas.

Whatever landscape or garden controls you use, we strongly urge that they not include pesticides or herbicides. Studies have shown that such chemicals not only have possible adverse health effects on humans and pets but affect all animals in the food chain, from the smallest insect to the largest carnivore—and those effects can be serious. Natural controls can be just as effective without the hazards. Also, organic fertilizers are preferable to chemical-based ones. Remember that whatever you use to feed edible plants ends up in the bodies of any creatures that eat them—including your family. (See Appendices for sources of further information.)

Gardening with wildlife in mind calls for a shift of consciousness on the part of most gardeners. In that spirit, we have reprinted the following "apologia" written by Wendy Johnson of the Zen Center/ Green Gulch Farm in northern California, where the Zen Buddhist community has operated a commercial organic farm for many years. Even though the people of this community grow produce for market, they take a broad view of how their activities impact the entire ecosystem where they live and work.

Plants and Animals in the Garden,

We welcome you—we invite you in—we ask your forgiveness and your understanding. Listen as we invoke your names, as we also listen for you:

Little sparrows, quail, robins and house finches who have died in our strawberry nets;

Young Cooper's hawk who flew into our sweet pea trellis and broke your neck;

Numerous orange-bellied newts who died by our shears, in our irrigation pipes, by our cars, and by our feet;

Slugs and snails whom we have pursued for years, feeding you to the ducks, crushing you, trapping you, picking you off and tossing you over our fences;

Gophers and moles, trapped and scorned by us, and also watched with love, admiration, and awe for your one-mindedness;

Sowbugs, spitbugs, earwigs, flea beetles, woolly aphids, rose-suckers, cutworms, millipeds and other insects whom we have lured and stopped;

Snakes and moths who have been caught in our water system and killed by our mowers;

Families of mice who have died in irrigation pipes, by electricity in our pump box, and by predators while nesting in our greenhouses;

Manure worms and earthworms, severed by spades, and numerous microscopic lifeforms in our compost system who have been burned by sunlight;

Feral cats and raccoons whom we've steadily chased from the garden;

Rats whom we poisoned and trapped and drowned. Deer, chased

at dawn and at midnight, routed by dogs, by farmers, by fences and numerous barriers;

… We invoke you and thank you and continue to learn from you.

Home Building and Remodeling

Before beginning construction on a new home or remodeling an existing one, think about the possible effects these activities may have on wildlife. For example, use of heavy equipment can completely disrupt biosystems found on the site. Historically, only government agencies and business construction projects were required to prepare environmental impact reports, but now these reports are often a required part of residential construction planning.

Toxic or hazardous materials used in construction can contaminate groundwater and find their way into the wildlife food chain. If improperly stored on the site, they can injure wild animals more directly. Take the time to educate yourself on proper storage of toxic materials. Also, insist that your building contractors satisfactorily answer questions about the use of toxic materials and properly clean up the building site throughout the construction process.

When planning designs with an architect or designer, consider the location of windows, decks, and enclosed porches or sun-rooms for wildlife views, and the possibility of incorporating built-in structures such as an eaves birdhouse. Architectural design focusing on wildlife concerns and enhancement is a new area and one with some interesting recent developments. (Ask your architect-designer to educate him- or herself on wildlife issues, and apply that information to your designs.) When planning placement of windows, consider siting and/or marking them to help birds avoid injuring themselves on impact. (See the Birds section of the Reference Guide for more information on this.)

General Maintenance

PERIODIC HOME MAINTENANCE: Semiannual maintenance—often done in spring and fall—should always include inspecting for and repairing any exterior holes that permit wildlife access into the house. All such openings should be securely closed with wire mesh, shingles, sheet metal, or other appropriate materials. (The sections on specific

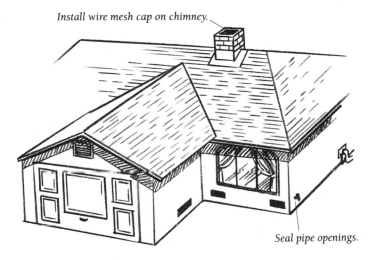

Install wire mesh cap on chimney.

Seal pipe openings.

Take the time to identify and secure openings where wildlife may enter your home, and recheck protection devices regularly.

species in the Reference Guide contain detailed instructions for making such repairs.) Open-sided porches should be fenced from floor level to ground, if this has not previously been done, with fencing buried slightly underground, if you choose not to have wildlife neighbors nesting under your porch. Wood siding and shingles should be treated according to the product's directions with nontoxic compounds that limit insect infestation and woodpecker damage. Maintain outbuildings, such as garages, woodsheds, and barns, in the same way if you are concerned about keeping wildlife out of them.

During periodic household chores such as cleaning gutters and eaves and overhauling garages, basements, and attics, carefully inspect these areas for signs of any animals in residence. If you find one, try to identify the creature and then follow the directions for that animal in the Reference Guide for exclusion or capture and relocation (either by you or a local wildlife agency).

YARD MAINTENANCE: General yard maintenance often includes clearing or relocating weeds, tall grasses, wood- or brush piles, and other items that provide cover for wildlife. Depending on the size of your yard and neighborhood considerations, you might leave some of these areas to encourage wildlife. When doing cleanup chores like pruning, raking, and mowing—especially in spring—take care to avoid injury to wildlife and nesting sites.

POOLS AND SPAS: Maintaining swimming pools and hot tubs involves some special care to avoid harm to wildlife. Keeping them covered at all times when not in use is the surest way to prevent possible drownings or injuries to animals and contamination of water with their droppings.

Nontoxic chemicals that keep the water safe for humans but will not contaminate groundwater when pools and tubs are drained are available; use these whenever possible. If you do, the drained water can be allowed to cool and used for watering plants and lawn rather than wasted. But be sure the chemicals are safe; otherwise they can seriously damage plantings and pollute groundwater.

Trash Disposal

Among the most common cases of human-wildlife interaction are the foraging of wild creatures for food in garbage cans. Raccoons and other animals have identified these repositories as convenient "fast-food outlets." To keep the animals out, purchase cans with clamps or other mechanisms to secure the lids. If your present cans lack such devices, you can secure lids with chains and locks or a stout bungee cord or two. Building storage areas that raise cans off the ground and securing them to the structure can prevent access and keep cans from being toppled over.

It's important to dispose of toxic substances in the safest way possible. Most local disposal companies and recycling centers provide special locations to which you can bring toxics such as paint, antifreeze, motor oil, and household solvents. Do not leave these materials stored anywhere that children, pets, or wildlife might get at them, and do not pour them into sewers, on the ground, or into bodies of water, because they seriously contaminate groundwater.

Pets and Wildlife

Domestic pets, unfortunately, cause much harm to wildlife. A recent study in England revealed that cats kill an estimated 70 million native animals, half of them songbirds, each year. A simple measure is to put a bell on the breakaway collar of any cat that is allowed outdoor access. The bell will alert birds and other small animals to the cat's presence and give them a chance to escape. Accept the fact, however, that your yard will never attract as many birds with a free-roaming cat, belled or not. If you are trying to attract birds to nesting boxes or feeders, it is best either not to have cats or dogs, or to protect the nesting and feeding areas with fencing if possible.

Dogs allowed to run loose prey on many wild creatures, ranging from birds to deer (if the dogs are large enough). They also are in danger themselves of being bitten by a creature they harass (with the chance that the creature may have rabies), sprayed by a skunk, or stuck by a porcupine (depending on the location). Dogs should be leashed or under positive voice control when outside. Keep a close eye on both cats and dogs in spring and summer (nesting season), when ground-nesting birds are easily disturbed. Pets should be neutered or spayed, which tends to limit their urge to roam, and their vaccinations should be kept up to date to protect them and wild animals from rabies and other communicable animal diseases.

Many irresponsible owners who tire of their pets just release them to the wild. Those animals cause serious damage to wildlife populations either by directly killing the wild animals or by competing with them for food and other resources. Further, domestic pets released to the wild often suffer, and many starve to death because they are not trained to survive in the wild. Find a good home for unwanted pets or take them to your local animal shelter if you are no longer able to care for them. Releasing nonnative animals to the wild is unethical, cruel, and illegal.

Pet doors installed in your home conveniently allow pets to come and go as they please, but they also provide easy access for wild creatures. Many reports of wildlife in homes are related to the use of pet doors by raccoons, opossums, skunks, and others. If you are willing to risk a wild animal inviting itself in, a two-way pet door can be used. As an alternative, you can install a one-way door that allows pets to exit, but neither they nor wildlife to reenter. If you prefer to avoid any chance of a wild neighbor getting inside, completely seal or remove pet doors.

For some new models of pet door, the cat or small dog wears a magnet-equipped collar that opens the door for that animal only. These doors can be adjusted so that the access is temporarily one way or blocked altogether if you want pets kept outside while you are away. However, we have no reports on how well these doors work.

Educating Neighbors

Wildlife issues can easily become neighborhood issues—either because you wish to encourage wildlife and your neighbors do not, or because someone is inappropriately feeding wild animals that can become a general nuisance. The best approach is to talk directly with your neighbors about your wildlife concerns, and try to forge some consensus about encouragement or control techniques. You might even want to invite a group of neighbors to meet and discuss these issues, refer them to this book and other sources, and/or create a neighborhood association focused on safe and healthy interaction with wild residents.

When Wildlife Must Be Removed

Though you may welcome wildlife in most cases and have taken the necessary steps to seal your home from would-be animal guests, there may be occasions when a wild animal must be removed from your home or yard. In general, unless an animal appears to be injured or ill, the best course is to leave it alone. Wild animals prefer to avoid direct human contact and eventually will depart on their own.

If the situation threatens imminent harm to family or pets, however, you can use certain techniques to remove and relocate a wild animal to more suitable habitat. Inside the home, capture techniques vary with the species; for example, catch small birds with a long-handled net or cover them with a cloth or tissue to quiet them. Then carry them outside for release. If a mammal or snake is inside the house, cover it with a box to quiet it and keep it in one place, and call a nearby wildlife care agency for assistance.

As a technique of last resort to remove animals from your yard—nesting raccoons or skunks, for example—you can use live traps available from hardware stores. Use them with diligence. Also take care in relocating animals. Relocating a nursing female without her young, or releasing an animal in an unsuitable location, can cause serious problems for the animal and other people. Again, if you contemplate using a live trap, it's best to get advice from experienced wildlife agency personnel.

Protecting Wildlife from Roads and Other Hazards

Automobiles are the single largest cause of wild-animal death in the United States. To understand why they cause so much harm, we need to understand wildlife behavior.

Wild animals move about to find food, water, and shelter by following the contours of the ground. They share established trails with each other and adapt to many different terrains and conditions. People, on the other hand, like to go straight from one point to another in the shortest distance possible, so our roads have little relationship to animal trails. Highways often cut directly across long-established animal trails to water and feeding grounds. When animals try to cross them, they are not prepared to encounter scent-free, fast-moving automobiles.

Roads create unnatural boundaries of other kinds, too. Wild animals have flexible territories, marked by scent and controlled by the animal's ability to defend its turf. Animal territories can be passed through and are not off-limits to other species. Human territories, however, are often divided by roads and fences: "property lines" that give people the idea that everything inside is theirs. They feel free to do anything they want with the land, including polluting the groundwater and discharging chemicals into the air, and often consider certain animals and plants intruders.

Roads also become garbage dumps for human trash. Roadside waste—equal in bulk to half of the food products bought by Americans each year—can seriously harm wildlife. Plastic six-pack rings can catch and strangle, animals can get their heads caught in small containers, and they can eat what appears to be food but is really plastic or other potentially fatal substances.

Humans also create "highways" on water. On inland lakes and rivers, coastal bays and wetlands, and the open sea, boats and engines cause great damage to wildlife from pollution, garbage, and habitat destruction, as well as physical injury in some cases.

So what can we do to reduce or eliminate these adverse consequences on wildlife? When driving on highways, pay close attention to road signs advising of wildlife crossing zones. (If you know of such locations that have not been marked by road or highway departments, request that signs be installed.) Slow down in those areas, especially in early morning and early evening hours, and stay alert. If you spot an animal—usually by the light reflecting in its eyes—slow down further and be prepared to stop and yield the animal the right-of-way. Often, automobile lights blind a wild animal, and it may become disoriented. Give it time to recover its vision and move on.

Do not litter from cars. Consider taking part in roadside cleanup activities: Many areas now have highway litter programs, in which local individuals and businesses help sponsor cleanup efforts.

Do whatever you can to avoid polluting waterways. Pack out all garbage. Plastics are even more damaging to seabirds and marine mammals in waterways than to land animals along highways. Limit the use of engines, such as outboard and inboard motors and jet skis, because of fuel and noise pollution. Use nonmotorized boats like canoes, sailboats, and rowboats where possible. Keep engines out of shallow, critical wetland habitats, where propellers can easily damage the fragile ecosystem.

Using Consumer Power for Wildlife

Human beings are consumers, especially in this country, and U.S. consumption patterns greatly influence those in other parts of the world. The power of your consumer dollars can help protect wildlife. For example, habitat can be preserved by reducing human demand for and waste of land, paper and wood products, electricity, petroleum products, and metals. Wildlife can be directly protected by reducing the demand for products made from wild animals, such as animal hide boots or clothing.

We can make many specific buying decisions that will protect wildlife and habitat. Make sure that the products you buy, such as souvenirs, jewelry, or leather goods, are not made from endangered species (crocodile skin and tortoiseshell are common examples). For gardening, buy only plants or bulbs that have not been collected from the wild. Plant native rather than exotic species wherever possible. Check labels to choose the least toxic products available for cleaning, pest control, and other household jobs.

Minimize the use of pesticides and herbicides, and try mo ural, nontoxic control methods. Buy organic produce to lessen demand for agricultural products grown with huge amounts of p cides. Conserve energy: Reduced demand for energy will result in wer efforts to drill for oil in sensitive wildlife habitats, to dam rivers for hydroelectric power, and to strip-mine for coal. When purchasing a car, make fuel efficiency one of your chief criteria.

Expanding your "wildlife consciousness" to make choices such as these may not bring the sort of immediate, firsthand gratification you experience from watching squirrels scamper through your backyard trees or finding a nest in the nesting box you have built. The wild animals you are helping may live far away; they may even be generations not born yet. But all these steps, directly personal or more removed, will contribute to improving our species' relationship with our fellow creatures, and our role as earth's stewards.

CHAPTER 3

Caring for Wildlife:
When Humans Can Help

E ncountering a wild animal that is hurt, helpless, or trapped can elicit a sympathetic response even from people who have never felt any personal interest in wildlife before. Children often get their first lessons about wildlife from such situations that occur around the family home: when a bird finds its way inside and can't get out, falls from its nest, or is injured by the family cat; when a litter of baby raccoons is discovered under a porch, apparently abandoned; when a sick or injured sea lion is spotted on a local beach. Children may even learn the hard way that wild creatures are not pets—for instance, by trying to rescue a mouse from the cat or dog and being bitten by the victim for their trouble.

Wildlife rehabilitation centers such as the California Center for Wildlife exist in large part to provide trained care for injured wild creatures and knowledgeable advice to concerned individuals who call to report a situation and who bring in hurt or orphaned animals. Usually closer and more accessible sources of advice than state wildlife agencies, rehabilitation centers have become primary sources of wildlife education for many citizens, a trend that should continue to expand as long as the public perceives the need for and supports such services. Certainly, as people continue to expand their living areas into lands occupied by wildlife, the need for wildlife education and care will grow.

We'll take a brief look at the history of wildlife rehabilitation— and how interested persons can get involved—later in this chapter. First, here are some guidelines based on the experience of CCW for what to do when you encounter "animals in distress."

Injured or Ill Wildlife

If you encounter a situation where a wild animal is clearly disabled and cannot care for itself, almost always you should secure trained care for it—either by transporting it to a facility yourself or by summoning personnel from a wildlife agency to remove it (while you control or keep an eye on its whereabouts).

It's sometimes tempting to try to "play doctor" for a hurt animal, and children are often fascinated with looking at or handling wildlife at close range—a rare event in the course of normal interaction. But it is illegal for private individuals to possess or attempt to treat wildlife without a permit from state or federal regulatory agencies, among whose mandates is public health.

There are good reasons for this. Wildlife rehabilitation centers use special diets and medical techniques. Without adequate training, you can easily harm the animal by feeding it an unsuitable diet, giving it inappropriate medication, or just stressing it through human contact.

Untrained caregivers may inadvertently promote malnutrition and illness by improper feeding. (Such food as bread and cookies, for instance, can seriously compromise the health of wildlife.) They also run the risk of imprinting or socializing the animal to humans, which dooms it for future release back to the wild. They may inadvertently spread animal diseases to humans or other animals by inappropriately releasing a sick creature. Depending on the species, the would-be helper may also risk injury in handling creatures armed with teeth and claws or carrying a disease communicable to humans.

Whom Do You Call?

Whom to call if you come upon an injured or ill wild animal depends on the wildlife agencies found in your area. Generally, three levels of government and private agencies are involved in wildlife protection in the United States:

1. The U.S. Fish and Wildlife Service has authority in matters regarding migratory birds and raptors, as well as federally designated endangered species.

2. Each state has its own state department of fish and wildlife, conservation, or environmental protection that oversees all wildlife not federally protected.

3. On the local level, some cities and/or counties have animal control agencies, which usually focus on domestic animals. Also at the local level are private wildlife rehabilitation and humane societies, funded chiefly through private monies. In places where no locally operated control agency exists, these societies may receive some government funding.

If you have found a wild animal that needs care, check the phone book first for a local wildlife rehabilitation or humane society. They are typically listed in the yellow pages under Animal Shelter and Support Services, Animal Associations, or Humane Societies. These organizations tend to have more expertise with wildlife than do local animal control centers oriented toward domestic pets. If no rehabilitation center or humane society is nearby, ask the animal control shelter if it accepts wildlife.

If it cannot assist, look under state government listings for your department of fish and game, conservation, or environmental protection. State agencies usually have regional offices with field officers who can give you advice about caring for the animal until it can be trans-

Transport small injured or ill wild animals to a care agency in a covered box with cloth or paper lining and a heat source.

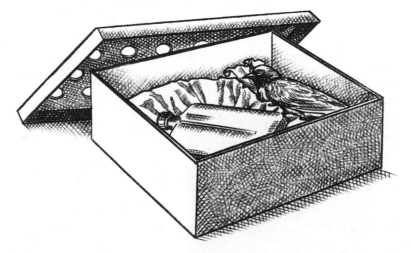

ported to another location for care. A last resort may be to call a local veterinarian, who may know if any veterinarians in your area are licensed to treat wildlife.

Appendix A in this book is a fairly comprehensive listing of wildlife rehabilitation centers throughout the United States, as well as all state wildlife agencies, with addresses and some phone numbers. This should be helpful, but remember that published information can go out of date, so you may have to do a little research on your own.

What Can You Do?

Keeping in mind all the caveats noted about caring for wild animals yourself, you can do some things to prepare the animal for being moved to a care facility and to make it more comfortable in the meantime.

If necessary, and with as little stress to the animal as possible, put it in a box (large enough to hold the creature without cramping it but not so large that it can run or fly around inside), cover the box to keep the stress level down, and transport the animal to a wildlife clinic. If you have a heating pad, heat it up and place it in one part of the box (avoiding direct contact with the animal); it will provide warmth for quite a while. A heating pad can't be kept warm in transit, obviously, so if you have some distance to travel, a hot-water bottle—securely stoppered and wrapped in a towel—may be more effective.

When capturing a small, immobile bird, approach it slowly with a tissue or soft cloth and pick it up in your hand. Place it in a box padded with towels, tissues, or toilet paper—but not cotton wool, which can tangle in the bird's feet and wings—and cover the box. Also put in the box a small jar lid or similar container of water, large enough so the bird can drink but not deep enough that it could drown.

For larger birds and other animals—again, if they are immobile or nearly so—approach with a blanket and gently cover the entire creature to keep it quiet, then lift and place it in a covered box that contains a source of warmth and water.

Do not attempt to feed any injured wild animal. Most are hardy enough that they can survive overnight without food, as long as they have water, and CCW recommends that wildlife not be kept at home longer than overnight before transport to a care facility, unless the home caregiver is properly trained and licensed.

When handling a wild animal of any size and strength, such as a mammal or large raptor, wear protective clothing—sturdy gloves, long sleeves, eyewear, and boots. Also, the possibility of exposure to rabies or other wildlife-carried illnesses is real, so protecting yourself from contact with the saliva or other body fluids of mammals is imperative.

Many wildlife rehabilitation centers offer training in wildlife care techniques and need volunteer assistance. If you want to care for injured wildlife, do so with proper training in conjunction with a well-organized, professional-level wildlife rehabilitation center.

Orphans

If you come upon an apparently orphaned animal in the wild— this happens most often in the spring—it's usually best to leave it alone. Most often, the parents of the "orphan" are close by. Wildlife parents often conceal their young during the day while they feed, returning periodically to feed and check on their babies.

If you interfere with the young animal, it can suffer serious consequences. In the case of all species except birds (but including turkey vultures), human scent can scare the parent away, so once you have touched the baby, it will truly become an orphan and will starve to death. Also, leaving a human scent trail makes it easier for predators to find the young animal. It is better not to disturb the animal, then, unless it is directly imperiled by an unsafe situation or location. If you are concerned about it, take the time to wait and observe for the parent's return before taking other action.

Even if you *have* left human scent with an "orphan," the first treatment effort attempted by many rehabilitators is to try to reunite it with its parent. So if you take home an apparent orphan and call a wildlife care center, don't be surprised if you are advised to return the animal to where you found it so that the parents can reclaim their young. After you have brought the animal back to the original location, observe it from a distance for several hours. If the parent does not show up, then you should probably take it to a care agency.

Except for turkey vultures, birds have no sense of smell and are not affected by human scent. So babies that have fallen from nests can be returned to the nest (if it can be safely reached) without rejection by the parents. Baby birds found on the ground that cannot be replaced in the nest should be placed in a protective box and taken to a wildlife care center. Fledglings (young with feathers) need some time on the ground while they are learning to fly. This is when they are most vulnerable to predators, but that is part of the natural order. Remove a fledgling only if it is in imminent danger.

About Wildlife Rehabilitation

Wildlife rehabilitation—the treatment and care of injured, orphaned, or sick wildlife for release back to the wild—started in the United States between 30 and 40 years ago. (Great Britain's history in wildlife rehabilitation goes back even further.) Caring humans who witnessed the harm done to wild creatures began trying to help restore their health and well-being. Such people recognized the right of wildlife to life and health and responded to the emotional urge to help with practical action.

Before the early 1970s, most wildlife rehabilitation was done by individuals in their homes. Between 1970 and 1975, as environmental awareness rose, organized wildlife rehabilitation centers were founded. In 1974, approximately 60 to 80 rehabilitation centers (organizations with a designated wildlife care building that treated over 100 animals per year) existed, mostly on the East and West coasts.

Since then, organized rehabilitation efforts have undergone amazing growth. There are now well over 1,000 rehabilitation centers throughout the country that belong to one or both professional associations: the National Wildlife Rehabilitators Association and the International Wildlife Rehabilitation Council. These associations sponsor conferences, work on developing wildlife care standards, and help member centers share care techniques and other information.

Despite the growth of wildlife care as an organized profession, individuals still undertake much of the effort. Only an estimated 50 percent of all "permitted" rehabilitators belong to the professional associations, and only 50 to 75 percent of all people doing rehabilitation work in each state hold required permits. Wildlife rehabilitation continues to be very much a grassroots effort.

Wildlife Care Training for Veterinarians

One reason for the growth of wildlife rehabilitation as a separate endeavor is that, traditionally, veterinarian training has not included wildlife care. Veterinarian schools grew up around the food-animal industry and continue to be closely tied to agricultural interests. In the early years of this century, veterinary practices did not even include care for household pets such as cats and dogs. After World War II, in response to economic incentives—people would pay for care of their pets—veterinary schools started training students in small domestic animal care. However, until recently, there were no incentives to train or study wildlife care, because virtually no jobs were associated with the practice.

Interest in wildlife care programs in veterinary education has arisen just in the last 10 to 15 years. For the most part, students volunteering their time in wildlife clinics started such programs with little if any faculty involvement. In some veterinary schools, wildlife care programs are now extensive, and participation is mandatory; in others, no program exists at all. Most schools fall between those extremes. Faculty involvement is gradually increasing as interest and economic incentives grow. Although economic incentives for wildlife care professionals remain limited, that situation appears to be changing as society places greater emphasis on the need to protect the natural abundance and diversity of wildlife.

Permits for Wildlife Rehabilitators

All individuals and organizations that want to work in wildlife rehabilitation—including veterinarians in some states—must obtain permits to do so from the appropriate government agency: state or federal, depending on the animals treated. The U.S. Fish and Wildlife Service controls all permits for rehabilitation work on migratory birds. State wildlife agencies issue permits for all other types of wildlife. Some state agencies do not allow the rehabilitation of certain species that they consider pests or nuisances.

To obtain a permit for migratory bird rehabilitation from the U.S. Fish and Wildlife Service requires a written application. If granted, the permit is valid for three years and must be renewed upon expiration. Any person or organization issued such a permit must keep written records of the number and species of birds treated, the dates of receipt and disposition of each bird, and the name and address of the person bringing the bird in for care. There is currently no requirement to demonstrate skill, training, or expertise in wildlife care to obtain these permits.

State requirements for wildlife rehabilitation permits vary widely. Some state programs—for example, New York's falconry program— have sophisticated testing, qualification, and inspection requirements. Others require no proof of training or knowledgeability before granting a permit.

The Future of Wildlife Rehabililtation

A consensus has emerged that wildlife rehabilitation needs to focus on three avenues for continued improvement: increased training, better documentation of research data and analysis of results, and recognition of the vital educational role played by rehabilitation centers.

TRAINING: Because of limited resources for training in the past, many rehabilitators have had to learn mainly from experience and thus have not always provided the best possible care to the animals they have attempted to aid. To improve wildlife care treatment and the success rate for the numbers of animals able to be released back to the wild, individuals and rehabilitation centers need more and improved training.

Improved training requires expanded availability of programs for veterinary students and access to training for individuals who now perform rehabilitation without training or licenses. This is already happening to some extent: Some rehabilitation centers provide training to volunteers, and some—such as the Wildlife Center in Weyers Cave, Virginia—actually operate as teaching hospitals and provide professional-level training to all interested (including veterinarians).

DOCUMENTATION AND SHARED RESEARCH: Because of its grassroots origins, wildlife rehabilitation has so far focused on actual caregiving rather than on scientific research; thus there has been little contact and professional recognition between rehabilitators and other wildlife professionals such as biologists, pathologists, veterinarians, refuge managers, and endangered species workers. Unfortunately, poor work by a few unpermitted and untrained rehabilitators has negatively affected the attitude of game officials toward wildlife rehabilitation.

Yet wildlife rehabilitation centers are sources of a vast amount of information that could be effectively utilized by management officials—information related to population trends, epidemiological data (diseases and traumas suffered by wildlife), and migratory patterns. Because rehabilitators function with such limited funding, however, little if any of their data has been documented in ways that enable it to be readily analyzed. Efforts are currently under way to develop uniform methods for recording such information on computer and to establish on-line telecommunication networks linking wildlife rehabilitation centers.

In addition to the need for wider access to information about wildlife treated by rehabilitators, there is an ongoing need for those who have developed wildlife care techniques to document and share them with other rehabilitators. Support should be developed for professional writing and publication of information about successful care projects, so that the experience of those who have been involved in wildlife rehabilitation for years can be shared with new volunteers and built upon. Such steps will contribute greatly to improved training for wildlife care volunteers.

PUBLIC EDUCATION: Rehabilitation centers play an important educational role, which the general public and government agencies responsible for wildlife management need to recognize. They answer millions of questions annually from people who need help in dealing with wildlife issues, saving state wildlife agencies large sums they would otherwise have to spend to respond to such calls. (New York has actually started to quantify the amount of money its wildlife centers are saving the state.) And these centers are, for the most part, nonprofit organizations with little or no government funding. Some state agencies have begun to work with rehabilitation centers, providing them with information that the agency wants released to the public.

Rehabilitation centers also educate the public directly about wildlife. Because they are a community resource that encourages the public to visit, call, and bring in wildlife for care, centers can reach people who might not otherwise be concerned with wildlife. They provide firsthand education not only about the care of injured wildlife, but also—probably more importantly—about how people can live in ways that avoid injury to wild creatures in the first place.

To Those Interested in Rehabilitation Work

Because of the recent growth in this field, excellent resources now exist for obtaining training in wildlife care. We strongly encourage those who are seriously interested to seek out training and to become licensed by the applicable agency or agencies. While licenses may still be obtained in some areas where organized rehabilitation work and training are limited, anyone providing care is encouraged to join the professional associations, share information, and visit the better-developed centers and teaching hospitals, where one can take part in internship programs and get as much training as possible within personal time constraints. See Appendix A listings for rehabilitation centers near you.

Introducing the Reference Guide

The early chapters have provided some general information about protecting and preserving wildlife, on both the public and the personal level. The Reference Guide, following, identifies some of the more common North American wildlife, describes basic natural history to help you understand the animal's lifestyle and habits, and suggests specific humane control methods to protect your homes, lands, and families from what some people consider wildlife damage or nuisance. We hope this information helps you and your family to harmoniously share your lives and space with those wonderful creatures.

REFERENCE GUIDE

*to Common North American Wildlife
with Situations and Solutions
for Human-Wildlife Interaction*

Small Land Mammals

The animals covered in this section include raccoons, skunks, opossums, weasels, badgers, moles, hares and rabbits, armadillos, bats, and a variety of rodents. They are grouped together based on their general size and how they interact with humans.

[RACCOONS]

Raccoons (*Procyon lotor*) belong to the Procyonidae ("those who came before dogs") family. This highly intelligent mammal has a rounded head with short nose, small ears, and a sturdy body with minimum-length, thick, grayish brown fur. Raccoons are easily identified by (1) a distinctive pattern of alternating black and yellowish white rings around a large, bushy tail and (2) a unique narrow black face mask with two white patches above the eyes. They average 3 to 3½ feet long (including the tail) and 12 inches high, weigh 15 to 48 pounds, and live for 10 to 13 years.

Females produce one litter a year, numbering from one to six kits and averaging four or five.

Range and Habitat

Over most of the U.S. and southern Canada, except in the western mountain ranges, raccoons are found in many different habitats, especially near streams, ponds, and marshes in mature wooded areas. Their range is expanding farther north into Canada, because of habitat lost to agriculture and the apparent warming of northern weather. As humans have moved into raccoon habitat, this mammal has proven more adaptable than most. For nesting sites it prefers warm, dry, dark, easily protected areas. In the wild, it dens in tree hollows, hollow logs, or sometimes rocky caverns. In urban areas, raccoons may nest in drainpipes, basements, crawl spaces, and house attics. Raccoon populations now are actually densest in suburban and urban areas.

Other Characteristics

Raccoons will eat whatever their environment provides. In their natural environment, they eat insects, nuts, worms, frogs, shellfish, fish, small mammals, birds, eggs, grubs, snakes, and fruits. In agricultural areas, they may feed on corn crops, poultry, and garden and orchard vegetables and fruits. In urban settings, an easily opened garbage can is hard for them to resist. They are nocturnal but are occasionally active in daytime.

They are fairly sociable and often den with other raccoons. In colder regions, raccoons may sleep for a good portion of the winter; in the summer, they find shady, cool places to rest. They are territorial with limited private ranges, approximately 1 mile in diameter. Often their territories overlap with those of other raccoons, but boundary clashes are rare. When confronting each other, they often grunt threateningly but seldom fight.

The species' scientific name, *lotor*, means "the washer," because raccoons have been observed dunking their food in water before eating it. This behavior in captivity is thought to mimic behavior in the wild, where raccoons hunt in or near water and hold their catch submerged before eating it. In the wild, they do not wash all food before eating.

Raccoons have keen senses of smell and hearing. They are strong and agile, hence good tree and fence climbers. Each foot has five long and slender digits, which operate with remarkable dexterity. In the wild, they use their front feet for finding food in water, opening shellfish, and conveying food to the mouth. In adapting to human habitat, they often apply this dexterity to opening garbage cans and pet food storage containers.

Zoologists attribute the raccoon's adaptability to "transmission of culture," a mammalian trait this creature has developed to a high level. The young quickly pick up new skills from adults and then can make their own adjustments or adaptations to new circumstances.

Enemies and Defenses

The raccoon's primary enemies are humans, dog packs, traps, and automobiles. Many would-be larger predators know better than to take on an adult raccoon, a tough fighter with razor-sharp teeth. If threatened, the raccoon will often try a counterthreat, fluffing out its fur so that it appears larger and uttering a throaty growl or cry. Raccoons may appear bold but usually are not aggressive except during mating season or when defending their young. However, their strength, teeth, and claws equip them to defend themselves effectively.

How to Observe

Raccoons are so common that you need not look far for them, and as their natural habitat shrinks, they are increasingly found in urban areas. They are night creatures and will be shy in areas where they are hunted.

Where people do not pursue them with rifles and dogs, they are curious animals. Their tracks are easily identifiable, looking much like a human handprint.

Situations and Solutions

Raccoons Raiding Garbage Cans

WHY IT HAPPENS: Raccoons have learned, through adapting to human habitat, that garbage cans are excellent sources of food.

SUGGESTIONS:

1. To "raccoon-proof" a garbage can, fasten the lid securely with rope, bungee cords, chain, or even weights. To prevent cans from being knocked over and rolled around, secure the handle to a metal or wooden stake driven into the ground.
2. Store garbage cans in wooden bins or in a shed or garage to limit raccoon access.
3. As a last effort, place an inch or so of ammonia-soaked newspaper or rags in the bottom of the garbage can and sprinkle cayenne pepper on top of the garbage to discourage raccoons. Handle ammonia carefully, and keep in mind that it is toxic to children and animals. The ammonia is intended to deter raccoons with its odor, not to injure them.

Raccoons on Porch or in Yard: Fear of Threat to Humans or Pets

WHY IT HAPPENS: Raccoons, like humans, are constantly tending to their basic needs for food and shelter. They find both near us. While they may be just curious, they are probably in search of food and usually are not aggressive unless cornered, mating, or with young.

SUGGESTIONS:

1. Send them off with a good dousing of water from the hose or a bucket.
2. Instruct and remind children not to approach, touch, or feed them.
3. Keep pets in at night when raccoons are most active. Raccoons may attack dogs if cornered; they seldom bother cats unless the cat is territorial and aggressive. Kittens, especially if out at night, may be seen as prey. Store pet food in heavy-duty plastic containers with tamper-resistant lids.
4. Try talking to your neighbors, one or more of whom may deliberately feed raccoons because they are so cute. Try to discourage this practice

by reminding neighbors not to leave out pet food dishes and to store pet food securely.

5. Use pet doors at your own risk. Lock them at night, if possible, or you may be surprised to discover that a skunk, opossum, or raccoon has invited itself into your home. Some newer models can be opened only by pets wearing a special magnetic collar.

Raccoons easily feed from unsecured garbage cans.

Raccoons under the House or Deck

WHY IT HAPPENS: In the mating and nesting season, these animals are especially attracted to warm, dry, dark, and easily defended areas for temporary homes.

SUGGESTIONS:

1. Limit and eliminate access by following these steps:

   * Close off all but one access route to the den area.
   * Gather all materials to close the remaining entrance and place them outside the opening. Sheet metal works best, or you can use sturdy wire mesh or wood; you will also need hammer, nails, and so on.
   * Toss ammonia-soaked rags into the space; the pungent odor annoys the animals with their keen sense of smell. Check daily to ensure that the odor is present; replenish as needed. Place small bowls of ammonia on either side of the entryway; refill daily for at least two weeks. Use ammonia carefully, however, because it can be toxic to children and to domestic and wild animals. The aim is strictly to drive away the raccoon with the odor.
   * Brightly light the area, day and night. This is annoying to nocturnal animals; it is easily accomplished by taping a mechanic's droplight or trouble light to a long two-by-four and sliding it into the space. Or try placing a radio near the opening and playing it loudly day and night. (This may annoy your neighbors more than the raccoons, however.)

- Spread a light layer of flour on the ground outside the entrance, covering an area large enough to record footprints as the animals exit. After sunset, begin checking the flour every 45 minutes for exiting tracks. When you see tracks, seal the opening tightly, unless you hear sounds that indicate the presence of kits.

- If you do hear kits, leave the access open so the mother can tend her young; repeat the flour-tracking process when they begin to follow their mother hunting (at about eight weeks). It is kinder and less stressful to all concerned to wait for the ammonia smell to finally force the mother to move her young than to directly confront and try to remove the animals. Be sure to continue the ammonia treatment at night so the nocturnal mother will look for a new den site. *Do not approach the den when the mother is inside, as her protective instinct can make her dangerous.*

- If you hear noise after closing the entrance, determine where it is coming from. Check outside the blocked entrance, as a determined raccoon will scratch and pull at the barrier to regain access. If the sound is coming from inside the enclosure, an animal is trapped inside; reopen the area and repeat the process until all the den residents have departed.

2. If you are sure there are no kits that would drown, flood the area of occupation, if this can be done easily and without concern for water damage or contact with electrical wiring.

3. Consider live-trapping as the last alternative. It is rarely a permanent solution, because raccoons are usually plentiful enough that others will soon replace those trapped; also, live traps are expensive. Check with local wildlife agencies regarding live-trapping of raccoons and appropriate release sites.

Raccoons in the House

WHY IT HAPPENS: Occasionally a raccoon will find its way into a house through a pet door or chimney and be unable to find its way out.

SUGGESTIONS:

1. A panicked raccoon can cause extensive damage, so close doors to all other rooms in the house, open doors and windows to the outside, and leave the house. Wait quietly for the raccoon to find its way out. Do not use food as a lure; this will make wildlife associate food with

humans and return for more.

2. If the raccoon has not left in a reasonable period of time, call your local wildlife agency. Only professionally trained wildlife workers should attempt capture (as opposed to live-trapping) of raccoons.

Raccoons in the Attic or on the Roof

WHY IT HAPPENS: Attics and roofs can be good nesting locations from a raccoon's point of view.

SUGGESTIONS:

1. Limit access by following the steps under "Raccoons under the House or Deck." Unless the roof is easily accessible to you, you may have to forgo the flour tracking and depend on the other steps. Be sure to keep replenishing the ammonia until you no longer hear sounds in the attic; then close the opening.

2. Remove trellises, vines, shrubs, tree limbs, or other objects that may give animals a route to the roof or attic. Wrap tree trunks with 2-foot-wide sheet metal, positioning it at least 2 feet above the ground to prevent raccoons from jumping over the barrier and climbing trees for access to buildings.

3. Replace shingles, repair holes near eaves, and cover the chimney with heavy mesh wire.

Raccoons in the Chimney

WHY IT HAPPENS: Raccoons will den in uncapped chimneys and even sometimes bear young there. They will use the fireplace flue because of the smoke shelf.

SUGGESTIONS:

1. Prevent entry by capping chimneys with a commercial chimney cap, wire mesh, or other cover.

2. If a raccoon is in your chimney, place a small bowl of ammonia at the base of the chimney so the fumes will carry upward. (Close fireplace doors or set a barrier across the opening to control odor and prevent the raccoon from exiting via the house.) Or lower a bag filled with mothballs or rags soaked in ammonia from the top. Be sure to leave the top open so the animal can climb out. Make sure that kits too young to climb are not left in the chimney; given the opportunity, the mother

will move her young to a new den site. Once the chimney is cleared, put a screen over the top.

Baby Raccoons "Orphaned"

WHY IT HAPPENS: It is normal for raccoon mothers to leave their young in order to hunt. It is also normal for kits to whine and cry like puppies.

SUGGESTIONS: Unless you can observe the area for many hours, it is difficult to determine whether the mother is truly missing or just temporarily away. If the young cry continuously, with no quiet periods during which the mother may be feeding them, call your local wildlife agency to get further information on evaluating the situation.

Raccoons in the Garden or Fruit Trees

WHY IT HAPPENS: Raccoons are good climbers and relish fruit, but they may break branches and compete with the grower's enjoyment of his or her crop. Raccoons also like to help themselves to grapes and corn just before they are ready for picking.

SUGGESTIONS:

1. Keep the yard free of fallen fruit. Wrap a strip of sheet metal (about 2 feet wide) around the trunk of the tree, positioning it at least 2 feet above the ground so the animal cannot jump over it and continue up the trunk.
2. Use extra vigilance in chasing animals away, using lights and loud noises, to deter raccoons long enough for crops to be harvested.

Raccoons in Ponds, Hot Tubs, and Pools

WHY IT HAPPENS: Raccoons are attracted to water because they associate it with fish and other prey in the wild.

SUGGESTIONS:

1. Cover hot tubs and pools at night when animals are active.
2. If the pond isn't too large, submerge a 2-foot-wide wire mesh horizontally around the edge. Roll out the mesh, leaving it lightly secured under water. Raccoons can't reach over the wire and tend not to stand on it because it is unstable. See also suggestions about use of electric fencing, number 6 in the following section.
3. If you are so inclined, leave open access to the pond so the raccoons

can share the water with you.

Raccoons Digging up Garden Plants and Lawn

WHY IT HAPPENS: Raccoons dig in search of worms, insects, and grubs—tiny, wormlike larval stages of insects that live in lawns. The good news is that they won't eat your plants. The bad news is that they will dig them up to get at the food source in the soil below.

SUGGESTIONS:

1. Sprinkle lawns or planters with cayenne pepper to discourage grub hunters.
2. Control grub populations so that raccoons will not be drawn to your lawn in the first place. A commercial product called Grub Attack is an effective organic control.
3. Fasten bird netting over garden plants. It is easier for raccoons to dig elsewhere than to remove the netting.
4. Improve existing fences by enclosing any open area between the bottom of the fence and the ground. Or install fence extenders facing outward at a 45-degree angle on top of each post, with two or three strands of wire strung between them.
5. If the area is fairly small, try sinking jars filled with ammonia into the ground, with sponges as wicks. Be sure the jars are anchored in the soil to prevent spilling. Or hang socks filled with mothballs.
6. Serious gardeners might consider an electrified fence. String ordinary, 2-millimeter galvanized wire along insulator posts around the perimeter. The wire should start about 8 inches above the ground to prevent crawling underneath, and lines should be spaced close together so animals cannot reach through. Connect the wires to an approved fence charger with alternating current not exceeding 12 volts, which can be purchased relatively cheaply at feed stores. Be sure to check with your local building inspection department for installation guidelines and/or limitations.

Concern about Rabies and Other Diseases

FACTS: Raccoons, like many wild animals, carry fleas. Like other animals, including both domestic and wild, they may be infected with certain diseases that are transmittable to humans and pets. These diseases include rabies, tuberculosis, and canine and feline distemper. Any warm-blooded animal can contract rabies; in the U.S., skunks, raccoons, foxes, and bats are the most likely wild candidates. The incidence within a species varies from one part of the country to another.

SUGGESTIONS:

1. Keep children away from wild animals.
2. Keep your pets' vaccinations up to date. If you see an animal acting erratically, have someone keep it in view and call your local wildlife agency. Any wild animal bite that breaks the skin must be reported to your state or local health department. The raccoon or other animal should be captured, if possible, to be checked for rabies, which necessitates destroying the animal—all the more reason to avoid close encounters.

Continuing Raccoon Problems

WHY IT HAPPENS: Using the techniques described here has not completely stopped troublesome raccoon visits to your home and yard.

SUGGESTIONS:

1. If you cannot resolve problems with raccoons by other means, a final alternative is to use live traps to capture the animals. Consult your local wildlife agency to determine whether trapping raccoons is allowed under state law. In some states, wildlife relocation is illegal.
2. Do not trap between October and March, except in mild climates, because relocated raccoons may be unable to find suitable dens and will die from exposure or lack of food. Also, take care not to relocate a female raising young, which are highly unlikely to survive her loss.
3. Live traps are available in most hardware stores and should be baited with apples, dog food, oatmeal and honey, or other aromatic bait. Once caught, the raccoon should be released right away in any area distant enough (at least 5 miles) to ensure against its return. It should not be released where it can trouble other people.
4. Live-trapping will not necessarily completely stop raccoon visitation, because others may move into the area. Ultimately, as long as they are kept out of the home and their interaction with children and pets is limited, consider raccoons friendly visitors with whom you can share the natural setting of your home.

[SKUNKS]

Skunks are members of the weasel family (Mustelidae). There are four species of skunk in North America: striped skunks (*Mephitis mephitis*), hooded skunks (*M. macroura*), spotted skunks (*Spilogale putorius*), and scarce hognosed skunks (*Conepatus mesoleucus*). Although their markings vary, these bushy-tailed creatures are always black-and-white and absolutely unmistakable.

The most common are striped skunks, measuring 20 to 30 inches long (including the wide, bushy tail) and weighing 6 to 10 pounds (about the size of a house cat), with two wide, white stripes on its back that meet on its head; and spotted skunks, about half that size, with white spots instead of stripes. All skunks have small heads and eyes, pointed snouts, and short legs that make them seem to waddle. Their strong forefeet and long nails make them excellent diggers. They tend to be slow-moving animals, never in much of a hurry, and are generally poor climbers.

A litter of from one to seven young, averaging five, is born from late April to early June.

Range and Habitat

Striped skunks range throughout the U.S., Canada, and Mexico, in all types of terrain. An individual's territory may span 30 to 40 acres. In the wild, skunks tend to den in shallow burrows or hollow logs. They prefer semiopen country and bushlands and are hardly ever found more than 2 miles from a water source. Where urbanization has occurred, skunks have adapted to denning beneath buildings, decks, dumps, and woodpiles and are capable of burrowing a den a foot or so underground, with well-hidden entrances. They like warm, dry, dark, and defensible areas; most house basements and crawl spaces qualify.

Other Characteristics

Skunks are generally nocturnal and begin foraging at sunset. (With their black fur and sensitivity to light, they try to avoid hot, sunny days.) Skunks are omnivorous and help keep the rodent population in check. They often travel 5 to 10 miles within their territory at night, looking for field mice and other small rodents as well as lizards, frogs, birds, eggs, garbage, acorns, and fallen fruits. They also dig for insects, especially beetles, larvae, and earthworms. An estimated 70 percent of a skunk's diet consists of insects considered harmful to humans.

Skunks can find ideal shelter under your front porch.

Skunks do not seem to maintain well-defined territories, but they do regularly use the same pathways between their burrows and hunting areas. The western spotted skunk is even less territorial, with different individuals using the same burrows at different times. While not true hibernators, skunks take long winter naps, during which groups consisting of many females and only one male may den together in the same burrow. To prepare for the winter slowdown, skunks increase their food intake during the fall.

Enemies and Defenses

The skunk's chief enemies are automobiles and great horned owls, both of which kill skunks in large numbers. Skunks rarely attack unless cornered or defending their young. If approached by an intruder and unable to flee, a skunk will usually fluff its fur, shake its tail, stamp the ground with its front feet, growl, stand on its hind legs, turn its head and spit to scare the potential attacker. If those techniques do not work, it will lift up its tail and spray.

The chemical skunks spray at their enemies is a sulfur compound called N-bulymercaptan. It is ejected in a fanlike pattern from two small openings near the animal's rectum. The glands that produce the chemical hold enough for five or six full-powered sprays, but skunks seldom spray without warning or cause. Although they have sharp teeth, they rarely use them in defense, because their spray is most accurate and effective at a range of up to 15 feet.

How to Observe

Striped skunks are everywhere. Anywhere in skunk country, a nighttime stroll with a flashlight is likely to turn up a skunk. Since they like carrion, they often walk along country roads looking for carcasses, and this contributes to their high mortality rate caused by cars. If you see a skunk in the wild, stay far away (at least 20 feet) to avoid being sprayed.

Situations and Solutions

Skunks around the Home

WHY IT HAPPENS: Nearly as adaptable as raccoons, skunks find food and nesting sites around human habitations. The best protection against them is to modify your habitat to limit resources available to them.

SUGGESTIONS:

1. Control garbage cans and pet foods as food sources.
2. Close openings in buildings with boards or wire mesh that extend at least 8 to 10 inches underground.
3. To prevent skunks from digging under a structure, dig a trench 1½ feet deep and six inches wide along the exterior wall. Place wire mesh vertically so that it extends 1½ feet down, and bend the bottom 6 inches outward at an angle. Backfill the trench with dirt or cement once the wire is positioned.

Skunks Living under the House

WHY IT HAPPENS: Skunks choose the same general living areas as raccoons, but they are not good climbers and therefore cannot enter attics. Instead they may burrow under foundations or where decking enclosures meet the ground.

SUGGESTIONS:

1. You usually smell a skunk before you see it. A persistent, faint skunk odor around a 4- to 6-inch-diameter hole indicates that a skunk may be living inside. To find out, cover the hole with loose dirt; if a skunk is in residence, it will dig out during the night. Allow three days for this test; if dirt remains undisturbed, then close the opening with masonry, boards, or hardware cloth.
2. If you determine that a skunk is in residence, use the ammonia method described in the section about raccoons.

3. Installing one-way doors on entrances to skunk dens can also be effective, allowing the skunk to leave at night but barring it from re-entering. Leave the door in place for two to three nights to make sure that the skunk has left, and watch for any new holes nearby. Do not use one-way doors during May or June, when babies may be in the den. If the mother cannot return, the babies will starve. This is inhumane and can also cause odor problems. A one-way door can be constructed of a wooden frame the size of the opening, rigid wire stakes to hold the frame in place, and a double layer of hardware cloth "hinged" at the top. See illustration.

Skunks Digging Up the Yard

WHY IT HAPPENS: Insects and grubs are a primary food source, and skunks have strong front claws adapted for digging them out of the soil.

SUGGESTIONS:

1. Place mothball-filled socks and/or sprinkle cayenne pepper around your yard.
2. Start a nontoxic insect-control program (especially for grubs).

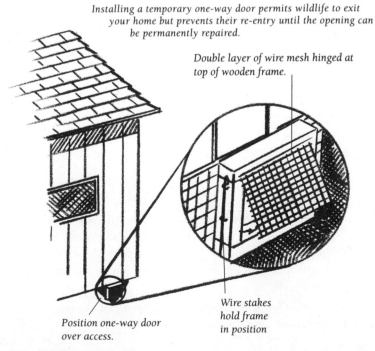

Installing a temporary one-way door permits wildlife to exit your home but prevents their re-entry until the opening can be permanently repaired.

Double layer of wire mesh hinged at top of wooden frame.

Wire stakes hold frame in position

Position one-way door over access.

3. Fences are effective as long as they are buried at least 1½ feet in the ground.

4. As a last resort, live-trap and release skunks. Bait traps with chicken parts, cat food, tuna, or peanut butter. Wooden traps are better than wire because they provide more protection from spray. Cover wire traps (except the entrance) with some kind of heavy cloth to help keep the animal calm and protect against spray. If you find a skunk in an uncovered wire trap, move slowly toward the trap holding a tarp or other heavy covering in front of you to shield against spray. If the skunk appears agitated, back off and approach when it is calmer. When you can get close enough, place the tarp over the trap; skunks in a dark, covered trap usually remain calm if handled carefully. Captured skunks should be released as soon as possible, at least 10 miles away in suitable habitat. Live-trapping is only a temporary solution, because other skunks may move in, so take steps to deter skunks from frequenting your yard.

Skunk Odor in the House

WHY IT HAPPENS: Skunks may be fighting under your house or be frightened by another animal, perhaps your pet.

SUGGESTIONS:

1. Air the house out thoroughly. Use fans, under the house if necessary (where the odor usually originates).

2. Spraying acidic solutions such as diluted vinegar can help counteract skunk spray, which is alkaline.

3. Use chlorine bleach, ammonia, and commercial products containing neutroleum alpha to clean odor from inanimate objects. *Do not use bleach or ammonia on pets.* When cleaning skunk-sprayed items, be sure to protect your eyes and wear a mouth mask.

Skunks Straying into the Garage or Basement

WHY IT HAPPENS: Skunks most likely have been foraging for food and mistakenly entered a garage or basement.

SUGGESTIONS:

1. Leave a door to the outside open and let the skunk exit on its own. If you try to make it move, it will probably spray and create many more

problems than if left alone.

2. If you think the skunk is sick, follow the directions for dealing with diseased skunks.

Skunks in the Window Well

WHY IT HAPPENS: Skunks in search of food or denning area may get into a below-ground-level foundation window well and then be unable to get out.

SUGGESTIONS:

1. The skunk needs a means of exiting the window well. The best approach is to place a rough board (so skunk feet can grip) in the well at no more than a 45-degree angle to allow the skunk to climb out.

   • When approaching the window to position the board, stay low and out of the skunk's sight. If possible, a second person should observe the skunk during this procedure; if it exhibits any defensive behaviors, such as raising its tail or stamping its feet, the humans should retreat.

   • Another way to get the board in the well is to dangle it from string attached to a long pole, which keeps people well away from a possible spray.

   • Once the board is placed, keep all people and animals away from the well until after dark. The skunk will leave on its own then.

2. To keep skunks and other wildlife out of window wells, either leave permanent exit ramps in the wells or cover them with tight-fitting wire mesh.

Skunks in a Chicken Coop

WHY IT HAPPENS: Through adapting to human habitat, skunks have learned that unprotected poultry are a ready food source.

SUGGESTIONS: The only solution to poultry predation by skunks is to securely enclose poultry, especially at night. Repair all openings in coop or fencing. Fencing should extend 6 to 8 inches underground to prevent skunks and other animals from digging under.

Humans Sprayed by Skunks

WHY IT HAPPENS: If a person surprises a skunk in a situation where neither can retreat, the skunk will spray in self-defense. Skunk spray in human eyes is extremely irritating and can cause temporary blindness, but no permanent damage.

SUGGESTIONS:

1. Flush eyes liberally with cold water to ease irritation.
2. Wash skin with carbolic soap and water, tomato juice, or vinegar.
3. Depending on the severity of the spray, you may be able to save clothing by washing repeatedly in vinegar water and/or hanging it outside for a month or so before dry-cleaning. For the worst sprays, however, it may be best to discard or burn the clothing because it will hold the skunk odor for a long time.

Pets Sprayed by Skunks

WHY IT HAPPENS: Skunks spray in defense against attack or to protect their young.

SUGGESTIONS: The quicker you take action, the more completely you can remove the odor. Wash your pet with tomato juice or diluted vinegar to counteract the chemical makeup of the skunk spray. Skunk Off and similar preparations containing neutroleum alpha, available from some wildlife agencies and pet stores, are effective.

Concern about Rabies and Other Diseases

FACTS: In some parts of the country, rabies in the skunk population is a serious problem. Although skunks are usually nocturnal, exceptions can include newly weaned skunks who are still mastering skunk behavior. However, rabies can also cause skunks to be active during daylight hours. Typical behaviors of a rabies-infected skunk are walking in circles, falling, and being overly friendly or lethargic. See also the section on Concern about Rabies and Other Diseases under Raccoons.

SUGGESTIONS:

1. *Stay away from the skunk!* Keep children and pets indoors.
2. Call your local humane society or other wildlife care agency *immediately.*
3. If possible, have someone stay in visual contact with the animal until help arrives.
4. If a person or pet is bitten, report the incident to your state or local health department. The skunk must be caught by the authorities to

determine if it is rabid. Contact a physician or veterinarian immediately. If capture of the animal is not possible, the human victim must undergo the postexposure preventative rabies inoculation series— the only sure protection against contracting this fatal disease.

5. Keep pets inside at night, when skunk encounters most frequently occur.

6. Keep pet rabies vaccinations up to date, and if your pet has a run-in with a skunk, check to determine whether the pet has been bitten. Even pets with current vaccinations may not be completely immune; dogs bitten by potentially rabid animals are usually held in quarantine (and sometimes euthanized). Capturing the biter may be the only way to avoid such extreme measures.

[OPOSSUMS]

The intriguing opossum (*Didelphis virginiana*) is the only marsupial (that is, mammal with a pouch for carrying and nursing young) native to North America. This mammal has grayish white fur, weighs 4 to 15 pounds, and is 2 to 3 feet long, including its ratlike tail. Males are commonly larger than females. The opossum's head is white; the pointed snout, feet, and legs are black; the toes are whitish pink; and the ears are naked flaps of skin. Opossums have 50 sharp teeth, the most of any mammal. Because of its body type, the opossum is sometimes mistaken for a large rat.

After a 12-day gestation period (probably the shortest of all marsupials), 5 to 25 young no bigger than bees are born blind and naked. They instinctively crawl the 2 inches from the birth canal to the mother's pouch (it takes about 10 minutes), where they attach themselves to 1 of 13 nipples. The nipples swell in their mouths, providing secure attachment and a constant food source for more than 2 months.

Range and Habitat

Before 1800, opossums in North America were found only in the southeastern U.S. The animal's range today includes the eastern two-thirds of the country, excluding the upper plains states and the Pacific coast. Their range is limited northward by cold temperatures and westward by hot, arid climates. They thrive in temperate foothills, farmland, woodland, and rural and urban areas. An individual's home range varies from 3 to 40 acres, and opossums will use a number of dens within their home range.

Most opossums stay near water, creating dens in hollow trees or taking over other animals' vacated burrows. In urban areas, they may den in brush piles and culverts and under buildings and decks.

Other Characteristics

Opossums are among the most primitive mammals. They lived during the time of the dinosaurs and have survived by adapting to human habitat and being able to eat just about anything. They dig roots, beetles, ants, grasshoppers, and earthworms. They also scavenge for carrion and eat eggs, vegetables, and fruits, including corn, persimmons, berries, and grain. Garbage, mice, frogs, and venomous snakes are also in their diet. Opossums love snails.

They have a life span of three years in captivity and up to three years in the wild. Another unusual trait of opossums is that they continue growing throughout their lifetimes. They have a high mortality rate at all stages: 10 to 25 percent of young still in the pouch do not survive, and of those that survive weaning, fewer than 10 percent live longer than one year. Opossums are nest builders and nocturnal, spending much of the day in their dens and foraging for food at night. Occasionally they are seen during the day.

In winter, opossums sleep for long periods of time but do not truly hibernate. Unlike other mammals, they lack methods for storing food or energy, so they need ready food sources year-round. They are susceptible to cold and may become torpid, lying in the den for days at a time during extreme cold spells. In the northern part of their range, it's common to see opossums with frostbitten ears and tails.

Opossums have strong prehensile tails and opposable "thumbs" on their hind feet, which make them clever tree climbers; the tail is also used as a fifth limb to carry items such as grass to line a nest site. Contrary to myth, opossums do not sleep hanging upside down by their tails. They can hang from the tail only for short periods and use it primarily for grasping.

Enemies and Defenses

Opossums are preyed on by every carnivore found in their range. Dogs, foxes, hawks, and owls are some of their chief natural predators. Humans take a large toll on opossum populations through automobile kills and, in some areas, hunting and trapping for meat and fur. Opossums are also susceptible to malnutrition and diseases caused by worms, fleas, and ticks.

The opossum's first defense when threatened is to try to escape by climbing the nearest tree, although it is a very slow runner. If cornered on the ground, it will growl, hiss, and bare its 50 sharp teeth. It may also emit a smelly substance from its anal glands, drool, and defecate. But its primary defense against predation is "playing possum": The animal's brain and nervous system react to fear by automatically throwing the opossum into a catatonic state, which lowers heartbeat and respiration.

How to Observe

Seeking an opossum in the wild is best done at night. Many thousands are killed each year by cars when the animals venture onto roads to feed on other highway victims. A nighttime walk along a country path bordering a stream or marsh will occasionally turn up an opossum.

Situations and Solutions

Opossums in the Yard, in Garbage, or under the House

WHY IT HAPPENS: Opossums often look for food or for a nesting site around human dwellings. Opossum sightings around the home tend to be reported more often than sightings of other animals, perhaps because people cannot identify them and so are fearful. Unless cornered, these animals are not dangerous.

SUGGESTIONS:

1. Refer to the sections on Raccoons and Skunks for effective methods of removing these animals from dwellings.
2. Fence in your backyard or garbage can area. Secure can lids and take pet food and pets in at night.
3. If you catch an opossum raiding pet food or a garbage can, do not attempt to pick it up or corner it. When threatened, opossums can—but rarely do—attack with their sharp teeth. Use bright lights; make loud noises by banging pans, rustling paper, opening/closing doors, or playing radios; and/or squirt water to frighten them away.
4. Carefully place ammonia-soaked rags, mothballs in socks, and/or cayenne pepper in strategic places surrounding the area most frequented by opossums.

Opossums Raiding Poultry Yards, Corn Crops, or Gardens

WHY IT HAPPENS: Opossums have learned that unsecured poultry pens and gardens are ready food sources.

SUGGESTIONS:

1. Proper maintenance of enclosed poultry yards and houses will deter opossums. Basic poultry fencing or electric fencing works well, and all buildings should have access holes covered.

2. Opossums will help themselves to ripe fruit. Use tree wrap, wire mesh, or hardware cloth to prevent animals from climbing fruit tree trunks.

3. As a last resort, live-trap opossums with 9" x 9" x 32" traps baited with fish, apples, or canned pet food. If there is a chance that the trap may attract a skunk instead, cover it with burlap so the animal inside can be handled safely. Transport opossums at least 5 miles away for release in suitable habitat. Avoid trapping during early spring and summer, when young may be orphaned by the capture of their mothers.

Young Opossums "Orphaned"

WHY IT HAPPENS: The mother may be temporarily away hunting, or the young may truly be orphaned.

SUGGESTIONS: If opossums seem healthy and are 7 inches long or more (not including the tail), they are mature enough to survive on their own. Smaller ones are not yet self-feeding; either take them to or call a wildlife care agency.

[WEASELS]

Weasels *(Mustela* spp.) are members of the Mustelidae family, which also includes badgers, wolverines, skunks, and river otters. Mustelids have in common the characteristic of anal musk glands that they use for marking territory and defense. Treated here are long-tailed weasels *(Mustela frenata)*, black-footed ferrets *(M. migripes)*, and American mink *(M. vison)*. Generally, members of the weasel genus are long and slim with long necks and short legs. They weigh less than 4 pounds, are purely carnivorous, and sport luxurious fur coats sought after by trappers. The North American long-tailed weasel *(Mustela frenata,* hereafter referred to just as "weasel") measures 11 to 17 inches, including the tail. Adult males weigh 7 to 10 ounces, females 3 to 7 ounces. Weasels have small eyes set into an elongated, tapered skull. Their coat is reddish brown above with white to yellowish white underparts in the summer; the brown tail is tipped with black. They molt from October through November, their fur color changing to winter white in regions of heavy snow and cold. In the spring molt (February through April), their brown coloring returns.

Minks resemble weasels but are larger, and their dark brown coats do not change color seasonally. Black-footed ferrets are the same size as minks, with a buff-colored coat, brown black face mask, brownish head, black feet and legs, and black-tipped tail. (Ferrets sold in pet stores are a European strain; the black-footed ferret native to North America is a separately evolved species, currently endangered.)

Litters of four to nine young are born blind, naked, and helpless during late April to early May.

Range and Habitat

Weasels are found throughout North America in habitats from conifer forests to farmland to open, dry grasslands. They prefer open woodlands, brushland, and rocky areas near water. Minks prefer water-related habitat. Endangered black-footed ferrets originally were found primarily in the plains and eastern Rocky Mountain regions, where they preyed on prairie dogs and lived in their burrows. (See Conservation Note below.)

Other Characteristics

Weasels feed primarily on mice, rats, moles, rabbits, chipmunks, frogs, snakes, worms, small birds, and eggs. Insects and plants contribute a small portion to their diet. They consume up to 30 to 40 percent of their body weight in a single night. Minks eat a similar diet but can take larger prey, including their favorite, muskrats. Black-footed ferrets prey chiefly on prairie dogs; they may supplement their diet with rabbits, mice, and ground squirrels.

Weasels are accomplished predators, relying on acute senses of smell, sight, and hearing. They are fearless, often attacking rats and young rabbits much bigger than themselves, and are well adapted for hunting burrowing prey by sliding their bodies into the burrows. They also swim to capture water prey and climb trees after bird eggs and fledglings. Their extremely strong jaws with strong canine and shearing teeth can penetrate the skulls of their prey with a single bite.

Weasels live and hunt alone. They are curious, active year-round, and generally nocturnal, although they are sometimes seen during the day. Their "speech" includes hisses, screeches, purrs, and chatters. Their burrows, which often have several entrances, are found in abandoned rodent dens, hollow logs, and rock crevices; the sleeping and birthing chamber is lined with leaves and fur from their prey. Long-tailed weasels live an average of one to two years and a maximum of four to five.

Weasels are territorial, using scent signals to mark boundaries. Males tend to be more territorial than females, and they regularly cover all of their territory in search of food. (They may travel as much as 2 to 3 miles in search of food during a single night.) Territories may overlap, especially in good weather when the food supply is plentiful. Territories are kept for years by the same individuals, who are only replaced if they die or move away on their own. Depending on the species, male weasel territories range from 12 to 40 acres; those of females are smaller and not as well defined.

Enemies and Defenses/Conservation Note

Weasels' enemies are mainly raptors, including eagles, hawks, and owls. Minks and house cats also prey upon them. Humans have been a potent foe of weasels and minks, through extensive trapping for fur and poisoning to protect domestic livestock. Channelization of streams and rivers has destroyed important water habitat that weasels and minks rely on. Weasels' primary defense is escape, but when annoyed or frightened, they may emit a foul odor from anal scent glands.

The extermination of prairie dogs during the settlement of the West almost resulted in the extinction of the black-footed ferret. By 1972, it was thought to be extinct, but sightings continued to be reported. A captive breeding program in Wyoming has resulted in the increase of the black-footed ferret population to 300 in captivity; the goal is to establish 200 breeding adults and start returning the species to the wild in several populations spread over their former prairie range.

How to Observe

Weasels, black-footed ferrets, and minks are not easily seen in the wild, because of their nocturnal habits and their tendency to stay away from human habitat. If you are lucky enough to catch sight of one in the wild, it will likely hide quickly. If you do observe one, stay clear and do not attempt to approach.

Situations and Solutions

Weasels in a Henhouse or Other Stock Enclosure

WHY IT HAPPENS: Weasels in the wild normally do not kill more than they need to eat. However, prey movement triggers their predatory behavior, so if a weasel makes its way into a henhouse, for example, and the hens are unable to escape, their panicked movements trigger the weasel's instinct and it ends up killing all of them.

Weasels perform a valuable service to humans by helping to control the small-rodent population. Usually that benefit far outweighs the occasional damage they may cause. Whether a domestic animal was killed by a weasel can be determined by observing the carcass. Weasels kill by biting at the base of the skull or under the wing, and they usually eat the back of the head and the neck. Also, the tops of eggs are bitten off and the contents eaten.

SUGGESTIONS:

1. To protect domestic animals from weasels, make sure the henhouse or other enclosure is well protected by using heavy-gauge mesh wire to cover up holes in the structures. This will keep out most potential predators. If it appears that predators are burrowing to get in, fine mesh screening can be buried vertically several feet deep around the outer perimeter of the structure.
2. Weasels can be caught in live traps baited with fresh meat. Once caught, they should be released as soon as possible in suitable habitat at least 5 miles away. Live-trapping alone will not solve the problem, because other individuals may move into the area.

[BADGERS]

Badgers *(Taxidea taxus)* are members of the Mustelidae family. They have fat, low-slung bodies with long hair, and short, stout, strong legs with five toes and strong claws on each foot for digging. The badger has been described as looking like "a miniature wagon load of hay as it trundles along on its short legs." Badgers are about 2 feet long and weigh 12 to 25 pounds.

Range and Habitat

In North America, badgers prefer open grassland. They range from southwestern Canada into the northern Great Lakes region, spreading throughout the prairie, mountain, and desert states to the Pacific coast and south into Mexico. They prefer loose, sandy soils for easy digging.

A litter of one to five cubs (averaging two or three) is born from March to May.

Other Characteristics

Badgers eat a wide variety of foods, mainly seeds, berries, and other wild fruits. They also feed on worms, beetles, bees, honeycombs, wasp nests, rats, lizards, snakes, ground-nesting birds and their eggs, and young rabbits and will eat carrion from the kills of larger predators. They are skillful predators, using their acute smell, sight, and hearing. They search for food both above and below ground, digging with their strong feet and claws. Their jaws are extremely strong, with well-developed canine and shearing teeth, so they can penetrate the skulls of their prey with a single bite. They sometimes bury kills for later eating.

Unlike other mustelids, badgers have a complex social organization. After mating is completed, several families will use the same burrow, or sett, and entrance. When the young are born, the males move to a separate part of the sett. They are territorial and use scent signals to mark their boundaries. Badger territorial behavior outside the burrow is still being studied.

Badgers are nocturnal animals, hunting and inspecting their territories at night, so it is difficult to keep track of their whereabouts. They become inactive and go into a deep sleep during the winter, though this is not a true hibernation state.

Badgers are known for their ferocious fighting behavior and dangerously sharp teeth and claws. They have been known to fight off as many as four dogs at once. Coyotes, which know better than to attack badgers, have learned to use them to help flush out prey. When a coyote sees earth shooting up from a hole, it knows a badger is digging after prey and will stand by in hopes of catching whatever escapes.

Enemies and Defenses

The badger's chief enemies are humans because of habitat lost to human development and trapping for pelts. Badger fur was once used for making shaving brushes. While these animals are considered pests, they actually are an asset to farmers, keeping down rodent, snake, rabbit, and insect populations. Because of their fighting abilities, badgers were severely persecuted in Great Britain, where, in a long-illegal activity called badger baiting, the jaw or leg of a badger was broken and the handicapped animal was thrown into a pit to defend its life against a pack of dogs.

Although badgers normally may appear lumbering, they can move quickly when threatened, either to attack or escape.

How to Observe

Badgers are extremely shy and often can be more easily heard than seen. Because of their ferocity, do not attempt to approach or touch a badger. One that feels at all threatened will attack.

Situations and Solutions

Badgers Preying on Poultry

WHY IT HAPPENS: If a natural food source is not available, badgers may learn to take available domestic poultry.

SUGGESTIONS: Follow suggestions described in the section on Weasels for controlling access to poultry enclosures.

[MOLES]

Although they have burrowing habits like rodents, moles (*Talpa* spp., Talpidae family) are considered members of the shrew order. Moles have thick, heavyset bodies 4 to 6 inches long; long, naked snouts; short, sparsely haired tails; and short, powerful legs. Their front legs are sickle shaped with five-fingered clawed "hands" to help with burrowing and earth moving. Their short, almost velvety coats are brown or blackish brown above with lighter colors underneath. Their small, almost blind eyes are hidden by a skin membrane or their coat; the ears also are not visible.

Range and Habitat

Several species of moles range throughout Canada and the U.S. They prefer soft soil close to rivers, streams, and other waterways and spend most of their time underground in their tunnels.

Only one litter, ranging from two to seven young, is born per year, in nesting chambers situated deeper in the tunnel system than the mother's living area.

Other Characteristics

Moles live and feed primarily underground in their complex system of burrows and tunnels. They come to the surface only occasionally to gather nesting materials. When on the surface, they are vulnerable to predators due to their poor eyesight and slow movement.

The mole's tunnel system can be from just a few inches up to 3 feet deep. The main tunnel runways are usually no more than 2 inches in diameter. Vertical shafts to the surface are marked by characteristic mole-hills, mounds of earth created from digging the tunnel and pushing the loosened dirt out of the hole. Molehills tend to be circular, with a center entrance hole plugged with earth, as distinct from gopher holes, where earth is pushed out in more of a fan shape, with the entrance hole to one side. Moles may also create surface-feeding burrows that look like ridges by pushing rather than digging through the soil just below ground level. Surface-level tunnels or ridges are used only temporarily and may never be reused. Deep runways are part of the mole's permanent territorial complex.

Moles are capable of moving forward or backward through their tunnels. They dig with their front feet while pushing the loose soil behind them with the hind limbs to keep the tunnel clear. To establish territory boundaries, they scent-mark their tunnels. Solitary creatures, moles rarely leave their individual territories, avoiding overlap and contact with neighboring moles as much as possible. When contact occurs, aggressive conflicts usually result. Unless displaced, a mole occupies the same territory throughout its lifetime.

Tunnels are used as living and food storage areas. Moles feed on earthworms, insects, larvae, and slugs; they have also been known to eat some roots, bulbs, and seeds. They can consume their own body weight in one day and are active feeders day and night.

Enemies and Defenses

Moles' natural enemies are large predators, including badgers, wolverines, and coyotes, which can dig them out of their burrows. More often, however, they are killed by humans, who have historically poisoned and trapped moles. Although moles seldom eat plant materials, their burrowing can damage gardens and lawns. Often plant damage is attributed to moles when, in fact, other creatures that use the mole's tunnels, such as mice and voles, are to blame.

How to Observe

Because they live underground, it is extremely rare to observe a mole directly. Usually the molehills of dirt marking their tunnel shafts indicate that a mole is nearby.

Situations and Solutions

Moles Burrowing in a Garden or Lawn

WHY IT HAPPENS: Burrowing, especially near the surface, is the mole's way of searching for food. These animals play an instrumental part in keeping down the insect population.

SUGGESTIONS:

1. Use nontoxic methods of insect and grub control to help control mole populations. Moles are drawn only to areas that provide sufficient food.
2. Erect barriers around small flower or garden beds by burying quarter-inch mesh hardware cloth 12 inches deep, with a 12-inch extension at a 90-degree angle.
3. Use chemical repellents that include any product containing thiram, a protectant for bulbs. Do not use naphthalene, moth flakes, or moth-balls as mole repellents.
4. Sound repellents—including "mole wheels," vibrating windmills, children's pinwheels, or similar devices—can be pushed into the tunnels to carry vibrations disturbing to the moles. Currently available are some battery-operated sound repellents that claim effectiveness over limited areas; be sure that such products can be returned for refund if they are not effective.
5. Live-trapping of moles should be attempted as a last resort, because moles survive only a few hours without feeding. A simple method is to use a coffee can or similar container.
   - Identify an active tunnel by tamping down on surface runways and then observing areas where the ridges and molehills return. The re-building or reuse of those areas indicates that they are active, major runways in the mole's system.
   - Bury the container. Then collapse the tunnel in front of and behind the can. Moles will dig through any temporary collapse of loose soil in the tunnel, so they will dig through and become lodged in the can.
   - Monitor the trap frequently to ensure that any trapped animal is removed and relocated immediately.

[HARES AND RABBITS]

Hares and rabbits belong to the mammal order Lagomorpha and the family Leporidae. Because their chisellike front teeth are so similar to those of mice, rats, and beavers, at one time hares and rabbits were thought to be rodents. Although they are in separate genera, the terms *hare* and *rabbit* sometimes are used interchangeably. True hares (*Lepus* ssp.) found in North America include the European or brown hare (*Lepus europaeus*), the black-tailed and white-tailed hares (*L. insularis* and *L. townsendii*, respectively, both known as jackrabbits), the Arctic hare (*L. timidus*), and the snowshoe hare (*L. americanus*). True rabbits found in North America include the eastern cottontail (*Sylvilagus floridanus*), the desert cottontail (*S. audubonii*), and the swamp rabbit (*S. aquatius*).

HARES: The hares known as jackrabbits have extremely long hind legs for fast running and long leaps. The Arctic hare, weighing 2 to 2½ pounds, is the smallest hare and looks more like a cottontail rabbit than a jackrabbit. Its black-tipped ears are shorter than its head. In the winter, it is white, but the underside of its tail is brown, not white like the cottontail's. Summer color is dark brown, whitish under the tail.

The black-tailed jackrabbit is brownish gray with an off-white underside. The tail has a black strip above extending to the rump. It is 19 inches long, with a 2- to 4-inch tail and 4- to 7-inch-long ears, and generally weighs 4 to 8 pounds. The white-tailed jackrabbit is the largest of the native hares, weighing from 6 to 9 pounds. It is 18 to 20 inches long and light brownish with a white tail. This hare changes color to white or pale gray in cold climates.

Snowshoe hares have gray brown coats in summer that turn pure white in winter. In western coastal zones, where snow rarely falls, these hares remain gray brown all year.

European hares have been introduced into parts of North America. They are 20 to 30 inches long and weigh up to 13 pounds. Their coloring is grayish brown with black on the top of their tails and the tips of their long ears. The antelope jackrabbit ("jackalope"), found in some desert areas, has extremely large ears that help regulate its body temperature. It maintains necessary fluid levels by living off succulent plants like cactus.

Black-tailed jackrabbits breed year-round, averaging two to four litters of two to five leverets each per year. The white-tailed species may have more than one litter a year during late spring to summer. Arctic hares have two to three litters a year with an average of three per litter. Hares have a life span of 5 to 6 years.

RABBITS: Cottontail rabbits are small animals, usually under 12 inches in length and 6 to 7 inches tall at the shoulder. As with hares, the females are larger than the males. Adult cottontails usually weigh 2 to 3 pounds. Their coats are grayish brown with a reddish cast in places and white markings underneath. Most cottontails also have a white spot on the forehead between the eyes. Rabbits shed their hair twice a year but do not change color seasonally. They have large hind feet and long ears. Their distinctive trait is a short tail with a white, fluffy underside that looks like a ball of cotton.

Swamp rabbits resemble cottontails but are larger, sometimes weighing 2½ to 6½ pounds. They have darker coloring and shorter, more rounded ears.

Eastern cottontails are extremely prolific, producing two to five litters a year of four to six "kittens" per litter. The life span of rabbits is 2 years in the wild and up to 10 years in captivity.

Range and Habitat

Rabbits and hares occupy a great variety of habitats, from the Arctic north to high mountains, prairie flatlands, and deserts. White-tailed jackrabbits live from eastern Washington south to northeastern California and east through Minnesota, Iowa, and Kansas, in habitat that includes grasslands, mountains, and hills. The black-tailed species prefers flat, open country, grasslands, and deserts. The Arctic hare is found in Alaska. The snowshoe hare is found throughout most of Canada south to northern California, and in the northern parts of Minnesota, Michigan, and New Jersey south through the Allegheny Mountains.

Rabbits, especially the eastern cottontail, are probably the most widespread and familiar of the lagomorphs, ranging throughout the eastern two-thirds of the U.S. into the eastern plains of the mountain states and the desert Southwest. Eastern cottontails prefer wooded bushy upland areas bordering on fields and farmland and rarely venture far from brushy cover. They seldom occupy forests but are among the first species to colonize newly cut timberland. Desert cottontails prefer open shortgrass country above the floor of stream valleys in the western states.

Swamp rabbits live in dense cover of canebrake and thickets in bottomland hardwood swamps and along stream borders. Strong swimmers and divers, they seldom venture far from water. Because of their dependence on water, this species' future depends on that of our wetlands. Swamp rabbit populations have been declining because of habitat lost to development, including drainage ditches, dams, river channelization, and the planting of rice fields.

Other Characteristics

The diet of hares and rabbits consists 90 percent of grass, although they will eat almost any vegetable matter. During summer, rabbits feed on grasses and broad-leafed weeds. They also like garden crops such as beans, peas, cabbages, and lettuce, as well as farm crops such as alfalfa, clover, and vine leaves and tendrils. In the winter, they subsist on tree buds, twigs, and bark. Swamp rabbits eat cane, grasses, sedges, and dock and, in winter, cross vine, poison ivy, greenbrier, tree seedlings, and bark.

Jackrabbits prefer herbaceous plants and grasses but also eat cultivated crops like cabbage, alfalfa, clover, and soybeans. In winter they eat twigs, buds, fruits, roots, and dry grasses, including stacked hay. They seldom drink surface water but get their moisture from food.

Because grasses are difficult to digest, rabbits and hares have developed digestive systems that process their food twice. The first digested food emerges from the animal as soft black pellets, which they then eat a second time. The final digestive waste material is passed as small, hard, fibrous pellets from which all nutritional value has been extracted.

Habitat choice among rabbits and hares seems connected to each species' ability to run. Cottontail rabbits need to live in areas with plenty of protective cover. Faster species can live in open areas and still escape predators. Black-tailed jackrabbits can run 30 to 35 mph and can leap about 20 feet; white-tailed jackrabbits can maintain speeds of 35 mph, occasionally exceeding 40 mph. Snowshoe hares can jump up to 12 feet and reach 30 mph.

Rabbits tend to be more social than hares, grouping together in colonies; hares tend to be more solitary and territorial, but they do share feeding areas. Rabbits seldom stray far from their birthplace. Females especially tend to stay in their home territories, usually no more than a few hundred square yards, up to 3 acres. The larger male territories—up to 8 acres—will usually encompass those of several females. Once a territory is chosen, the rabbit grooms it inch by inch, to establish boundaries and pathways. When chased by a predator, it avoids straying into unknown territory by continuously running in a circle until it can escape into a burrow.

Rabbits ordinarily do not dig their own burrows. For shelter and refuge from predators, they usually take over and use burrows dug by woodchucks, badgers, prairie dogs, or other burrowing animals. They do build "forms," which are trampled-down grassy areas above the ground where they rest occasionally at night and throughout the day.

Both hares and rabbits are nocturnal. Rabbits forage for food in the early evenings and early mornings. Their large eyes are adapted for seeing well in the dark and provide an almost 360-degree range of vision. Hares and rabbits also have excellent hearing, and their ears can be moved separately to focus on distant sounds. The ears appear pink because the very thin cartilage is tinted by blood flowing through the veins. Hares and rabbits are generally silent, making few sounds except when fighting, mating, or in extreme danger.

Enemies and Defenses

HARES: Coyotes are the primary predator of jackrabbits. Other predators include humans (hunters kill an estimated 2 million jackrabbits every year), large carnivores, reptiles, and raptors. The primary predators of Arctic hares are lynxes, weasels, foxes, minks, bobcats, owls, and hawks.

Since they must contend with so many predators, hares have many survival devices, including acute senses of hearing, smell, and sensitivity to motion, as well as fast reactions and running speed. If a hare is alerted to danger, it will remain upright and still, ears up, eyes wide and unblinking, nose twitching until the danger has passed. It may make warning sounds by pounding its back feet on the ground. If suddenly surprised, it will freeze, pressing its body to the ground, ears flat on its back. When it flees, a hare will leap high and away from its hiding place, bounding away with long, graceful leaps. Jackrabbits have the unique skill of "spy-hopping"— leaping higher than normal (up to 6 feet) every five to six strides—in order to pinpoint a pursuer. White-tailed jackrabbits can also swim to escape capture, but snowshoe hares avoid water.

RABBITS: Rabbits are preyed on by almost all carnivores, including weasels, minks, skunks, raccoons, cats, dogs, foxes, bobcats, coyotes, hawks, owls, and snakes. Their high reproductive rate produces many more young than the habitat can ordinarily support, providing an important food supply for predators. It has been estimated that 85 percent of all rabbits die or are killed every year. Rabbits' other chief enemy is humans, who kill millions in the U.S. each year, both for sport and because of damage. Hunters take more cottontails than all other game animals combined.

Native rabbit populations have also suffered from the loss of woody cover growth; removal of hedgerows; farming along roadsides; and over-grazing on pastures, streambanks, and lakeshores.

Rabbits use several defense techniques. If the danger is far away, a rabbit will freeze and remain motionless to blend in with its background. If the danger is near, it runs quickly to heavy brush or down a borrowed burrow hole. Rabbits can run up to 20 mph and leap up to 10 feet; they often zigzag to confuse a pursuer. They are strong swim-

Cottontail rabbits may help them-selves to unprotected garden plants.

mers when necessary and, when cornered, may strike the pursuer with a hind foot to stun it. When captured, they make a shrill, high-pitched sound and may go into shock.

How to Observe

The best time to observe rabbits and hares is at night or early in the morning when they are feeding and most active along the edges of woods and fields.

Situations and Solutions

Rabbits Damaging Gardens or Crops

WHY IT HAPPENS: Eastern cottontails tend to be present in high densities, therefore causing focused damage to crops and shrubs—as opposed to hares, which choose more isolated habitat, such as open prairie, and avoid humans as much as possible. The cottontails may uproot young seedlings and eat crops as well as strip the bark from shrubs and young trees. Rabbit damage can be identified by a clean, angled cut on the end of their browse. (Deer leave a rough, jagged cut.) Also, browsing and debarking by rabbits usually does not extend more than 2½ feet above ground.

SUGGESTIONS:

1. Restrict cottontails from gardens and crops by erecting a 3-foot-high fence made of 1-inch wire mesh ("poultry wire"). Rabbits are not good climbers or burrowers and ordinarily do not jump fences, but a 1-foot

extension (bent out at a 90-degree angle) can be added to the top of the fence to discourage animals that do climb fences, and a 1-foot or deeper extension can be added below ground to discourage burrowers.

Existing deer fences can be rabbitproofed by adding fine wire mesh to the lower part. Tight-fitting gates with sills will keep rabbits from digging below the bottom rails of the gate. Keep gates closed and inspect fences regularly for signs of digging. If rabbits are the only damage problem, a smaller fence—2 feet high, of 1-inch mesh wire stretched between posts and staked to the ground—may suffice. Since rabbits mostly favor young shoots in gardens, the fence may be moved as the plants mature. It also may be more practical to fence the entire perimeter of a small lot rather than individual garden beds.

2. Protect individual trees and shrubs by wrapping plastic tubing or ½-inch wire mesh around the trunk. These guards should fit loosely to allow for growth; they should extend at least 4 inches into the ground and 2 feet above the normal snow line. Tree prunings can be left as a decoy food source during the winter; rabbits much prefer twigs and buds to tree bark.

3. Some odor and taste repellents are available, though not particularly effective when rabbits are hungry or the garden contains highly preferred foods. Repellents must be constantly replenished, especially after

A garden can be protected by wire mesh, with the bottom edge buried to keep rabbits and other creatures from burrowing underneath.

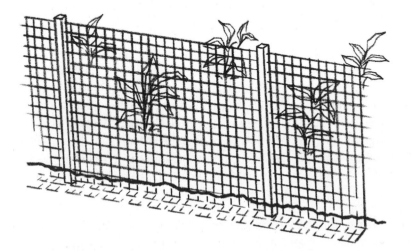

rains or heavy watering, and should not be used on edible parts of plants once those develop. Carefully follow directions when using any repellent.

4. Rabbits avoid areas with little cover, so mowing lawns around gardens and orchards will help reduce damage.

5. Attracting natural predators such as hawks and owls helps control rabbit populations.

6. Live-trapping is of limited use, because other rabbits may soon replace those trapped. Traps are not effective with jackrabbits, who are reluctant to enter traps. Check with your local wildlife agency to determine whether trapping and releasing of rabbits and hares is allowed; releasing trapped rabbits is sometimes prohibited because the animals may carry disease or be considered agricultural pests. If trapping is allowed, bait traps with a combination of apples, carrots, and rabbit droppings. Trapping is best done during the winter or during rainy or foggy nights in warmer times. Trapping in spring or summer may result in starvation of young. To protect the rabbit from self-inflicted injuries, release it as soon as possible, at least 5 miles away in suitable habitat.

Managing Habitat for Rabbits

WHY IT HAPPENS: To ensure the survival of rabbit populations, which are an important link in the food chain, humans can encourage and create suitable rabbit habitat.

SUGGESTIONS: Maintain small areas of different types of cover, to create extensive and varied "edges" (places where two or more different types of vegetation meet, much favored by rabbits). Rabbits need grass of sufficient height around escape cover to build their "forms" and nests, but large fields of grass are not as useful as grass intermixed with low-growing woody cover. This can be a variety of shrubs, particularly thorny shrubs like Osage orange, multiflora roses, and blackberry thickets. Maintain the cover so it grows low to the ground and spreads out from the center. Brush piles can temporarily replace living cover until new plantings are established. Good food plots for rabbits include timothy, clover, orchard grass, cowpeas, soybeans, and grain sorghum.

Exposure to Disease from Dead Rabbits

WHY IT HAPPENS: Rabbits (and other animals such as muskrats) are subject to a disease called tularemia, which can be transmitted to humans through openings in the skin when dead animals are handled. The disease, fatal to rabbits, is transmitted to them by ticks, fleas, and deerflies; its signs are rabbits acting sluggish, tame, or unable to run when disturbed. It usually occurs in autumn, seldom in winter, because freezing temperatures kill the insects that carry it. In humans, it causes chills, headaches, fever, and aching pains, but it is treatable with antibiotics.

SUGGESTIONS: To avoid the possibility of contamination, always use rubber gloves to handle any dead rabbit, whether it was killed by hunting or found dead. If you find white spots on the liver of a rabbit while cleaning it for food, discard the entire carcass by burying or burning it.

[ARMADILLOS]

Armadillos are members of the Edentata order and the Dasypodidae family. There are 20 species in 8 genera. These unusual mammals are distinguished by their hard, jointed outer covering ("armor") that evolved to aid their survival in arid lands. The common, or nine-banded, armadillo (*Dasypodidae novemcinctus*) is about 15 to 20 inches long, with short, sturdy legs and claws well developed for digging. It has a long, pointed snout, a narrow head, and erect, funnel-shaped ears. The shoulders and hips are protected by stiff, hornlike hoods, and the midsection is covered with strong, bony plates that overlap to form a large shell over the back and sides. Face, tail, and feet are also armored. Joints in this bony structure allow the armadillo to curl up for protection. Above, it is brownish black with widely scattered hairs and yellowish spots on its sides. Heavy for its size because of its armor, the armadillo weighs from 8 to 17 pounds.

Armadillos give birth to genetically identical quadruplets in each litter, born in late March to early April in an underground burrow.

Range and Habitat

While 20 different species of armadillos are found in Central and South America, only the nine-banded armadillo is found in North America, where it lives in the southern U.S. in temperate or hot, semidesert areas, ranging from central Texas across the Gulf coastal states up into portions of Arkansas and Oklahoma. This species' northward expansion appears limited by its low tolerance for cold winter temperatures: Armadillos cannot tolerate frost, and freezing temperatures both eliminate their insect food and make it hard or impossible for them to dig. They prefer habitats with dense ground cover but can live in areas with less cover as long as there is moisture and loose, easily dug soil in which to burrow.

Other Characteristics

Armadillos like to burrow for protection from predators and for shelter from extreme temperatures. In summer they are nocturnal, staying in their burrows during the heat of the day. In winter, they reverse this routine and come out during the day to warm in the sun.

Armadillos are timid, and their only well-developed senses are hearing and smell. They tend to move slowly but can become more lively when digging for food. The armadillo eats a wide variety of foods, including large quantities of beetles, wild bees, wasps, caterpillars, crickets, grasshoppers, ants, millipedes, snails, slugs, earthworms, grubs, wild berries, and, sometimes, freshwater shellfish, frogs, and salamanders. It competes for food with few other creatures except lizards, birds, and moles and serves an important role in keeping down insect populations.

Nine-banded armadillos have the unique ability to cross small waterways by holding their breath and walking across the bottom, weighted by their heavy shells. If the waterway is too wide for this technique, the armadillo can also float across by drawing air into its stomach and intestines and swimming with only the end of its nose out of the water.

Enemies and Defenses

When threatened, a nine-banded armadillo will jump straight up in the air, then run for cover in the nearest burrow. If it cannot find one, it may wedge itself into a rocky crevice. As a last resort, it may fall on its side and curl up into a ball, protected by its shell. It also may emit a strong odor from scent glands near the base of its tail.

Armadillos' main enemies are large predators and humans. Due to their poor eyesight, they are easily struck by automobiles, and humans kill them because they burrow in lawns and golf courses. Armadillos are also used in medical research because of their unique quadruplet reproduction and their susceptibility to leprosy. (Although they can suffer from leprosy themselves, they do not transmit the disease to humans.)

How to Observe

Because they are nocturnal creatures, and slow, armadillos are easily viewed by humans. In some areas, like Texas and Florida, they have adapted to human habitats and may be observed on roadways and in suburban lawns. You may also see one while hiking in the desert.

Situations and Solutions

Armadillos Burrowing in a Lawn or Garden

WHY IT HAPPENS: Burrowing is instinctive to armadillos and necessary for their self-preservation. Because they are insect eaters, they also must burrow to obtain their food.

SUGGESTIONS: In some states, armadillos are protected, nongame animals. If you are having trouble with burrowing armadillos, contact your local wildlife agency for advice and assistance. If allowed by local laws, control techniques include the following:

1. Construct fencing, with special adaptations to prevent climbing, to exclude armadillos from yards and gardens. Consult local wildlife agencies for plans and suggestions.
2. Remove brush when it is thick enough to provide cover or where burrows exist.
3. Control insects with nontoxic methods to limit the armadillo's food source. (Alternatively, view the armadillo as a natural insect-control mechanism and share your yard with it.)
4. Bait live traps with spoiled meat or overripe fruit. Place traps around burrows and release the captured armadillo at least 2 miles away in suitable habitat. Avoid trapping during breeding season (March through September) so that young are not orphaned and starved. As with most live-trapping, this should be considered a last resort.

[BATS]

Almost 1,000 species of bats are found worldwide. The most common in North America are from the order Chiroptera and the families Vespertilionidae and Molossidae. They include the little brown bat, big brown bat, big-eared bat, red bat, Brazilian free-tailed bat, Indiana bat, and gray bat. They are 3 to 6 inches long, with wingspans ranging from 8 to 16 inches; consult a specialized guidebook for accurate identification.

The only mammals capable of true flight, bats have "wings" that are really membranes of skin stretched between their flanks and extended finger bones. Most species also have small tail membranes, small eyes, short snouts, and complex noses with numerous folds and flaps called "leaves." Except for the big-eared bat, most bats have small but complex ears with an extra lobe in front of the ear cavity. They have poorly developed hind limbs used to hang upside down when they roost.

Each female produces just one young per year.

Range and Habitat

In North America, bats range throughout most portions of the U.S. into southern Canada. They are insectivores and choose habitat that provides plentiful food, often near lakes and streams. But they also need quiet, dark caverns or rocky outcroppings in which to rest during the day and hibernate in winter.

Other Characteristics

Bats are nocturnal, feeding primarily on night-flying insects. It has been estimated that one gray bat may eat up to 3,000 or more insects, including many mosquitoes, in a single night. Large bat colonies, like the 20 million free-tailed bats that congregate in the Texas Bracken Cave colony, eat up to 250,000 pounds of insects nightly.

Contrary to myth, bats generally have good eyesight, which they use for long-distance orientation. For short-distance navigation and catching food, bats use a sophisticated method of echolocation similar to that used by dolphins and in marine sonar. Bats first find their prey by flying through dense vegetation or above ponds and lakes where mosquitoes congregate. In towns, they will gather around street lamps and other light sources that attract insects. Then they send out high-pitched sounds that bounce off their prey and other objects, returning to the bat's complex ear formations. For an object 6 inches from the bat's mouth, the time delay in hearing the returning sound is only a thousandth of a second. Typically, the whole process of detection, pursuit, and capture of prey takes about one second. The prey is scooped up by the mouth, the cupped membrane of the tail, or the wing skin.

Most bats hang upside down when hibernating or resting. Their hind limbs function as "hooks" that tightly grip their roosts. Roosting sites vary among species; each prefers a specific location in and around trees, houses, or caves. Because they are nocturnal, bats spend the daylight hours hanging in their roosts.

Many bats save energy by lowering their body temperatures when outside temperatures cool and insects are scarce, sometimes spending days in their roosts waiting for warmer conditions. In winter, some bats truly hibernate, significantly reducing their heart rate and body temperature. In some species, body temperature can even drop below the freezing point, because blood freezes at a lower temperature than water. When hibernating, bats use only a small amount of energy provided by fat stored between their shoulders. However, they remain aware enough to awaken if disturbed and can use the equivalent of 10 to 30 days worth of food to rekindle their heart rate and body temperature while they relocate to a new hibernation site.

Hibernating bats usually congregate in large groups, for reasons unknown. It has been suggested that dense crowding helps keep their body temperatures stable, but they all may simply choose the best available location. Bats that do not hibernate migrate to areas where food is more plentiful in the winter. Some species travel long distances and others no more than 30 miles.

Enemies and Defenses

Bats' greatest enemy is humans. Sometimes people intentionally kill bats, but others unintentionally cause harm by disturbing their roosting and hibernating sites. Each time humans enter a winter hibernating cave, bats arouse and use valuable energy. In summer, entering a roosting site can cause young to be dropped or abandoned.

Habitat loss is the other primary harm. Three endangered species, the gray bat, big-eared bat, and Indiana bat, have all suffered drastically in various ways attributable chiefly to habitat loss and degradaton, as well as human disturbance. Generally, bats are not dangerous to humans or other animals. Like any mammal, they can carry rabies, although less than 1 percent of all bat populations actually do carry the virus. More people die annually from dog attacks, bee stings, lightning, or household accidents than from bat-transmitted rabies.

Conservation Note

Pesticides in the food chain harm many bats. In the early 1960s, it was estimated that 150 million free-tailed bats annually fed on .25 million metric tons of insects over farms in the southwestern U.S. and Mexico. Since that time, bat populations have drastically declined—some as much as 99 percent—through eating insects contaminated by agricultural pesticides. A contaminated diet and a slow reproductive rate have had serious impacts on bat populations in the U.S.

How to Observe

Because disturbance can cause such harm to the remaining bat populations, check with your local wildlife agency about bat observation locations, opportunities, and techniques. The best way to observe bats may be by attracting them to your property by installing a bat house (see below); they will return the favor by consuming mass quantities of annoying insects.

Situations and Solutions

Bats in the Attic or a Wall

WHY IT HAPPENS: In nature, bats roost in rock and tree crevices. They are attracted to warm and dark areas, like openings in houses.

SUGGESTIONS: Most colonies of bats are small and remain unnoticed for years. Large colonies residing in an attic or wall may become a problem because of noise and unsightly accumulations of droppings. Since bats can squeeze through openings the size of a quarter, you may have to do some investigating to find out where they are entering. Check especially for cracks under eaves. Outside the house, bats will hide under shingles, roofing, awnings, and ivy and behind shutters. Stains from body oils or bat droppings may help identify exits. Noise from large colonies may also reveal their presence.

Once their entrance location has been found, eliminate access by following these steps:

1. Close off all but one access to the den area.

2. Gather all materials needed to close the entrance—sheet metal works best, or use sturdy wire mesh, or wood, hammer, nails, and so on— and place them outside the opening.

3. Do one or more of the following to clear bats from occupied space:

   • Brightly light the area day and night, which is annoying to nocturnal animals. The easiest way is to tape a mechanic's drop or trouble light to a long two-by-four and slide it into the area.

   • Cool the attic with fans to make the temperature unsuitable for bats.

   • Certain mechanical repellents, which tend to be safer than chemical repellents, may help discourage bats. Mixed success in dispersing roosting bats has been achieved through the use of ultrasound devices, such as an aquarium pump attached directly to and blowing on a high-frequency dog whistle (not submerged in water). Such a device should not be used in a home with pets.

- Chemical repellents can be useful but may be more harmful to humans and pets. Mothballs (naphthalene) in mesh bags or socks may be hung in attics; however, this is less effective in well-ventilated spaces. Aerosol dog and cat sprays, applied to specific roosting spots when bats are absent, can also work. Never spray such an aerosol directly on the bat—the chemicals can injure it or cause it to fly at you in an effort to escape.
  - Attach bird netting or flexible plastic strips above the opening, using staples or duct tape, to form a temporary one-way exit. The sides may also be attached, but leave the bottom loose. As bats leave to feed, they will drop out of the roost but will be unable to get back in. Leave nets in place two to three nights to ensure that no bats remain inside.

4. When you think the bats have finally left, close up the opening with caulking, screening, wood, or sheet metal, as appropriate for the location.

5. Exclude bats from Spanish or concrete tile roofs by installing a simple rain gutter flush against the attachment surface. The upper edge of the gutter should be even with the lower edge of the tile, extending out about 8 inches. Bats dislike climbing on the slippery metal gutter and usually will not return.

6. Do not attempt to exclude bats during summer months because young unable to fly may be trapped and die. Not only is this inhumane, but it may cause a severe odor problem.

7. If you seek professional help, keep the following in mind:
   - Seek a bat exclusion expert and get more than one estimate.
   - Bats do not multiply like rabbits, nor are they attracted in hordes by the scent of other bats.
   - Even sick bats rarely attack people or pets. Bats have few parasites, so additional spraying is not necessary.
   - Permanent physical exclusion is necessary for any bat control job.
   - Use of poisons to eliminate a bat colony is illegal without a special permit in most states.

Bat Droppings in Indoor Roosts

WHY IT HAPPENS: Once bats have been excluded, the area must be cleaned of any remaining droppings.

SUGGESTIONS: Wear a respiratory mask whenever handling bat guano. It contains a fungus that causes histoplasmosis, a respiratory disease transmitted when the guano is disturbed, causing fungal spores to become airborne and inhaled. Hot, dry conditions, such as in attics, usually kill the spores; more likely locations for exposure are chicken or barn roosts, where temperatures and moisture aid the fungus. The best protection is to wear a dust mask and rubber gloves whatever the location, sweep up droppings, and wash clothing immediately after use.

Single Bat Trapped in the House

WHY IT HAPPENS: A bat may become disoriented and accidentally enter a home through an open window or door.

SUGGESTIONS:

1. Close off all doorways to the room and open a window. The bat will usually depart on its own.
2. If the bat does not exit by itself, remove it in a large jar or can. Approach the bat slowly so it is not startled, and place the jar or can over the bat. Then slide a piece of stiff paper or cardboard under the opening, using it as a lid when removing the bat. Use protective clothing on all exposed skin when approaching a bat.

Sick Bat on the Ground

WHY IT HAPPENS: The bat may be diseased, possibly with rabies. When lying on the ground or stuck on a screen door or window, especially with its wings folded, a bat may look like a mouse or rat.

SUGGESTIONS:

1. Unless you are fairly sure it is dead, avoid approaching a bat on the ground and, if you must, use great care. Bats, like all wild animals, may bite when handled and should never be removed bare-handed. The rabies virus is found in saliva and may be transmitted through an infected animal's bite. Nonbite exposure can occur when saliva or brain tissue from an infected animal enters open skin or mucous membranes (nose, eyes, mouth).

2. To have a sick bat removed, call your local wildlife care agency. If for some reason you decide to remove it, use heavy leather gloves and cover all other exposed skin for protection. If you are accidentally bitten, make sure the bat is saved for examination, immediately wash the bite with soap and water, and seek medical assistance.

Providing Roosting Sites for Bats

WHY IT HAPPENS: Because of continued loss of bat habitat and growing knowledge of bats' role in controlling insects, many people are beginning to install bat houses on their land.

SUGGESTIONS:

1. Sources of designs for bat houses are included in Appendix C. Ready-made houses are available through some garden catalogs.
2. Bat houses must be secured to a tree trunk or the side of a building at least 12 to 15 feet above ground. Bats cannot tolerate inside temperatures above 90 degrees F, so the house should be sited to receive morning sun but afternoon shade. Bat houses should be located within half a mile of a water source such as a river, lake, bog, or marsh, where insect populations are high.
3. Although sometimes occupied within a few weeks, bat houses usually are not inhabited for a year or two after they are in place. Installing the house by early April and adjacent to areas where bats already live (in barns or attics, for example) increases the chance of early occupancy.

Rodents

Forty percent of all mammal species are rodents. There are 30 families of rodents, containing 1,700 different species. All are small animals with powerful, gnawing teeth for eating tough vegetable matter, and they can close their mouths while leaving their front teeth exposed for digging. Their other distinguishing feature is that their teeth never stop growing. They must continue gnawing to wear them down so that (1) they can close their mouths (otherwise they would be unable to take in food and would eventually starve) and (2) the teeth do not grow into their skulls, eventually killing them.

The rodents described here are grouped into three general categories according to their jaw muscle structure. First are the squirrellike rodents, including squirrels, chipmunks, prairie dogs, woodchucks, and beavers. The second group is the micelike rodents, including mice, rats, voles, muskrats, and lemmings. The third group is the cavy family, which in North America includes only the porcupine.

[SQUIRRELS]

Members of the squirrel family (Sciuridae) include tree squirrels, flying squirrels, ground squirrels, chipmunks, prairie dogs, and woodchucks (marmots). All are primarily vegetarian, eating roots, stems, bark, shoots, leaves, flowers, fruit, and nuts from a wide range of plants. Some include a few insects in their diets. Most have long, cylindrical bodies with large bushy tails that provide balance and slender toes with sharp claws that aid in climbing. The burrowing species (ground squirrels, prairie dogs, and woodchucks) have strong front paws and short tails.

Squirrels are known for their tendency to hoard seeds and other food either in their nests or in caches nearby. Squirrels often store more than they need and lose or forget where it is stored; in doing so, they help scatter seeds to take root and grow in new locations.

TREE SQUIRRELS: The several species of tree squirrels in North America include the eastern gray, the fox, the American red, and the flying squirrels. Gray squirrels (*Sciurus carolinensis* and *S. griseus*) are usually grayish above with white or light gray on their bellies and white-tipped tail hairs; they are 8 to 10 inches long (excluding the equally long tail) and weigh 12 to 24 ounces. Fox squirrels (*S. niger*) have rusty yellow fur interspersed with gray and a pale yellow or orange belly; they are 10 to 15 inches long (excluding the tail) and weigh 20 to 48 ounces. The American red squirrel is smaller than the gray squirrel, with brownish red fur and white underparts.

Tree squirrels have litters of three to eight pups.

FLYING SQUIRRELS: These squirrels (*Glaucomys* ssp.) are similar in shape to other tree squirrels and also have thick fur and long, bushy tails but generally are more delicately built. Their limbs are connected by loose skin covered in soft, gray brown fur attached to the "ankles" and the base of the tail. These winglike membranes enable the creatures to glide from tree to tree. Their undersides are usually a whitish color. Small North American flying squirrels weigh only 5 ounces and are 8 to 10 inches long. Nocturnal

Squirrels rarely damage gardens and trees, so make sure they are the real culprits before taking any action.

animals, they have large protruding eyes that help them see in the dark.

GROUND SQUIRRELS: Squirrels in this genus (*Spermophilus* ssp.) are 16 to 19 inches long, including the bushy tail, and weigh 1 to 3 pounds. Their coloration is grayish brown with buff flecks. They have short ears and legs and strong front claws.

Litters range from two to eight.

Range and Habitat

TREE SQUIRRELS: These species occupy similar types of habitat but are not usually found in the same areas. Gray squirrels like hardwood forests with mixtures of oak, hickory, and other trees that supply edible nuts. They are often seen in urban parks and yards. Fox squirrels prefer mixed hardwood and conifer forests including spruce, hemlock, pine, or fir trees and are less common in urban areas than grays. Timber management practices that create broken stands of middle-aged and mature trees provide the most food and den sites for gray and fox squirrels.

FLYING SQUIRRELS: These species are found primarily in mature hardwood forest areas throughout North America.

GROUND SQUIRRELS: The den of this type of squirrel—found in the eastern U.S. and throughout the West except in California's southeastern deserts, western Oregon, western Nevada, and the Baja Peninsula, Mexico—is an intricate burrow with several entrances.

Other Characteristics

TREE SQUIRRELS: These species spend most of their lives in trees. They use their large, bushy tails for shade from hot sun, warmth in cold weather, balance in climbing and jumping, and slowing their descent when falling or jumping to a lower limb. They build nests high up in trees, in hollow trunks or forks between thick branches, using moss, twigs, and dry leaves to make loose nests. Some tree squirrels are ground dwelling and nest in burrows. A colony of squirrels may construct and share several nests each year. Of these, some are used for several years and some may never be used.

Tree squirrels feed on acorns, hickory nuts, walnuts, buds, seeds, fungi, and fruit. They sometimes also eat insects and bird eggs. Unlike other members of their family, they have no stripes or internal cheek pouches. Gray squirrels, while basically tree dwellers, will venture to the ground to collect and bury nuts at random. They find their caches not by memory but by their keen sense of smell, though many buried seeds and nuts are never found and generate into new trees. Gray squirrels are considered major tree planters in hardwood forests.

Fox squirrels are larger, less active, and less agile than gray squirrels, and they tend to spend more time foraging on the ground. They eat a variety of nuts and seeds, preferring the green seeds of conifer trees, and do not bury their food at random but store it in large underground caches for winter. The contents of such caches are available to whichever squirrel finds them.

Both species ordinarily do not roam more than 200 yards from their nesting tree, although they may build nests in different trees over a several-acre area during abundant food seasons. Gray squirrels are somewhat sociable and can tolerate other squirrels nearby. Fox squirrels are unsociable, very territorial, and aggressive; they do not tolerate other squirrels in their territories.

Tree squirrels do not truly hibernate and can withstand severe weather conditions, but they spend long hours in their protective nests during winter.

Squirrel populations fluctuate dramatically based on food supply. As many as 80 percent of individual fox squirrel populations die and are replaced each year. The average life span of tree squirrels in the wild is five to eight years.

FLYING SQUIRRELS: These species' unique and distinguishing characteristic is their ability to glide over great distances, sometimes even changing direction in midair. Some species can glide up to 1,500 feet in one flight. They control their airborne movements by changing the tension of the gliding membranes and their tail position.

North American flying squirrels live mainly on nuts, seeds, fungi (mushrooms), and lichens, though they occasionally also eat fruits, insects, and small birds and their eggs. Like other squirrels, they store food in hidden places—climbing down their trees headfirst to dig a hole in the ground—and often forget or abandon those supplies, thus aiding regeneration of plants and trees. Flying squirrels do not truly winter hibernate, but they do spend long, inactive periods in their nests, sleeping in large, sociable family groups and using stored food supplies only occasionally.

GROUND SQUIRRELS: Primarily herbivores, ground squirrels eat plant material, including wild fruit plants, seeds, succulents (such as ice plant), and grasses. They also prey on insects, the eggs and young of ground-nesting birds, and, occasionally, small mammals. They eat much food where it is found but also carry seeds in cheek pouches to build up large stores underground.

Ground squirrels are active during the day and sleep at night. Northern ground squirrels are also true winter hibernators that put on weight during the summer to get them through their winter sleep in underground nesting chambers. These animals also estivate (summer hibernate) during dry summers. Southern ground squirrels do not truly hibernate but remain inactive in their burrows in winter. Ground squirrels are not as social as prairie dogs but may group together and live in large colonies where food is abundant. They live from 5 to 12 years.

Enemies and Defenses

Tree squirrels are often prey for large carnivores such as coyotes, owls, and wolves, but their main enemies are humans and automobiles. In many states, tree squirrels are extensively hunted for food and pelts, and destruction of woodland habitats for development adversely impacts squirrel populations. The ground squirrel's chief enemies are coyotes, foxes, weasels, badgers, and hawks. Its primary defense is sighting an approaching predator at a great distance and escaping to the protection of its burrow.

How to Observe

Tree squirrels, especially gray squirrels, are readily observable in city parks and suburban yards. Fox squirrels tend to be more reclusive and occupy remoter wooded areas. Because flying squirrels are nocturnal, they are difficult to observe in the wild. Ground squirrels are most easily seen during the warm seasons in open spaces, where they have a good view of the surrounding territory. Check with your local nature museum or wildlife agency to identify the species of squirrels indigenous to your area and the likely areas for observation.

Situations and Solutions

Attracting Squirrels to Your Land

WHY IT HAPPENS: If you wish, squirrels can be attracted to your property by providing adequate natural food sources and living spaces.

SUGGESTIONS:

1. Most importantly, have a ready source of tree-produced nuts and seeds. Manage timber to provide sufficient food and nesting sites by creating broken stands of mature nut-bearing trees, thinning timber to develop better leaf crowns, leaving trees with rotted cavities and hollows for denning purposes, and preventing forest fires.

2. If you lack enough tree cavities for nesting sites, place squirrel nesting boxes in suitable habitat. Obtain construction plans from local wildlife agencies.

Squirrels Damaging Gardens and Fruit Trees

WHY IT HAPPENS: Squirrels are feeding on their natural food sources.

SUGGESTIONS:

1. Squirrels rarely do signficant damage to plantings, so try to determine the real culprits. Because squirrels are active during the day, it is relatively easy to observe whether they are feeding on your garden or fruit trees. If the damage occurs at night, squirrels are not at fault.

2. Because squirrels are such excellent climbers, fencing is not a particularly effective control. One way to protect trees is to wrap a 2-foot band of sheet metal around the trunk about 6 feet off the ground. Trim any branches below 6 feet. Also, make sure no other trees are close enough to provide jumping access. Some taste repellents applied to the food source may be effective; be sure to follow instructions carefully.

3. Some gray squirrels strip bark from trees, usually low to the ground, to get at the sweet sap under the outer layers. The trees most vulnerable to this are young sycamore, beech, and oaks. If this occurs, wrap the damaged area with sheet metal to protect it from further damage. If the problem continues, contact your local wildlife agency for further assistance.

Squirrels Living in a Building

WHY IT HAPPENS: Squirrels, like other rodents, raccoons, and skunks, will readily take up residence in a building if access is available.

SUGGESTIONS:

1. As with the procedure for raccoons, it is important to block all holes with wood or wire mesh to prevent entry. To remove a squirrel from an attic or other similar space, do the following:
   * Block the entry and set a live trap baited with peanut butter, fruit, or nuts.
   * Remove the captured animal in the trap immediately and release it at a different location with suitable habitat at least 5 miles away.
   * Be careful not to block holes if young are still inside. Adult squirrels can cause significant damage gnawing to get back inside to their young. If a hole is blocked, open it long enough for the adult to rescue the young; then cover it again.
   * Remember that live-trapping is not a final solution. Be sure to close all possible access areas to prevent repopulation.
2. Prune overhanging tree limbs, shrubs, and vines that may provide access to attics and other areas. Cover telephone and electric wires near the house with long plastic tubing to discourage use of the wires for entrance and exit.

Squirrel Trapped Inside a Home

WHY IT HAPPENS: A squirrel may accidentally enter a home looking for food or may be chased in by a predator, such as a dog.

SUGGESTIONS: Squirrels are excitable and can cause severe damage if trapped inside a home. When badly frightened, they tend to run recklessly in circles and will knock over anything in their way. Quickly and quietly open a door or window to the outside and leave the room. The squirrel wants out as much as you want it out and will leave as soon as the threat of your presence is gone.

Squirrel Trapped in a Chimney

WHY IT HAPPENS: A squirrel may fall in a chimney while climbing on the roof.

SUGGESTIONS:

1. Do not remove the squirrel through the fireplace, as it may escape into the room. Secure a heavy rope from the top of the chimney and drop it down to the fireplace. The rope provides a perfect escape route during daylight hours. After the squirrel has exited, remove the rope and properly cap the chimney.

2. If a squirrel is trapped behind a fireplace screen or doors and is unable to exit up a rope, carefully set a live trap baited with peanut butter inside the fireplace.

Squirrels Interfering with Bird Feeders

WHY IT HAPPENS: Easily accessible bird feeders provide a source of food for squirrels.

SUGGESTIONS: Install only free-standing (not hanging) bird feeders in sites where squirrels cannot get access; keep them away from shrubs and overhanging tree limbs. Put the feeder on a metal pole at least 6 feet high. Attach a metal cone to the pole to prevent squirrels from climbing up it. Hanging feeders are not recommended, because squirrels can climb down the hanger line or shake the line until food falls to the ground.

Squirrels as Carriers of Fleas, Ticks, and Lice

WHY IT HAPPENS: Parasites reside in the fur of squirrels and use the rodent as a host environment. These parasites may carry diseases that can affect humans. For an extreme example, fleas found on some California ground squirrels may carry bubonic plague.

SUGGESTIONS: *Do not attempt to handle squirrels.* Any handling of these excitable creatures causes intense stress. When releasing a live-trapped squirrel, avoid touching it, and wear gloves and long sleeves to prevent contact with any squirrel parasite. Place the trap on the ground, open the door, and allow the squirrel to exit on its own.

[CHIPMUNKS]

Chipmunks (*Eutamias* and *Tamias* ssp.) resemble tree squirrels with their bushy tails and visible ears. They are smaller, weighing 1 to 5 ounces, and their fur is reddish brown with black-and-white stripes down their backs. They carry their short tails erect when they run for cover.

Two litters of four or five young are produced each year.

Range and Habitat

Chipmunks are found throughout North America in deciduous forests and bushland. They have adapted to suburban gardens and natural landscaping. Although they are good climbers, chipmunks prefer to live in burrows dug at the bottom of tree stumps, fallen logs, woodpiles, retaining walls, and rock piles. Chipmunk burrows are 2 inches in diameter, plunge steeply downward, and have little loose dirt on the surface.

Other Characteristics

Chipmunks live on acorns, nuts, berries, and seeds and occasionally eat insects, small amphibians, and birds. They have extremely large cheek pouches that can become as wide as their shoulders when filled with seeds. These pouches enable them to gather large quantities of food in the fall for storage near their sleeping nests. Northern species of chipmunks truly hibernate (that is, their metabolic rate, heartbeat, and body temperature decrease significantly). Southern species enter winter sleep but awake periodically to eat their stored foods.

Enemies and Defenses

Large carnivorous predators like wolves, coyotes, foxes, eagles, owls, and hawks all take chipmunks. Humans are also a primary enemy because of perceived impact on food crops. Actually, chipmunks do not usually cause property damage, except for some ornamental bulbs they may eat. Damage blamed on chipmunks is more likely caused by mice or voles. Some people object to chipmunks burrowing in flower beds or under sidewalks or porches, but these small burrows rarely cause structural damage.

How to Observe

Chipmunks are found primarily in wooded areas. While shy, they are readily observable. Check with your local wildlife agency to determine good observation locations. It is better not to "tame" chipmunks on your property by feeding them peanuts and other things but to provide natural sources of food, such as nut-producing trees.

Situations and Solutions

Chipmunks Burrowing in Flower Gardens or under Sidewalks or Porches

WHY IT HAPPENS: Chipmunks are making their homes in locations that they consider safe and that provide sufficient food.

SUGGESTIONS:

1. Because chipmunks are responsible for so little real damage, consider adopting a tolerant approach and sharing your land with them.

2. To prevent burrowing around retaining walls, sidewalks, and porches, bury hardware cloth vertically 10 inches below surface level with 8 inches flaring out horizontally at the bottom.

3. Protect flower bulbs by covering the planting area with a wire screen (coarse-gauge, not fine mesh). Plants can grow up through the wire, but chipmunks cannot burrow through it.

4. Discourage chipmunks from coming into your yard by removing their favorite dwelling places, like rock and woodpiles, brushy hedges, and dense ground cover.

5. Live traps are not recommended for use with chipmunks, because trapping a few individuals will not really affect the neighborhood population. Trapping females during spring and summer months almost guarantees the death of their young, and releasing a chipmunk in new territory with no burrows will likely result in its death from predation, accident, or starvation.

[PRAIRIE DOGS]

Four species of prairie dogs (*Cynomys* spp.) are found in North America, including black-tailed and white-tailed species. Prairie dogs are small, slender, pear-shaped creatures that weigh 20 to 50 ounces and are 13 to 17 inches long, depending on the species. They have small ears, speckled gray yellow coats with white undersides, and short tails. Their eyes have orange pigmentation that allows them to withstand glaring sun. Their name comes from their barking cries.

After a 30-day gestation period, prairie dog litters of two to five hairless pups are born in early spring deep in their burrows.

Range and Habitat

Black-tailed prairie dogs are found on the open plains, where grass is plentiful and they can easily dig their burrows. White-tailed prairie dogs occupy more mountainous, rocky habitats. Prairie dog towns are found throughout the Great Plains, the Rocky Mountains, Texas, New Mexico, Arizona, and Utah.

Other Characteristics

Although closely related to squirrels, black-tailed prairie dogs have developed a totally different lifestyle, living in large clans called *coteries*. Several coteries may live together in huge prairie dog towns with complex, interconnecting tunnel systems that cover over 160 acres. Although coteries do not generally interact, they do meet at boundaries within the town, and some interbreeding occurs. Unlike their "town-dwelling" cousins, white-tailed prairie dogs live in isolated, small family units.

Black-tailed prairie dog burrows extend vertically downward 4 to 10 feet to separate main and nesting chambers. The excavated dirt is stacked around the entrance hole to form a crater-shaped mound, which prevents water runoff into the burrow and provides a lookout point at least 6 inches tall. The animal whose turn it is to be "lookout" stands on its mound and barks a warning signal that makes all prairie dogs dive into their burrows at any sign of danger.

A few feet down the burrow is a "listening chamber," where the animals pause to determine whether the threat has passed or whether they should escape from the burrow. Their burrows continue 10 to 18 feet back toward the surface to an escape opening on the surface. This hole never has a mound and is normally hidden by a clump of brush or grass so it cannot easily be identified by a predator. Once the perceived danger has passed, the lookout returns to the mound and broadcasts an "all clear" signal.

Prairie dogs, like their tree squirrel cousins, eat leafy vegetation, grasses, seeds, and, occasionally, insects. They are social creatures, "kissing" and nuzzling each time they meet another prairie dog from their town. They play together and are always on the watch for danger to the entire community.

Many other animals depend on prairie dogs and their burrows. Buffalo wallow on the mounds to rid themselves of insects; pronghorn eat the forbs that appear when prairie dogs have removed grasses; and endangered black-footed ferrets rely chiefly on prairie dogs as their food source. Snakes, burrowing owls, cottontail rabbits, and box turtles use prairie dog burrows for shelter.

Enemies and Defenses

Natural predators of prairie dogs include wolves, coyotes, foxes, owls, hawks, eagles, bobcats, mountain lions, badgers, black-footed ferrets, minks, rattlesnakes, and other predatory carnivores. To protect themselves, prairie dogs stand guard at the entrances to their burrows and bark a warning alarm at the first sign of danger.

Humans, though, are the chief enemy. Prairie dogs tend to overgraze the areas they live in, but their burrowing also aerates the subsoil and enriches the topsoil with the fresh minerals they bring to the surface. Because of prairie dog damage to crops and grasslands, farmers and ranchers have extensively poisoned the rodents so that they now are restricted to remote areas. Poisoning affects all the animals that prey on prairie dogs and is a major cause of the black-footed ferret's near extinction.

How to Observe

Because prairie dogs have been relegated to such remote areas by human impact, it is best to check with the local or state wildlife agencies for observation locations. If you venture out for a day of prairie-dog watching, be sure to use binoculars or a long-range spotting scope. If you come too close, all the animals will scurry underground.

Situations and Solutions

Prairie Dogs Damaging Range or Cropland

WHY IT HAPPENS: In creating their burrows and grazing down the grasses around them, prairie dogs are performing their natural function.

SUGGESTIONS: If possible, share your range with the prairie dogs. Encouraging the plant life that supports prairie dog predators, such as foxes, weasels, and raptors, will help keep their populations under control. Do not use poison to control prairie-dog populations because of its serious adverse consequences on the food chain. If you feel some control measures are necesssary, consult your local wildlife agency for nonfatal control techniques.

[WOODCHUCKS]

Woodchucks (*Marmota monax*), also known as groundhogs, are the most common North American species of the marmot genus and part of the squirrel family. They have heavy bodies; short, strong legs; strong, curved claws on their front paws for burrowing; and short, furry tails. Adult males weigh 7 to 13 pounds and are 18 to 22 inches long (not including the tail).

Adult females weigh 5 to 10 pounds and are 16 to 20 inches long. Their coarse coats are grayish brown with a red cast; lighter guard hairs can give them a "frosted" appearance. The legs are dark brown with black feet. Litters of two to seven young are born in May to June.

Range and Habitat

Woodchucks are found in northern regions of North America, including Alaska, Canada, and the eastern U.S. They live in dry grasslands and stony mountain areas.

Other Characteristics

Woodchucks' home ranges span 40 to 160 acres. Unlike other marmots, they live alone in a complex tunnel system dug near the edge of a forest, along a riverbank, or in rocky meadows. They dig a series of tunnels but inhabit only one for several months before moving on to another. In winter, they tend to burrow in protected woods or bushlands; in summer, they choose more open grasslands. Their tunnel system is usually about 25 to 30 feet long, is 2 to 5 feet deep, and has two or three entrances. The main entrance is most conspicuous, with a large mound of dirt used as a lookout and as a place for sunning and grooming. Other entrances are less distinctly marked and are used chiefly as escape routes. Entrances are usually dug under a rock or tree stump, probably to keep them from being enlarged by predators such as foxes or wolves. The tunnels slope down to one or more nesting chambers lined with grass and, rare among burrowing species, a separate toilet chamber.

Woodchucks are primarily vegetarians, eating leaves, grasses, flowers, and young shoots of herbaceous plants. They also like cultivated plants like soybeans, peas, clover, and alfalfa. Adults are good climbers and can reach fruit hanging in trees. They feed mostly during the early morning and late afternoon, though they can be out most of the day. Even while feeding, woodchucks do not usually venture more than a few hundred yards from their burrows.

Woodchucks are true winter hibernators, lowering their metabolism for up to six months while living on fat stores built up during summer feeding. As spring approaches, they gradually awaken and eventually arise to the breeding season. Males usually awaken first and travel to nearby dens containing hibernating females, where mating occurs. A hibernating woodchuck loses one-third to one-half of its accumulated body fat through the winter.

Enemies and Defenses

Woodchucks' main enemies are large predators such as coyotes, bobcats, and owls. When alarmed, they make a whistling or chattering sound. They cannot run fast, so they rely on their keen senses of hearing and smell to give them enough time to reach their burrows. When cornered, woodchucks can be fierce fighters.

As with other members of the squirrel family, woodchucks' primary foes are humans. Because of damage to farmlands, crops, and gardens, woodchucks have been hunted and poisoned; however, they benefit the natural order, especially through their abandoned burrows, which provide shelter and den sites for other species such as skunks, raccoons, foxes, rabbits, opossums, weasels, and snakes. Those species in turn help control many rodent and insect species.

How to Observe

Woodchucks are most easily seen during warm months, when they feed near field edges or garden areas in early morning and late afternoon. Do not attempt to approach a woodchuck, as it will likely retreat to its burrow before you can get close; if cornered, it can attack and fight ferociously.

Situations and Solutions

Damage to Crops and Gardens, Burrows Impeding Operation of Farm Equipment

WHY IT HAPPENS: All the behaviors that result in what we see as damage from woodchucks are natural responses to needs for food, shelter, and survival. Woodchucks also may claw or gnaw the bark of ornamental and fruit trees to wear down the winter growth of their teeth and to sharpen their claws.

SUGGESTIONS:

1. Woodchucks are timid and easily frightened. Scarecrows or objects that move in the wind can often keep them from inhabiting an area.
2. In gardens, the most permanent method of woodchuck control is fencing. A sturdy fence at least 3 feet high will keep out most animals. If woodchucks burrow under, bury the fencing an additional 1 to 2 feet below ground level. If they can climb the fence, add a 1-foot extension to the top, bent outward at a 90-degree angle, or run a single strand of

electrified wire 4 to 5 inches off the ground just outside the other fencing.

3. Removing grass cover and undergrowth around buildings will discourage burrowing. If woodchucks do burrow under buildings, install over the opening a one-way door made of a double layer of hardware cloth hinged at the top on a wood frame. This lets the woodchucks exit but blocks their return.

4. No commercial repellents are registered as effective for woodchucks. However, some people recommend placing a can filled with a pungent substance, like pine oil, in the burrow, which may encourage the woodchucks to move out. Do not use volatile substances like gasoline, and avoid this method in the spring or early summer, when you risk stranding and starving young in the burrow. Insecticides sprayed on garden vegetables have limited success and potential harmful effects on humans.

5. As a last resort, live traps for woodchucks should be made of metal, not wood, and placed either near the entrance of the burrow or near the food source. Bait the trap with apple slices or other fresh fruit. Once trapped, release the woodchuck in a suitable area 5 or more miles away. Do not trap in the early spring, when the helpless young are restricted to the burrow, or in late fall, when a transplanted woodchuck may not have time to find or build a suitable hibernation den. Live-trapping and relocation is only a temporary control; if the habitat is good, other woodchucks will likely move in.

[POCKET GOPHERS]

Pocket gophers (Geomyidae family) resemble prairie dogs, with their stocky, short, powerful, brown-furred bodies; short legs and tails; and flattened heads with small eyes and gnawing front teeth. They weigh from 1 ounce to 2 pounds, are from 6 to 12 inches long, and are highly adapted for digging with their strong front claws and protruding front teeth. They are named for their distinctive large, fur-lined external cheek pouches ("pockets"), formed from folds of skin and used for carrying food and nesting materials.

Range and Habitat
Pocket gophers—both eastern (*Geomys* ssp.) and western

(*G. thomomys*)—are found only in North America. Ranging widely from Canada to Central America, they live in a variety of habitats, from deserts below sea level to high mountain meadows. Their chief requirement is light soil that they can easily dig.

Other Characteristics

Pocket gophers use their claws as their main tool to dig through and collect dirt, pushing it behind them; their hind paws then push the dirt out of the way. The front teeth are also used for digging in hard soils and, in softer soils, for raking the loosened earth. These teeth stick out over their lips like tusks, so they can close their mouths while digging and avoid swallowing any debris. They bring the soil they dig up while creating burrows to the surface through short side tunnels and leave it in a series of small mounds.

Although pocket gophers are sometimes confused with moles, the two animals leave different signs. Gophers deposit separate cone-shaped mounds at tunnel outlets; moles leave continuous trails of raised soil. Molehills tend to be circular, with a center entrance hole plugged with earth, while gopher holes appear fan shaped, with the hole to one side. Unlike the tunnels of prairie dogs, gopher tunnels run parallel with the land surface; some can be more than 50 feet long. When inside, gophers keep the burrow entrances blocked with earth.

Gophers are herbivores, feeding on grasses and woody plant materials. They often open tunnels to the surface in the early morning or early evening to feed. Their constant working of the soil helps promote the growth of herbaceous plants, some commonly thought of as weeds. They also like cultivated plants such as alfalfa, which brings them into conflict with farmers. Gophers will bite plants off from underneath so that plants appear to wither and die for no reason. They collect plants and young roots throughout the summer, cut them into small pieces, and carry them in their cheek pouches to storage areas near their burrows. Gophers have also been known to gnaw on underground plastic sprinkler pipe and buried cables.

Gophers do not hibernate, so they need food stores for winter survival. Whenever they are not feeding at the surface, they are in their burrows. Solitary creatures for the most part, they repair any holes in their burrows immediately, to avoid contact with neighboring gophers or other occupants of abandoned burrows such as snakes, nocturnal birds, amphibians, and other mammals.

Enemies and Defenses

Like most rodents, pocket gophers are a primary food source for many large predators, including bobcats, coyotes, owls, and hawks. Humans historically have been gophers' main enemy because of damage the rodent can do to lawns, gardens, and agricultural lands. Gophers are still widely poisoned and trapped in efforts to control their numbers. Their presence does benefit humans, however, because their burrowing helps aerate soils, improving plant habitat.

Gophers feed on the root ends of plants under ground.

How to Observe

Telltale mounds of dirt by burrow entrances and the plugging of burrows with earth and grass are the surest signs of gopher presence. Unlike prairie dogs and ground squirrels, gophers live primarily underground, so they are not as easily observed at a distance with binoculars or a spotting scope.

Situations and Solutions

Damage to Agricultural Lands, Gardens, and Landscaping

WHY IT HAPPENS: Gophers are just creating their living spaces in soils well suited for burrowing.

SUGGESTIONS:

1. Crop rotation and alternate plantings can help control pocket gophers. Consult with local agricultural extension agents to develop a management plan that eventually reduces damage to acceptable levels while not continually suppressing the gopher population.
2. Around gardens and homes, fencing generally does not work except in limited areas. Bury hardware cloth (½- or ¼-inch mesh) 18 to 20 inches deep around small plots of ornamental trees and plants.

Tree trunks can be wrapped with commercial trunk-wrapping materials.

3. Habitat modification may have some success. Reducing ground cover and weeds cuts down food sources. If water supplies allow, keep ground irrigated and constantly moist, which makes it unsuitable for burrowing. When installing new landscaping, consider laying wire mesh over the entire surface and then covering with topsoil; the wire prevents gophers from burrowing down through or up from underneath. Be sure to bury the wire deep enough that it does not interfere with root growth of grasses or ornamentals.

4. Use flooding to force gophers from their burrows, exposing them to predators.

5. No repellents are currently identified as effective with gophers. Some people recommend cultivating a plant called "gopher's purge," but its effectiveness has not been determined.

6. Unlike other creatures, gophers do not appear to be deterred by sounds, vibrations, or electromagnetic radiation.

[BEAVERS]

Two species of beaver are found in North America. The "North American," or dam-building, beaver (*Castor canadensis*) is the continent's largest rodent, averaging 3 to 4 feet in length, including a 9- to 10-inch tail, and weighing 30 to 70 pounds. Its fur has long, chestnut brown guard hairs with soft, reddish underfur. It has a naked, paddle-shaped tail that is broad, flat, and scaly and hind feet webbed for strength in swimming. Beaver teeth are orange and grow throughout their lifetimes, needing constant gnawing to keep them worn down.

Females bear one litter of two to four kits per year from April through July.

The mountain beaver (*Aplodontia rufa*) rarely impinges on human habitat, so it will not be covered in detail.

Range and Habitat

North American beavers are found throughout the U.S. and Canada, except for the lower Pacific Coast and parts of the desert Southwest, in habitats ranging from sea level to 9,000 feet. They live near streams and lakes with trees along the banks. Their typical habitat is a small dammed mountain stream. Some beavers construct dams and large houses of sticks; others den in burrows beneath riverbanks.

Other Characteristics

Beavers are vegetarian. In the summer, they live mainly on leaves, grass, and small herbaceous plants like duckweed, cattail, sedge, bulrush, water lily, waterweed, goldenrod, and arrowhead. In the winter, they eat mainly the soft, chewable bark and small twigs of aspen, poplar, birch, maple, cottonwood, alder, and willow trees. Beavers do not hibernate, but they do store large amounts of edible woody material on the lake bottom near their lodges, easily reached by swimming under the ice. Adult beavers can remain submerged for 15 minutes by closing their mouths behind their large teeth and using their protective eye membranes and earflaps.

Beavers can be active at all hours but mostly venture out during dusk and nighttime. They use their wide, flat tail chiefly as a rudder but also to aid rapid swimming and for balance on land. Beavers have good senses of hearing and smell but poor eyesight. Average life span is 3 to 4 years, though it is not uncommon for them to reach 8 years of age, and rare individuals may reach 15.

Beaver colonies usually number 8 to 13, including the adult pair, kits, and yearlings. In spring, yearlings leave the lodge to form their own colonies and may travel up to 7 miles to find new territory. A beaver family usually occupies a stretch of stream or riverbank about ½ mile long and 650 feet wide. They mark their territory with strong, musk-scented secretions and defend it against other colonies.

The wild kingdom's master mechanical engineer, the beaver sometimes builds its lodge on the bank, with an underwater entrance on the riverbank, especially in southern regions. More northerly beavers usually prefer to build lodges in a lake or pond so that a protective moat surrounds the home. If no pond or lake is available, beavers will dam a stream to create one. Lodges are constructed separate from the dam.

Beavers construct dams both as protection against predators and as storage centers for winter food supplies. They gnaw through small saplings and tree trunks from their riverbank territory to obtain their building materials, using small branches to create the framework, mud and stones to strengthen and fill in the gaps, and large logs to hold the dam in place. Damming a stream isolates the lodge and ensures that the beavers can reach their winter food supply.

The lodge, which can reach 5 to 10 feet high, is built with the living area above water and the entrance below. Beavers constantly replenish the twigs and mud used in their dams and lodges. During the winter, mud on the outside of the lodge freezes, which helps to insulate the interior living space.

Beavers have played a large role in the natural and human history of North America. Dammed streams make the land more fertile, and new plant growth enables other animals to live. In many areas, beaver dams have actually created mountain valleys, distributed water runoff, raised water tables, made new habitat for fish and waterfowl, and stimulated the regrowth of vegetation.

Enemies and Defenses/Conservation Note

Beavers have few natural predators, though they do provide food for some coyotes and bobcats. Most beavers create scent mounds (large piles of mud with grass that has been sprayed with urine or musk) to warn other beavers away. Beavers slap the water with their broad, flat tails to warn of approaching enemies. Their lodges are constructed so that the mud freezes in the winter, protecting them against large predators; dams also help protect against predators.

Beavers' primary enemies are humans. North American beavers were heavily trapped when the West was first explored and settled, exploited for their highly prized fur. Beaver pelts were even used as a form of currency in remote areas, and wars were fought over access to beaver habitat. From a population of millions, beavers almost became extinct by the beginning of this century; by 1900, only an estimated 100,000 remained in the wild. Though still hunted for fur and meat in parts of North America, they are now slowly recovering through reintroduction efforts.

How to Observe

Streams, lakes, and ponds are the places to find North American beavers, or at least signs of their presence: neatly constructed dams and pointed tree stumps. If you want to observe beavers, approach quietly and use binoculars. They emerge for work after sundown.

Situations and Solutions

Flooding Caused by Beavers Damming a Stream or Drainage Culvert

WHY IT HAPPENS: Beavers dam a stream or drainage ditch as a natural habitat modification to protect their lodges.

1. Beaver pipes and/or wire culvert pipes have been used with some success to control dam-induced flooding. One suggested design is illustrated here. Other designs may be available from your local wildlife agency.

   • Insert from pond side to stream side of dam a large-diameter (1- to 2½-foot) pipe made of concrete-reinforcing or welded-wire mesh — or galvanized, plastic, or aluminum irrigation pipe — long enough to reach from pond to stream (10 to 40 feet or longer). Place this culvert in the dam below water level on the pond side and position it at the water level you want to maintain in the pond. Keep it low enough to allow for continued water control regardless of the dam size.

   • To prevent beavers from damming the pond side of the culvert, or highway drainage culvert openings, install a protective cover called a "beaver baffler." This can be a triangular wire guard or an elbow-shaped guard bent at a 90-degree angle and protruding into the water 1 foot below the surface. Beaver bafflers can be made of wire mesh, plywood, or other solid material. The cover needs to be inspected and adjusted every day for proper drainage. One-inch holes, drilled about 1 foot apart along the first 10 feet of the culvert, will also aid in water flow and are hard for beavers to plug. If beavers succeed in plugging an improperly installed culvert, install a second pipe, about 4 inches smaller in diameter, inside the original culvert.

2. Encourage beavers to relocate by modifying the habitat around a stream or pond. Removing food trees, especially willows and cottonwoods, restricts sources of food and dam building material. If the only available trees are too far overland, beavers will move to a better site.

Installing a culvert through a beaver dam allows the dam and lodge to remain in place while preventing excess flooding or stream flow restriction.

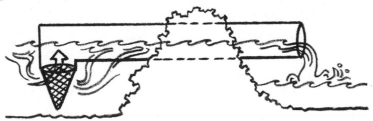

3. Spray or paint a homemade repellent made of 1 tablespoon of hot pepper in 1 gallon of water on tree trunks to reduce gnawing damage. Reapply periodically throughout warm seasons.

4. Live-trapping and dam removal should be a final resort. Live-trapping and removal just shift the problem to a new area, and constant vigilance is required to control new beaver occupancy. Dam removal alone is usually not enough to discourage beavers, because they begin rebuilding right away. Repeated destruction of dams and lodges may deter them temporarily but requires much work. Because of their size, strength, and sharp teeth, beavers can escape from standard cage traps. Specially designed beaver traps are expensive and complicated to set. If they are set too deep in the water, the beaver can drown; if not positioned properly, the jaws of the trap can cause fatal injury. Also, it is extremely unlikely that all members of the beaver family can be trapped and relocated. Trapping in summer risks leaving orphaned young in the lodge. If you choose to attempt live-trapping, consult your local wildlife agency for advice and assistance.

Beavers Feeding on Trees or Crops Adjacent to a Pond or Stream

WHY IT HAPPENS: Tree bark is beavers' primary food, though they sometimes eat corn and other cultivated crops nearby their dams and lodges.

SUGGESTIONS:

1. Exclude beavers by conventional or electric fencing. Conventional fencing needs to have small enough mesh to prevent beavers from passing through and should be buried a few inches below surface level to prevent digging underneath. Use a single strand of electric fencing suspended 1 foot off the ground. Once a beaver touches the fence several times, it will learn to stay away.

2. Protect ornamental trees from gnawing by wrapping them with hardware cloth, ¼- to 1-inch wire mesh, or tree wrap extending 3½ feet up from the ground. If the trees are in an area that occasionally floods, extend the barrier wrap at least 2 feet above the high-water mark.

[MICE AND RATS]

More than one-quarter of all mammal species belong to the suborder of mouselike rodents known as the Myomorpha, and 95 percent of the species in that group belong to two families: the Muridae, Old World mice and rats, and Cricetidae, New World mice and rats. Of all animals, mice and rats probably have the greatest impact on the environment, because of their feeding on seeds, roots, and foliage. They are also the main food source for many other animals, from birds of prey to weasels, coyotes, and other land predators.

Many species are highly adapted to coexist with humans by nesting in buildings behind paneling, beneath floorboards, or in lofts. They are most numerous in cities and on farms, where they can be serious pests because they can gnaw their way into almost any food storage container. They also spread diseases such as typhus, jaundice, and plague, because of parasitic fleas. Other members of the mouse families include voles and muskrats.

Mice

The most common types of mice found in North America are subspecies of the white-footed (also called deer) mouse *(Peromysus maniculatus)* and the house mouse *(Mus musculus)*. All species of the genus Peromysus are small rodents with grayish brown fur, large pointed ears, and naked tails. They vary in body size from 3 to 6.7 inches and in tail length from 1.6 to 8 inches. The tails of ground (terrestrial) mice tend to be shorter than those of tree (arboreal) mice.

House mice breed year-round, producing as many as eight litters of four to seven young per year.

The white-footed mouse can produce a litter of four to seven young five to eight times per year.

Range and Habitat

One subspecies of white-footed mouse, the deer mouse *(Peramyscus maniculatus)*, is probably the most common species of rodent in all of North America and is the most numerous mammal in the western U.S. from Oregon to New Mexico. Deer mice build their nests inside underground burrows, in

rocky crevices, or under old tree trunks.

The house mouse has spread all over the world from its origins in southern Asia. It will use any nook or cranny as a hiding place and tends to live close to human food supplies. It is also capable of living in the wild, however, and digs burrows with numerous underground chambers. It prefers freshly dug deep soil and can quickly take over newly cultivated farmland.

Other Characteristics

Mice are nocturnal and feed on seeds, grains, nuts, some insects, green plants, and tender bark. Because mice do not hibernate, they store large quantities of seeds in different locations to ensure sufficient food supplies during inclement weather. Nests built by white-footed mice are as intricate as some bird nests. These rodents weave dried grasses together and line the nest with thistledown, fur, or downy feathers to form a snug nursery. House mice tend to rely on humans for shelter and food, by breaking into stores of grains and seeds. They only need about 1/10 ounce of food per day to survive and can live without access to fresh water.

Mice have a social order with definite rankings among the males. The hierarchy is geared toward protection of individual territories that are scent-marked with urine. The less dominant feed and are active during the day while the dominant male is in its nest. When food is plentiful, territorial ranges are quite small, no more than a few square yards. Males tend to have larger territories than females, and each mouse investigates its whole territory to discover any changes that have occurred during the day.

Mice can transmit several diseases to humans, usually through food contamination. Great care should be taken not to eat any food contaminated by mice. Mice can also cause property damage by gnawing books, clothing, paper, wood, and other materials that they eat or use in nest building.

Enemies and Defenses

Mice, along with rats, are the most common food source for all predators, the mainstay for owls, hawks, eagles, coyotes, weasels, and many others. Humans are also their enemies for different reasons, considering them pests because of food raiding, damage, and the spread of disease. The problem they pose for farmers has been exacerbated by mechanized farming techniques: Combines that harvest and thresh grains all in one operation leave much straw and grain on the ground, and this abundant food and shelter source can cause mouse populations to boom. If the straw is burned in the field or otherwise collected, the problem is not so severe, and northern climates have a built-in control because the mice cannot survive outside in freezing winters.

Only one species of mouse is threatened, the salt-marsh harvest mouse (*Reithrodontomys raviventris*). The natural salt marshlands that used to be its habitat have rapidly disappeared to development. Often these lands are turned into salt ponds, leaving no high-tide mounds as refuges for the mouse. The only habitats in which this mouse is still found are in the San Francisco, San Pablo, and Suisun bays in northern California, where they have survived in small, isolated groups living in abandoned bird nests above high-tide levels.

How to Observe

Other than direct visual observation of mice in the house, the usual identification signs are ⅛-inch gnaw marks and 1/8-inch rod-shaped droppings, or scratching noises in walls or attics.

Situations and Solutions

Mice Living in Buildings

WHY IT HAPPENS: Mice, especially house mice, have adapted to live closely with humans. They can gain access through openings as small as the diameter of a dime. They can also climb interior walls, which can make getting rid of them difficult.

SUGGESTIONS:

1. To plug small holes, such as around drainpipes and small openings, use steel wool or quick-drying cement.
2. To plug larger openings, use ¼-inch or smaller mesh hardware cloth.
3. Remove exterior means of access, especially weeds and lower limbs of shrubs planted next to buildings.
4. Store all food in miceproof containers (metal, glass, or plastic) and properly dispose of all garbage, especially newspapers, paper, and cloth.
5. Limit spillage from bird feeders by installing spill trays, if possible, and limit access to pet food.
6. Live-trapping can be used, but unless all exterior access has been eliminated, mice will probably return.

Rats

Rats (*Rattus* spp.) found in North America include wood rats (*Neotoma* spp.), Norway rats (*Rattus norvegicus*, also known as common or brown rats), and roof rats (*Rattus rattus*, also known as black rats). Norway rats are large, stocky rodents with grayish dark brown fur, naked tails, and small eyes and ears. They weigh an average of about 1 pound. Roof rats are more slender, with pointed noses and tails as long as their heads and bodies combined. Wood rats (*Neotoma* spp.) resemble roof rats but have rounded noses and fine-haired tails.

In the wild, rat breeding is seasonal. Where provided with an abundant food supply, however, rats will reproduce year-round, being especially productive during spring and fall.

Range and Habitat

Wood rats are native to North America and are distributed across the U.S. Unlike other rat species, wood rats prefer not to live in close proximity to humans. They usually build their shelters or nests on the ground in wooded areas.

Both roof rats and the far more common Norway rat have colonized most of the world by stowing away on sailing ships traveling to new continents. Roof rats are found in the western, southern, and southeastern parts of the U.S. They prefer high, dry places for nesting, such as attics, warehouses, barns, and roofs. In the wild, the roof rat is a tree dweller. Norway rats occupy far-ranging habitats but tend to prefer damp places. They are most common in dense, urban areas of the eastern U.S. They are not good climbers so are usually found at ground level or below, in sewers and basements. They may burrow along building foundations and fence lines, under sidewalks, or in rocky debris piles. In the wild, Norway rats often live near beaches and riverbanks.

Other Characteristics

Most wood rats are nocturnal and mainly vegetarian, living on green plants and small woodland fruits; they particularly like acorns. Their ground or tree-built nests are intricately constructed of twigs and leaves with many emergency exits, designed to avoid surprise attacks, and difficult to break into. Some species build houses up to 5 feet tall. In addition to collecting natural materials for nest building, wood rats are attracted to shiny objects and will collect and hide small fragments of glass and metal, earning them the name "pack rats."

Roof rats are also nocturnal. They eat seeds, fresh and dried fruit, broad leaves, tree bark, and, when available, insects, snails, slugs, eggs, and bird nestlings. They also store excess food in hidden caches away from their nests. When living close to humans, such as in dark barns and warehouses, roof rats may be active most of the time and will feed on any human food supplies available. They live in small, hierarchical family groups led by one rat.

Norway rats are omnivorous: In the wild they eat seeds and vegetable matter as well as insects, snails, and crustaceans. In urban areas they tend to live more on garbage and other refuse, including spilled seed from bird feeders and animal carrion. They live in small, hierarchical family groups based on a female line of descent and including one or more dominant males. (Dominance is determined by body weight; the heavier the rat, the more deference is paid by others.) Norway rats are territorial and guard their boundaries jealously.

Enemies and Defenses

Wood rats are preyed on by many predators, including foxes, lynxes, coyotes, and raptors. When alarmed, they drum a warning signal with their hind feet, similar to rabbits and hares.

Rats, probably more than any other rodent, are a threat to humans because of disease carried by their fleas—most notably the bubonic plague that wiped out millions of Europeans during the Middle Ages. They also contaminate food with urine and feces.

How to Observe

The presence of rats is identified by ¼-inch wide, ½-inch long droppings; burrows along foundations or fence lines; grease or smudge marks on walls or pipes, indicating rat travel routes in the structure; signs of gnawing on doors, in corners, or in access areas to buildings; and the sound of rats in walls or attics during daylight hours.

Situations and Solutions

Rats Living in Buildings

WHY IT HAPPENS: Rats can gain access through holes no larger than ½ inch.

SUGGESTIONS:

1. Seal all holes with heavyweight material of ¼-inch or finer mesh. Be sure to check heat vents, which can be a prime location for entry.
2. Clear all brush away from foundations, where rats can be living or burrowing for access to the building. If necessary, install fine-mesh hardware cloth or pour concrete footings vertically a foot below ground level and then, at a 90-degree angle, another foot out from the foundation.
3. Maintain good sanitation in and around buildings. Dispose of all refuse, tall grass, and any debris, including woodpiles, lying around the grounds. All food sources, whether actual foodstuffs or garbage, should be kept in ratproof containers (strong plastic or metal—any material they cannot gnaw through) and pet food should never be left out.
4. If all other alternatives fail, rats can be live-trapped, but it is important to remove and relocate them quickly. Be extremely careful to prevent being bitten and do not relocate them anyplace where they could cause problems for other people.

Rat Bite to Human or Pet

WHY IT HAPPENS: Rats will bite, so great caution is recommended.

SUGGESTIONS: If a person or pet is bitten by a rat, wash the wound immediately with soapy water and see a doctor or veterinarian as soon as possible.

[VOLES]

Meadow voles (*Microtus* spp.), also known as meadow mice, and pine voles (*Pitymus* spp.) have thick, rounded bodies, blunt faces, and small eyes, ears, and tails. Adult meadow and pine voles usually weigh no more than 4 ounces, and their coats are of gray brown coarse hair. Red-backed voles (*Clethrionomys* spp.) are reddish in color.

Like mice, voles reproduce throughout the year, producing as many as 10 litters per year with an average of 5 young per litter.

Range and Habitat

Many species of meadow and pine voles are found throughout North America. Meadow voles live in open grassy areas such as meadows and hayfields, while pine voles tend to be found in coniferous forest areas. Red-backed voles are found throughout Canada and Alaska. Voles live primarily in agricultural areas but can also live in residential or urban settings.

Other Characteristics

Voles are vegetarian; their diet is made up chiefly of plant cuttings and grasses supplemented by seeds and fruits. They usually obtain their food by grazing or digging for underground roots. In winter, they do not hibernate and have been known to cause tree damage by gnawing on bark for food. Farmers sometimes have problems with vole infestations, which can damage vegetables and crops as well as fruit trees.

Enemies and Defenses

Like mice and rats, voles are a primary food supply for carnivorous predators such as foxes, owls, and hawks. Their main enemies are human beings because of damage they can cause to agricultural enterprises.

How to Observe

The presence of voles is identified by wide pathways made through grasslands in which clippings and droppings have been left. These runways often end at 2-inch-wide, open burrows. Voles tend to be less shy than other rodents and may sometimes be observed searching for food in open meadows.

Situations and Solutions

Voles Damaging Gardens, Crops, and Fruit Trees

WHY IT HAPPENS: Vegetables and grain crops are the primary food source for voles.

SUGGESTIONS:

1. Keep tall grasses and weeds adjacent to gardens and crops cleared.
2. Wrap tree trunks with ¼-inch or smaller mesh hardware cloth and bury it as much as 6 to 8 inches deep along the trunk.

3. For small vegetable or flower gardens, place ¼-inch wire screen or hardware cloth on the ground after planting. The plants can grow up through the screening but it keeps voles from burrowing to reach roots and tubers. Before planting flower bulbs, soak them in irritating repellents that contain the bittering agent thiram.

[MUSKRATS]

Muskrats (*Ondatra zibethica*) are the largest species in the vole and lemming subfamily Microtinae. The muskrat is a rabbit-sized, stocky rodent with a broad, blunt head, short legs, small eyes, and short ears. It has adapted to an aquatic life by developing a waterproof coat, partially webbed hind feet, and a naked, vertically flattened tail (beaver tails are horizontally flattened) used as a rudder. Its fur is dark brown above and silver tipped on the belly; it has long, coarse guard hairs and dense, waterproof, buoyant underfur. Muskrats range from 12 to 16 inches long (excluding the tail) and weigh 2 to 5 pounds.

Some females can produce as many as 3 litters of 1 to 10 young per year.

Range and Habitat

Muskrats are probably the most common small mammals in the northern areas of North America, ranging from the Arctic through Alaska, Canada, and the northeastern U.S. Muskrat habitat includes lakes, streams, canals, ponds, freshwater and brackish marshes, and drainage ditches. These rodents range throughout North America, except in the Arctic, the far southeast, central Texas, and the southwestern Pacific coast and deserts. Muskrats prefer still or slow-moving water with vegetation in the water and along the banks. Like beavers, muskrats build lodges in the water, or they dig burrows into the banks of the waterway.

Other Characteristics

The nocturnal muskrat is primarily vegetarian, feeding on aquatic plants such as algae, cattails, bur reed, duckweed, wild rice, sedges, and bulrushes. They also consume corn, clover, alfalfa, and fruits when available near their homes. When vegetation is scarce, they will eat small aquatic animals such as shellfish, frogs, insects, and slow-moving fish. Muskrat lodges, built of twigs, mud, and leaves, have the entrance below the water and the living area above water level; a lodge can measure

6½ feet at the base and be 2 to 4 feet tall. The tops of muskrat lodges are favorite nesting platforms for Canada geese. Muskrats may also burrow nests in riverbanks or pond dams, if the water is too fast for them to build a lodge midstream.

Muskrats are adapted to stay underwater for up to 20 minutes. Their front legs and feet are short with heavy claws for feeding, grooming, digging, and constructing a lodge; the partly webbed hind feet propel them while they swim.

Unlike beavers, muskrats do not store food for the winter so will eat nearly anything when ice interferes with their normal feeding. When feeding, muskrats prefer to take their food into the marsh or onto a stump or log, where uneaten portions soon pile up, creating feeding platforms. They use several of these throughout the year. In winter, they maintain under-ice tunnels from their lodges to their favorite feeding platforms; if other food supplies run low, the platforms themselves become their main food for the winter.

Muskrats get their name from two scent glands located on each side of the tail, which secrete a strong, yellowish, musky-smelling liquid used to mark their territories and to identify one another. Muskrats have small home territories and seldom travel more than 200 yards from their lodge, although they may range several miles overland to find suitable habitat. If muskrats overpopulate an area, they can damage their marsh habitat and may become vulnerable to disease epidemics that ultimately control their population. Also, when overabundant, they fight among themselves, reproduction decreases, and malnutrition increases. Muskrats rarely live more than one year.

Enemies and Defenses

Muskrats are preyed on by many carnivores, including foxes, weasels, minks, snakes, snapping turtles, coyotes, hawks, owls, and even other muskrats. Humans are also their enemy, as we continue to drain and destroy wetland areas and trap them for their pelts, for their musk scents, used in perfumes, and for food. More muskrats than any other furbearing animals are trapped in the U.S.

Some people consider muskrats pests because of the damage they can do to pond dams or dikes, though this is counterbalanced by their work in keeping down algae and other plant growth that can choke small ponds. By clearing pond plant life to construct their lodges, they make the pond accessible,which greatly increases wetland value for waterfowl and shorebirds.

How to Observe

The presence of muskrats can be identified by 5- to 6-inch burrow openings in dams or dikes at or below water level, aquatic plants cut off at water level, or dome-shaped mud and plant lodges in shallow water.

Situations and Solutions

Muskrats Burrowing into Pond Dam or Dike

WHY IT HAPPENS: Ponds are the muskrat's natural habitat, and an already-constructed dam or dike provides an excellent location for its nest.

SUGGESTIONS:

1. If dams or dikes are properly constructed—that is, built with an impenetrable core and thick enough—muskrats will not threaten their structural integrity. Gentle slopes (a 3:1 ratio or less) are less attractive to muskrats than steep slopes. Also, consider constructing a shelf by filling the impoundment pond with earth from bottom to water level, from the face of the dam 10 feet into the pond. This shelf will create a muskrat barrier as well as strengthen the dam against erosion.

2. Retrofit weak dams or dikes by placing a continuous layer of riprap (stones 6 inches thick), galvanized hardware cloth, or bird netting from 3 feet below to 2 feet above water level all the way across the dam or dike.

3. Burrows in riverbanks or lodges built in the pond are not a threat to the dam and should not be harmed. To discourage muskrat habitation of the waterway, you can attempt to control aquatic plant life, but using herbicides in water is strongly discouraged and hand removal of such plant growth is difficult, time-consuming, and repetitive. Alternatively, try to appreciate the balance muskrats maintain by keeping the pond plant growth under control.

4. If you choose to drive muskrats from existing burrows, do so by probing with a metal rod above the burrow entrance to locate the nesting chamber. Then dig down to expose the chamber. This will prompt muskrats to leave immediately. If young are in the chamber, stop digging but leave the chamber exposed. The mother will likely return to gather her young. Once the chamber has been abandoned, fill it in and install a barrier as described in number 2.

5. Because muskrats are considered furbearing animals, state wildlife agencies control trapping of them; be sure to check local restrictions

before undertaking any trapping. Even where allowed, it is unlikely that live-trapping will capture all family members. If you attempt it, place the trap, baited with apples, just outside the burrow and partially in the water. Make sure the trap is shallow enough that a trapped muskrat can breathe. Check the trap often, and relocate the muskrat to a larger body of water immediately. Do not trap during breeding season, because you may orphan many young.

Muskrats Feeding on Crops

WHY IT HAPPENS: Corn, alfalfa, clover, vegetable gardens, or fruit crops are planted immediately adjacent to waterways that form the muskrat's home territory.

SUGGESTIONS: A stone barrier or fence between the crop area and waterway may solve the problem, but the best solution is to plant more than 200 yards from the waterway, putting the crop outside the muskrat's territorial range.

[PORCUPINES]

The "New World" porcupine *(Erethizon dorsatum)* is the only member of the Caviomorpha suborder of cavylike rodents found in North America. Porcupines are the second-largest rodent on this continent, with strong bodies, compact heads, short, thick legs, and small eyes and ears. Their notable feature is the thick coat of hair interspersed with long bristles and stiff quills—approximately 30,000 light and dark-banded quills on the back and tail. Their underside is soft and relatively unprotected. Thick guard hairs on the front of the body are usually black or brown in the eastern U.S. and yellowish in the West. Porcupines have sharp front claws used for climbing and digging.

After the winter gestation, the female gives birth to one pup in April or May.

Range and Habitat

Porcupines are found throughout Canada and Alaska and southward to the deserts of New Mexico but are rare along the Atlantic coast. They prefer dry woodlands for bushy cover. They winter den in old trees, rock crevices, or ground dens.

Porcupines use their barbed quills for defense. Keep children and pets away from them, if possible.

Other Characteristics

The porcupine is primarily vegetarian. It spends most of its time in trees and mainly eats woody material stripped from trees with its large, strong front teeth, feeding on pine, fir, and spruce, among others. Porcupines also sometimes eat flowers and grasses, and they often chew on antlers discarded by deer, elk, and moose for the calcium and other minerals found in them. They are solitary creatures except during the breeding season and in winter, when several may share a den.

Porcupine quills are spongy and hollow, providing buoyancy to help porcupines swim. The tips are covered with many backward-facing, microscopically small barbs, which, once embedded in an enemy, begin to expand. The victim's muscles contract, pulling the quill deeper into its skin—sometimes fatally deep.

Enemies and Defenses

Porcupines' primary enemies are domestic dogs, mountain lions, wolves, coyotes, fishers (of the weasel family), and great horned owls. Porcupines are very slow moving and vulnerable to attack on their soft, unprotected underbellies. Their obvious and only defense is their formidable quills.

When a porcupine is scared or has been attacked, it turns its tail toward the enemy and erects its quills. Sometimes it swings its tail like a club, trying to strike its attacker to embed the quills; while it cannot throw the quills, it can drive them to the bone or even into vital organs. Often predators are unable to turn the porcupine over; they become covered with quills and break off the attack. Once embedded, the quills' barbs make them difficult to remove. A mouth and throat full of quills can result in slow death by starvation.

How to Observe

Porcupines in the wild have little fear of predators because of their effective protection and therefore are relatively easily approached. Be careful if you sight a porcupine on the ground: Do not purposefully approach or get too close, because if it feels threatened, it can embed its quills very quickly. Porcupines can often be spotted in trees during winter; look for a litter of twigs and droppings at the base. During breeding season, porcupines often can be identified at night by their unearthly screaming cries.

Situations and Solutions

Porcupine Quills in Dog

WHY IT HAPPENS: Domestic dogs often attack porcupines without realizing the danger of the quills.

SUGGESTIONS:

1. The only remedy is to pull the quills out, a painful procedure because of the hooked barbs on the ends. Quills are usually easier to remove if cut down so that only a short length is left protruding from the victim. Then pull them out using a pair of pliers.

2. Once you have removed the quills, disinfect wounds with hydrogen peroxide or other antiseptic. Allow the dog to nurse (lick) its wounds, which should heal relatively quickly.

3. If you do not want to attempt removal yourself, or if the wounds do not appear to be healing, consult a veterinarian.

Porcupines Chewing on Tools and Leather

WHY IT HAPPENS: Porcupines have been known to come around human homes, usually looking for salt. They will chew on shovel and broom handles, canoe paddles, saddles, and other wood and leather items because of salty sweat absorbed in these materials.

SUGGESTIONS:

1. Keep all tools, paddles, and leather goods picked up and locked away from access by porcupines.
2. Set out a salt lick in some remote part of your property for all wild animals to enjoy. This provides the salt animals need but helps keep them from coming too close. (See Appendix C.)

Large Carnivores

[BEARS]

Three types of bears can be found in the U.S. and Canada: the brown (grizzly) bear (*Ursus arctos*), black bear (*U. americanus*), and polar bear (*Thalarctos maritimus*). Bears are the largest and most powerful carnivorous mammals, with bulky heads and bodies and strong legs ending in nonretracting claws. They normally move slowly with a clumsy, flat-footed walk, but they can move quickly when necessary.

Brown bears are dark brown to blond in color and 7 to 9 feet in length. Males weigh 400 to 1,100 pounds, females 200 to 600. They are larger than black bears and have a more prominent shoulder hump and straighter claws. Black bears are brown to black, some with a white patch on the front of the chest, and are about 5 feet long; males weigh 150 to 400 pounds, females 125 to 250. Polar bears are all white and are 8 to 12 feet long. Males weigh 600 to 1,200 pounds, females 400 to 700.

Brown bears produce litters of one to three cubs (rarely four); polar bears produce one or two; and black bears usually have two but can bear from one to five young every two years.

Range and Habitat

Most bears are found in remote mountain areas, although some have become accustomed to the presence of humans and interact with humans directly in parks and wilderness areas. The most numerous and widespread of the North American bears, black bears live in forested and wooded areas from California to the Great Lakes, to the southeastern states of Kentucky, West Virginia, and Tennessee, up into Newfoundland in Canada. Grizzly bears are found in mountain forests mostly in Alaska and Canada. The Yellowstone National Park area is also home to a small grizzly bear population. Polar bears interact the least with humans, because they live on the Arctic ice pack.

Other Characteristics

Most bears are omnivorous, eating foods ranging from fruit, nuts, small mammals, and fish to large carcasses such as elk. Grizzlies are excellent fishers but have trouble catching large prey unless it is sick or injured; they do feast on carrion. Black bears are skilled climbers, finding nuts, seeds, fruits, and honeycombs, but they do not fish well. They do not ordinarily prey on large animals but have been known at times to attack sheep or goats. Polar bears are excellent hunters, feeding mainly on seals, walruses, small whales, fish, seabirds, and eggs; during summer, they also eat plants found along coastal waters. Little food is available to bears in early spring when they come out of their dens; however, they are voracious eaters during the late summer and fall, when they store body fat to help see them through the winter.

In years of short food supplies, bears may overcome their fear of people and venture further than usual into human territory. They have been known to bend open car doors, pry out windshields, and swim to island campsites. They also may adapt their habits, becoming nocturnal feeders instead of night sleepers to avoid contact with humans.

Bears tend to have poor eyesight and hearing, but their sense of smell is acute. (The polar bear has better eyesight and hearing than other species, because it depends more on hunting.) They use their sharp foreclaws to overturn stones to find food, to catch fish, and to climb trees. Because of their extensive food sources, bears seldom compete with other carnivores, which limits potentially harmful involvement with other large, dangerous species such as wolves.

Bears are generally solitary and territorial creatures but occasionally gather in groups if food is plentiful. Grizzly and black bears have distinct territories connected by pathways, including areas for feeding and resting. They mark their territories by rubbing throat scent glands against bushes, urinating on trees or rocks, and scratching tree bark. Polar bears cover the largest areas (up to 30 miles a day) looking for food and are not considered truly territorial.

Bear winter sleep is not true hibernation (metabolism and body temperature do not drop) but rather a response to winter food shortages. Bears living in areas with sufficient winter food supplies do not sleep, but those lacking food do. In winter, female polar bears enter dormancy, but males stay active unless weather conditions become extreme.

Enemies and Defenses

Bears' chief enemies are humans. Through hunting and habitat destruction, man has forced brown bears to retreat into the remotest parts of North America. Black bear populations have recovered somewhat in the southeastern U.S. where large-scale reforestation has occurred on old farm sites. Black bears used to be hunted for their fur throughout the U.S. but are now protected in many areas and are a favorite tourist attraction at national parks. (Some states still permit hunting of black bears.) Eskimo hunted polar bears for centuries using traditional methods, thereby living in balance with the bears. With the advent of guns, however, the polar bear population has dramatically fallen to a total of 10,000, and hunting is still permitted with more than 1,000 killed every year.

Although bears ordinarily pose no threat to humans in the wild (they actually avoid inhabited areas), a bear can be extremely aggressive and dangerous if cornered, injured, or defending cubs. Grizzlies tend to more aggressively defend cubs, while black bears will leave their cubs when fleeing from people. It is estimated that a person is 180 times more likely to be killed by a bee than by a black bear, and 160,000 times more likely to die in a traffic accident. Most reported black bear injuries result from a bear nipping or cuffing a human, as it would another bear, when it is being crowded, touched, or teased with food.

Due to their poor eyesight, bears may mistake humans for rivals. Though bears usually shun human smells, some have become acclimated to them through association with feeding at garbage dumps. Black bears that want food may use the same "bluff" threat they would use on other bears: They blow, clack teeth, lunge, lay back their ears, slap the ground or trees, and/or make a short rush. Rarely, though, does an attack follow this behavior, and usually even "blowing" bears can be chased away with loud noises.

How to Observe

Bears are rarely seen in the wild because of their remote habitats and tendency to avoid contact with humans. Their presence can be identified through tracks, droppings, and well-worn foraging trails with ripped-open decayed logs, claw marks on trees, long coarse hair imbedded in tree bark (bears love to rub their backs on trees), and stripped and broken berry bushes. Large flattened areas in cornfields are also a bear sign.

Bears are curious, intelligent, and potentially dangerous animals, and undue fear can endanger both people and bears. Many bears are killed each year merely due to human fear. Respecting bears and learning proper behavior in their territory will help lessen the fear and benefit both bears and humans.

Situations and Solutions

Hiking and Camping in Bear Country

SUGGESTIONS: When you visit areas where bears may be present, the following information can help prevent harmful interchanges between humans and bears:

1. Because bears do not like surprises, make your presence known by making noise while you hike. Sing, talk loudly, or tie a bell to your pack. If possible, travel with a group of people; groups are noisier and easier for bears to detect. Avoid thick brush. If possible, try to walk upwind (with wind at your back) so your scent is carried ahead of you.

2. Be careful not to set up camp near a well-traveled road or path that bears may also use. Avoid any sites where you observe carcasses of fish or dead animals, which may be a bear's personal supply and aggressively defended. When camping, cook away from your tent and avoid smelly foods so that odors do not permeate the tent and clothes. Store all food away from your campsite in airtight or specially designed bearproof containers, or hang food out of bears' reach. Some campgrounds have installed lines or horizontal poles in bear-prone areas. Hang food bags at least 5 feet below the line or pole, 10 feet from the nearest tree trunk, and 12 feet above the ground. Hanging food bags from tree limbs is not as effective, because bears can break small branches and climb out on large ones.

When camping, hang food bags in locations not accessible to bears.

3. Keep your camp clean and burn all garbage in a hot fire (if fires are permitted); carry out all garbage that cannot be burned. Do not bury garbage, because bears will likely locate the scent and dig it up. Bears have learned that containers such as coolers and backpacks may contain food; to minimize property damage, keep empty containers out of sight (in the trunk of a car), or leave them open so the bear can determine that they are empty. If the containers smell of food, hang them with the food bags. Reduce container smell by packing food in plastic bags that can be transferred to hanging bags. Leave tent flies open when out of camp so bears can easily see that there is no food inside.

4. Do not crowd bears. If attempting to view or photograph them, stay a great distance away and use long lenses. If a bear approaches while you are fishing, stop. If you have a fish on your line, do not let it splash—cut the line if necessary—so that bears do not learn that they can get fish just by approaching fishers. If you see a bear, avoid it and give it every opportunity to avoid you. If a cub appears abandoned, do not touch it. Leave the area immediately, and the mother will return for it soon.

Encountering a Bear in the Wild

SUGGESTIONS: If you find yourself within close range of a bear, stay calm. Attacks are extremely rare. Take the following steps:

1. Talk to the bear in a normal voice and wave your arms to let it know that you are human. If it cannot tell what you are, it may approach closer or stand on its hind legs to get a better look or smell. A standing bear is usually curious, not threatening. Try backing away slowly, but if the bear follows, stop and hold your ground.

2. Do not run from a bear. Like dogs, bears chase fleeing animals, and they can run up to 35 mph. Bears sometimes bluff by charging as near as 10 feet without making contact. If the bear gets too close, raise your voice, bang on pots and pans, use noisemakers of any kind to frighten it away. Do not imitate bear sounds or make a high-pitched squeal. A group making noise and chasing up to 15 feet from a black bear is usually effective in scaring it off—but do *not* chase a grizzly in this way. Do not try to pet bears; this can cause them to nip or cuff with their front paws.

3. If a brown (grizzly) bear actually touches you, fall to the ground and play dead. Lie flat on your stomach, or curl up in a ball with hands

behind your head. Once it perceives that the threat has been eliminated, a grizzly will usually stop an attack. If a black bear attacks, fight back vigorously. They are more easily frightened away.

4. Avoid use of guns unless you have no alternative. Handguns are generally not effective against bears. In most places where bears are protected, they may be shot only in self-defense in an unprovoked attack, and the hide and skull must be salvaged and turned over to authorities.

5. Defensive aerosol sprays containing capsaicin (cayenne pepper extract) have been somewhat successful with bears when used at a range of 6 to 8 feet. This is the same repellent long used by mail carriers against dogs. In research on the spray, no bear was angered after being sprayed; most just ran away, stopping to rub their eyes. The repellent irritates for several minutes but causes no injury to the bear.

Bear in the Yard

WHY IT HAPPENS: In settled areas close to bear habitat, black bears in particular may venture into yards in search of food.

SUGGESTIONS: Make sure that all possible food sources around your yard are properly stored or disposed of, especially garbage, pet food, and animal carcasses. If you are surprised by a bear on your property, *do nothing.*
The bear will wander away on its own without any need for you to interact with it. After it is gone, locate the food source that tempted the bear to come so close and eliminate it.

Bear Raiding Beehives, Orchards, or Corn Crops

WHY IT HAPPENS   Bears raiding beehives and crops are looking for food; they especially favor apples and sweet corn.

SUGGESTIONS:

1. Because brown and black bears prefer wooded areas, make sure beehives, apple trees, and cornfields are sited as far from woods as possible. Raise beehives above ground level on platforms or anywhere that bears cannot climb to. Electric fences, properly maintained, are effective in limiting bear access. Heavy-gauge, woven-wire fencing at least 8 feet high, with barbed wire on brackets, is also effective in discouraging bear intrusion.

2. Because bears often forage at night, surprise techniques such as loud radios, barking dogs, fireworks (be careful of fire danger), flashlights,

and scarecrows can be effective. It is important to vary techniques to ensure the element of surprise.

3. If bear crop damage persists, some wildlife agencies do live trapping and removal to remote areas. This technique is costly, however, and is not always a permanent solution, because a bear's strong homing instinct may cause it to return.

The Canid (Dog) Family

The wolves, the coyotes, and the foxes are the three different types of wild canids (dogs) found in North America. Wolves are absent from all but a few places in the lower forty-eight states, and are not covered here.

[COYOTES]

Coyotes (*Canis latrans*) are sometimes known as prairie wolves, though they are smaller than wolves and smaller than most people think. Their name comes from the Aztec word for the species, *coyotl*. They vary in size depending on location, but generally are 4 to 4½ feet long, including the tail, stand 18 to 25 inches tall at the shoulder, and weigh 20 to 50 pounds;

Coyotes have effectively survived human attempts at extermination and adapted to human development.

males are typically heavier than females. Their coloration is gray, brown, or tan above, whitish underneath. (Some coyotes are black with a white chest patch. Desert-living coyotes have yellowish red fur; northern coyotes tend to be more gray.) The reddish, bushy tail, tipped in black, is usually carried low, held straight out behind or between the legs. The muzzle is long, slender, and pointed, the eyes yellow with round pupils, the ears large and erect; like wolves and foxes, coyotes have black-pigmented lips. Eastern coyotes tend to be larger than their western cousins, probably due to cross-breeding with the now-endangered red wolf. The distinctive coyote call consists of long howls and yapping barks.

Females bear an average of five to ten pups annually.

Range and Habitat

Coyotes are adaptable; they can live in a wide variety of climates and conditions. Coyote habitat ranges throughout the U.S., Canada, and Mexico, in suburbia and wilderness, from sea level to over 10,000 feet. Once found only west of the Mississippi River, they now are found in all states except Hawaii, although they are still most abundant in the West. They live in deserts, lush waterway areas, rolling grasslands, high forests, cities, suburbs, rural towns, and agricultural lands. They favor brushy habitat, including sagebrush, chaparral, oak woodland, blackberry thickets, tall grasses, and the edges of fields near forests.

Other Characteristics

Coyotes are omnivorous and eat whatever is handy, including meat, garbage, insects, rodents, rabbits, birds, deer, pronghorn, and carrion. In late summer and early fall, fruits and berries can make up a large portion of their diet. Coyotes are important in controlling rodents; 80 percent of their diet consists of rabbits, squirrels, gophers, mice, and rats. Normally solitary hunters, they sometimes hunt in pairs and rarely in packs to bring down larger prey. When hunting, coyotes follow specific foraging routes reused throughout the year.

Coyotes can run up to 45 mph for short distances and swim well. They are active both day and night, though chiefly nocturnal. They have a life span of 10 to 15 years in captivity and 8 to 10 years in the wild. Like wolves, coyotes have been known to interbreed with domestic dogs. Hybrids are common in some suburbs and are hard to distinguish from pure-bred coyotes because they behave similarly; however, unlike purebred coyotes, domestic hybrids go into heat twice a year.

The scientific name *Canis latrans* literally means "barking dog," though the animal's most characteristic vocalizations are shrill yips and howls. Howling is often a group effort and may function as greetings between individuals or territorial claims. Not as social as wolves, coyotes do form family groups that share territories; they may also tolerate transient young coyotes living on the edges. Territories vary from 300 acres to 100 square miles, depending upon food supply and coyote population density. A normal home range is 25 to 30 miles in diameter. Coyotes have been reported to travel up to 400 miles in search of food, though when feeding young they do not range more than 5 miles from the den.

Coyotes' exceptional senses of smell, vision, and hearing, coupled with their evasiveness, enable them to survive both in the wild and in suburban areas. They adapt quickly to environmental changes and exploit new food sources, ignoring fast-moving automobiles to clean up road-killed birds and small animals, for example. The abundance of coyote populations adversely impacts fox and bobcat populations because these animals compete for the same prey.

Enemies and Defenses

Humans are the coyote's chief enemy. As settlers moved west and destroyed the coyote's traditional food sources, such as pronghorn, deer, mountain sheep, and even buffalo carrion, coyotes adjusted to hunting the young of domestic livestock. Because of this natural adaptation to a food source, humans declared war on the coyote, as on wolves, and have hunted, trapped, and poisoned them since that time. It has been estimated that 30 to 50 percent of all adult coyotes die each year from human-related causes.

Unlike the wolf, however, which was eliminated from the lower 48 states during this antipredator campaign, the coyote's adaptability led to the increase of its original range, as far north as Alaska and as far south as Central America. In fact, the coyote's reproduction level appears to be directly correlated to attempts to control its population. Larger litters seem to be born in areas where intensive efforts at eradication or control have been undertaken.

Coyotes are actually helpful to farmers and ranchers because they kill destructive, vegetation-eating rodents. And much of the poultry and livestock coyotes are unjustly accused of killing is already dead when the coyote finds the carrion.

How to Observe

In the wild, coyotes are shy and are best seen with help from professional guides. Be sure you have binoculars and patience. In most wildlife refuge areas, where a good supply of small mammals and ground-nesting birds exists and where hunting is not permitted, coyotes will appear— most often during the hours close to sunrise and sunset. In urban areas, coyotes may be more bold. *Do not attempt to approach a coyote.* It will likely run away, but any cornered or frightened wild animal can be dangerous and capable of attack.

Situations and Solutions

Coyotes Eating Garbage, Approaching House, or Attacking Pets

WHY IT HAPPENS: In urban areas, coyotes are less likely to fear people and more likely to associate them with an easy, dependable food source. Some have been known to come up to the doors of homes if food is regularly present.

SUGGESTIONS:

1. If you do not mind sharing your space with coyotes, enjoy observing them with binoculars when they visit. *Do not feed them, as they can easily become dependent on human food sources.*

2. Make sure your pets are inside whenever coyotes are seen or heard. Do not allow pets to run free. Always walk your dog on a leash and accompany pets outside, especially at night. Provide secure shelters for poultry and rabbits.

3. If you want to discourage coyotes from visiting, take the following steps:

   - *Do not feed coyotes.* Observe food sources that are attracting them and take steps to eliminate these. Never leave pet food outside or discard edible garbage where coyotes can get to it. Secure garbage containers and eliminate their odors. Use a small amount of ammonia or cayenne pepper in the garbage to discourage scavenging. Restricting use of birdseed may be advisable; coyotes are attracted to it and to the birds and rodents that use the feeder. If possible, eliminate outdoor sources of water.

   - Trim and clear near ground level any shrubbery that provides cover for coyotes or prey.

- Use fencing to help deter coyotes. The fence must be at least 6 feet tall with the bottom extending at least 6 inches below ground level.
- Actively discourage coyotes by making loud noises and throwing rocks to make them leave.
4. Ask your neighbors to cooperate in following these nonlethal steps to control coyote presence in your area.

Coyotes Preying on Domestic Livestock or Crops

WHY IT HAPPENS: Because coyotes have adapted to the spread of human development through their natural habitats, they have adjusted their food sources. Coyotes do kill *some* domestic livestock such as sheep, goats, calves, hogs, and poultry and damage some crops such as watermelons. However, studies have identified domestic livestock as a small percentage of coyote diets—and of that amount, much is discarded dead animals left out where coyotes can easily find them. This conditions coyotes to that food source and encourages them to raid the farmyard for more.

SUGGESTIONS:

1. Observe carefully to determine whether coyotes are truly responsible for the damage. Coyotes readily feed on carrion, so their tracks around a carcass do not necessarily mean the coyote was responsible for the kill. Predation on livestock occurs most frequently in late spring and early summer, when food demand is greatest, because adults have pups to feed. To help verify coyote predation, look for the following indications:
   - Trampled vegetation or other signs of a struggle.
   - Bite marks and bleeding, especially on the head and neck. This may require skinning the head and neck to look for tooth marks and bleeding. Coyote bites may penetrate the rear of the jaw bone and leave marks on even badly decomposed carcasses. Coyotes most often kill larger prey by biting the throat, causing suffocation, and frequently adjust their grip, leaving multiple bite marks. They may also attack from the rear, biting legs or tail to slow a fleeing animal.
   - Coyotes typically begin feeding behind the ribs, often eating the stomach of nursing animals. With calves, they may eat the nose and hindquarters, and they may attack a cow in labor, feeding on both calf and mother.

- Coyotes may carry off small animals such as chickens or newborn goats, leaving only tracks.

2. Try to distinguish between coyote and dog predation. Free-running dogs leave their victims mutilated; though they have the instinct to kill, they lack the experience to efficiently take down prey. Dogs also do not usually feed on the carcass. Feral dogs (those living entirely in the wild and independent of human care) may be efficient at killing for food and will leave sign similar to coyote. Dogs usually hunt in packs, while coyotes usually hunt alone or in pairs. Various-sized tracks around a killed animal may help to identify dog predation. Coyote tracks are narrower and more elongated than dog tracks.

3. Nonlethal methods to protect livestock include exclusion fencing, corralling animals at night, and using trained guard dogs. Fencing is generally the most effective. To exclude coyotes, use woven or welded wire fencing, no more than 4"× 6" mesh, at least 4 feet high with a barbed wire across the top for a fence 5 feet high. An outward overhang on top of the fence can prevent jumping over. Electric fencing can also be effective.

4. Make sure all small livestock, such as chickens and ducks, are securely inside at night.

5. Modify husbandry practices by confining livestock during birthing season; avoid using pasture where predation has been high; and use guard or herd dogs.

6. Dispose of all dead young livestock, such as chickens, lambs, pigs, and calves, by burying or burning. Do not leave carcasses in open fields where coyotes can feed on them.

7. Trapping is not particularly effective with coyotes. Nonlethal trapping, with padded jaw traps, should be attempted only with the advice and assistance of trained wildlife agencies.

[FOXES]

This canid has well-developed teeth; strong nonretractable claws; and acute senses of smell, sight, and hearing. Four types of foxes are found in North America: the red fox (*Vulpes vulpes*); the gray (or tree) fox (*V. cinereoargenteus*); the kit (desert or swift) fox (*V. velox*); and the Arctic fox (*Alopex lagopus*). Foxes have long bodies, relatively short legs, pointed noses, bushy tails, and large, pointed ears.

Red foxes, the largest, weigh 8 to 15 pounds and measure 22 to 25 inches long (excluding the tail). The thick coat is brownish red on top, yellowish white underneath. They have black legs, feet, and outer ears and black hairs mixed with red on the long, bushy tail. Some common color variations include the cross fox, which has a dark cross over the shoulders, and the black (silver) fox, which is black with white-tipped body hairs. Albino red foxes are not uncommon. All red foxes—unlike gray foxes— have white-tipped tails.

Gray foxes average 3 to 4 feet long, including the tail, and weigh 7 to 13 pounds. Their basic color is grizzled gray with a distinctive black streak along the top to the black tip of the tail. They are rusty yellowish on the feet, legs, sides, neck, and back of the ears.

Kit foxes are much smaller than red and gray foxes. They have thick, light yellow to pale gray coats and large ears, which appear to be a body heat–regulating feature. The oversize ears may also be more efficient at picking up sounds of prey in the dry desert air.

The Arctic fox strongly resembles the red fox but is much smaller and has shorter ears. There are two subspecies with different coloring that changes from winter to summer, starting tail first: one from white to silver-gray brown; the other from steel-blue gray to chocolate brown.

Fox young are born in early spring, in litters averaging three to five.

Range and Habitat

Red foxes are the most widespread species, found in a wide range of habitats from sandy coasts to mountain ravines. They tend toward more northern latitudes but occur all over North America, excluding the Rocky, Teton, and Cascade mountains, the lower Pacific coast, and the desert Southwest. They prefer a mixture of forest and open country.

Gray foxes tend to range in more southern latitudes but are found throughout the U.S. except in the central and northern Great Plains, the northern Rocky Mountains, the Great Basin, the Cascades, and the Coast Range; nor are they found in Canada or Alaska. They prefer chaparral and open forests and den in hollow logs, beneath boulders, or, sometimes, in ground burrows. One species lives on the islands off the southern coast of California.

Kit foxes are found in arid and sandy regions of North America, and Arctic foxes are found only in the Arctic regions of Alaska and Canada.

Other Characteristics

RED FOXES: Red foxes primarily eat rabbits and rodents but, like other foxes, also partake of insects and young roe deer (*Capreolus capreolus*). In coastal areas, foxes will eat crabs, stranded fish, and dead seabirds from the shoreline. In the summer, they include fruits, berries, grasses, and other plants in their diet. They bury excess food for later use. Unlike other canids, red foxes hunt alone. They usually do not eat their prey right away (unless it is very small); they take it back to their den to eat or cache it. They hunt mainly at night; red fox males can range from 12 to 30 miles a night, while females seldom range over 9 miles.

Territories range from 25 acres to 8 square miles, depending on the environment. Boundaries are marked with urine and feces. Red foxes also have scent glands on their feet to mark their regular paths. They either dig their own lairs or take over and extend abandoned badger, woodchuck, or rabbit holes; they often create "spare" dens for contingencies. The red fox marks the entrance to its lair, known as its "earth," by rubbing tail scent glands on the ground as it enters and exits. Dens usually have more than one entrance, with well-disguised escape holes.

Red foxes hunt alone and live as pairs or in small family groups that may include a number of unmated females who help care for the young in the den while the mother goes out to forage for food. Members of such groups often find each other's buried food by scent. Although fast and agile, red foxes also use their keen intelligence, sight, smell, and hearing for protection. Unlike gray foxes, they dislike being underground and will run from predators for long stretches rather than holing up. Their call is distinct from that of dogs, coyotes, and wolves: Males are said to yelp, females to yap.

GRAY FOXES: Gray foxes are omnivorous, eating small mammals, insects, fruits, birds, eggs, and carrion. They are timid, elusive, and primarily nocturnal. Unlike red foxes, they avoid contact with human areas. They are the only true tree-climbers among canids, climbing to sun themselves or to escape predators. Gray foxes are also good swimmers and can run up to 20 mph (slower than other American foxes).

Territories can vary from 100 to 2,000 acres, depending on habitat quality, food availability, population density, and competition with other species. Gray foxes can live to be six to eight years old, but most die within the first year from disease, predation, accidents, trapping, and hunting; they also are highly susceptible to rabies and canine distemper. They have a louder bark than red foxes, and also squeal and growl. Their anal scent glands give off a powerful odor.

KIT FOXES: Desert—or kit—foxes prey on rodents and other small mammals up to the size of a large hare. In order to catch such prey, they necessarily have great speed. They are generally solitary and occupy relatively small territories.

ARCTIC FOXES: These species are active year-round (despite their cold environment, they do not hibernate or have any dormancy period). They are tolerant of cold and do not start shivering until the temperature reaches −94 degrees F. In summer, they prey on small mammals, especially lemmings and mice, as well as insects, beached fish, seabirds, and the eggs and young of ground-nesting birds. In winter, they live on Arctic hares and leftovers from polar bear kills. In some areas, they compete for food with larger red foxes, which may explain why Arctic foxes have not spread into more southerly habitats.

Enemies and Defenses

Foxes' primary enemies are large predators, including eagles, large owls, bobcats, domestic dogs, wolves, coyotes, and humans. Foxes rarely fight except to defend their young. Their defenses include elusiveness; when threatened, red foxes run, and gray foxes climb trees. Many foxes are shot or poisoned by farmers concerned about their livestock, or are hunted and trapped for their fur. Another cause of recent declines in red fox populations apparently is competition with coyotes for food.

Because of dwindling natural habitat, red foxes have adapted to living more closely with people. Foxes in the wild normally do not kill more than they need to eat. However, prey movement triggers their predatory behavior, so if a fox makes its way into a henhouse, for example, and the hens cannot escape, their panicked movements trigger the fox's instinct and it ends up killing all of them.

Although many poultry farmers and game fowl hunters complain about red fox damage, studies have shown that such damage is actually slight. Red and gray foxes perform a valuable service to humans by controlling the small-rodent population, so they should be viewed by humans as an ally. Usually this benefit far outweighs the occasional damage they may cause.

Likewise effective in keeping down rodent populations, kit foxes also have been persecuted, so much so that they have almost disappeared from some of their native habitat. Arctic foxes have been so seriously reduced in number by hunting for pelts that they are rarely seen near any human settlements.

How to Observe

Foxes are not usually seen in open country. In areas where you suspect fox traffic, watch with binoculars for movement along hedges, fences, bushes lining streams, and other places where a fox would feel comfortable with cover close by. Foxes living in areas where hunting is forbidden tend to be less shy; they will even approach campsites to look for debris.

Situations and Solutions

Red Foxes Nesting in Empty Buildings

WHY IT HAPPENS: Foxes tend to den only during breeding season. If they are found nesting in an empty building, chances are high that the vixen is about to or has recently given birth.

SUGGESTIONS: If you can be patient and allow them to remain, the parents and young will abandon the den by the time the young are three months old. If you cannot wait that long, any kind of disturbance, such as dogs, loud noises, and human scent, will likely cause the vixen to move to another den. Once she is aware of the danger, allow her the opportunity to move her young without threat of harm.

Totally enclosing a chicken coop (including wire over the top) excludes foxes and other predators.

Foxes Preying on Domestic Animals

WHY IT HAPPENS: Foxes rarely kill prey larger than themselves. If red foxes do attack domestic livestock like fowl, rabbits, young lambs, goats, and even cats, it is probably because natural food sources are in limited supply.

SUGGESTIONS:

1. To protect domestic animals from foxes, make sure the henhouse or other enclosure is well protected. Use heavy-gauge mesh wire to cover up holes in the structures and keep out most potential predators. Since foxes can climb over or dig under fences, a completely closed-in structure is best. A watchdog may also help keep foxes away.
2. Foxes can be caught in live traps baited with fresh meat. Once caught, they should be released as soon as possible in a suitable habitat at least 5 miles away. Live-trapping alone will not solve the problem, though, because other individuals may move into the area. Always check with local wildlife agencies to determine rules or restrictions on live trapping.

Foxes Raiding Garbage Cans

WHY IT HAPPENS: As fox habitat is lost to human development, foxes apply their opportunistic feeding habits to raiding garbage cans.

SUGGESTIONS: To foxproof a garbage can, use rope, chains, or bungee cords to keep the lid closed and to secure the handle to a metal or wooden stake driven into the ground. Placing cans in wooden bins or in the garage may also limit fox access.

Sick or Disoriented Foxes

WHY IT HAPPENS: Foxes are susceptible to mange, canine distemper, and rabies. Distemper and rabies can cause symptoms such as walking in circles, disorientation, and drooling.

SUGGESTIONS: Do not attempt to touch a sick fox. One person should try to keep the animal in sight while another calls the local wildlife agency for assistance.

The Felid (Cat) Family

Felids found in North America include mountain lions, lynxes, and bobcats.

[MOUNTAIN LIONS]

Mountain lions *(Felis concolor)*, also called cougars, pumas, panthers, and catamounts, are large cats, ranging from 7 to 8 feet in length (including the tail) and weighing 150 to 300 pounds. Their body coloration varies from tan to gray as adults and is spotted when young. They have clear yellow eyes, a pink nose, and well-muscled, strong legs. The feet (four toed in back and five toed in front) have strong, hooked claws that retract into their paws.

Young are born in a den, in litters ranging from one to six, averaging two to three.

Range and Habitat

Mountain lions range from sea level to 10,000 feet in most of the western U.S., western Canada, Mexico, and South America. Typical habitat is steep, rocky canyon country, or mountainous terrain. They are primarily nocturnal, secretive, and rarely seen.

Mountain lions have been hunted almost to extinction in the eastern U.S., but a few remain in the southernmost areas, including the Gulf regions of Texas and Louisiana, and southern Florida. The Florida panther *(F. c. coryi)* is an endangered species.

Other Characteristics

Mountain lions are carnivorous. They prey on most other animals in their habitat, including pronghorn, hares, badgers, porcupines, skunks, coyotes, deer, bison, bear cubs, elk, moose, bighorn sheep, fish, and rodents. Male territories range from 15 to 30 square miles, and females range from 5 to 20 square miles, depending on the number of young they are providing for. They may hunt in a radius of 30 to 50 miles. A mountain lion's territory sometimes is not one large area but rather several separate ones connected by pathways. Mountain lions mark their territory and pathways with visible spots of feces and urine. Territorial pathways may overlap, but if the animals meet, one will always defer to the other rather than risk injury by fighting.

With few exceptions, mountain lions are solitary hunters and spend most of their lives alone. They have specialized teeth for killing and eating prey and, like many members of the cat family, enlarged and rough taste buds on their tongues to aid in scraping meat from bones. Individuals develop a preference for one type of prey (one may prefer hares, another deer), which limits competition with each other. They hunt by stalking, getting to within a few yards of their prey before lunging in for the kill. They have great speed for short distances and can leap 20 to 23 feet from a standstill.

Mountain lions have color vision and highly developed mental faculties to aid their acute senses in the hunt. In dim light, most cats see up to six times better than humans. They are generally quiet, although their vocalizations include growls, hisses, and roars, as well as high-pitched screams. Mountain lions in the wild live approximately 10 years.

Enemies and Defenses/Conservation Note

Mountain lions' chief enemy is humans, with whom they compete for food and territory. Once roaming over all of North America, the mountain lion, like the wolf, has been persecuted by those who believe all the myths about the damage they have caused people and livestock. Mountain lions climb well and take to trees if pursued. Most are shot out of trees by hunters after being chased by their dogs. When their wild food source is limited, they may prey on livestock, and their natural instinct is to kill many animals when the panic behavior of the prey provokes them. Mountain lions hardly ever harm humans, although they will attack in self-defense or to protect their cubs. Because they are territorial, they will defend their established ranges, particularly at courtship time. When they do attack, they kill, which has given them a reputation for savagery.

Mountain lions have greatly diminished in number because they have been bounty hunted (for sport, for their pelts, or to protect livestock), and because they have lost habitat large enough to support them. They are an important predator at the top of the food chain, focusing on deer and elk and thereby helping to keep these populations healthy and habitat from being overgrazed. But the more specialized a species, the less adaptable it is to change, and the cougar has proven relatively unable to adapt to habitat loss and competition with humans for large ungulate prey. Mountain lions are now a protected species throughout the U.S.

How to Observe

The mountain lion is secretive, and the sight of one is rare. Only by accident will you spot a mountain lion unless you are with an expert guide. Your state wildlife agency can direct you to the few places where mountain lions are completely protected. If you have the good fortune to see one, it will likely flee the minute it sees or smells you. Do not attempt to approach a mountain lion.

Situations and Solutions

Mountain Lions Preying on Domestic Livestock

WHY IT HAPPENS: If mountain lions lack a wild food source, they will exploit livestock or pets that are readily available within their hunting range.

SUGGESTIONS: If you have reason to believe a mountain lion has attacked livestock or a pet (for example, if you see pawprints around the carcass), report the incident to your local wildlife agency, which will advise you on steps to protect your livestock. Do not allow pets to run free—for their own protection and for the protection of the wild animals on which they might prey.

[LYNXES AND BOBCATS]

There are two species of lynx in North America: the common lynx (*Felis lynx*) and the red lynx (*Felis rufus*), otherwise known as the bobcat. Lynxes and bobcats are also called wildcats. Both lynxes and bobcats range in weight from 11 to 66 pounds. Lynxes have short coats, especially those that live far to the north. Their body coloration varies from tan to gray. Bobcat coat colors vary, but most are reddish above and pale underneath with some patterned dark stripes or spots. A distinctive characteristic of both lynxes and bobcats is the tuft of fur on each ear.

The head and body of the common lynx can be 28 to 43 inches long and the tail 7 inches. This lynx can be 20 to 26 inches tall at the shoulder and weigh up to 65 pounds. Bobcats are smaller, weighing 15 to 35 pounds, and have a short bobbed tail with black on the tip. Their ears are long with 1-inch black tufts at the end, and their large noses resemble rubber erasers.

Female lynxes have litters of one to four young; bobcats average three.

Range and Habitat

Lynxes prefer dense coniferous forests and swamps, while bobcats live in more varied habitats including rocks, brush, and dense vegetation. Lynxes range throughout Alaska, Canada, the Cascade Range, and portions of the Rocky Mountains. Bobcats are found below 8,000 feet in all of the western states and Canada. Although bobcats prefer rimrocks and gullies in the West, they also roam swamps and woodlands in other areas. They den in rock crevices and hollow logs. Their territories (small compared to those of mountain lions) vary with food supply, averaging 4 to 15 square miles.

Other Characteristics

While the diet of the lynx includes rodents and birds, and lynxes have been known to bring down young deer, their primary prey is the snowshoe hare. Bobcats eat a varied diet, including rats, mice, rabbits, squirrels, carrion, and insects, so they rarely encounter food shortages. Like mountain lions, both species use stealth in hunting their prey, often waiting for hours near a game trail for prey to come within their 10-foot springing range.

Lynxes and bobcats are solitary and active both day and night. They see well in darkness because their eyes have a special light reflector behind the retina; they also have extremely well developed hearing for locating prey. They are expert tree-climbers and swimmers and powerful fighters. Their large scent-marked territories are traveled daily. They have a life span of 15 to 20 years.

Enemies and Defenses/Conservation Note

As with all large carnivores, the lynx's and bobcat's main enemy is humans. People have been killing these animals (hunting and trapping them for pelts) for profit since 1730. In some parts of the country, hunting them is still permitted, though they are valuable to farmers because they eat many rodents. Lynxes and bobcats have few natural enemies, and their primary defenses include speedy escapes and tree-climbing.

Bobcats are the most common wild felid in the U.S. and Canada, but their numbers are decreasing due to hunting and habitat loss. In 1977–1978, more than 85,000 bobcat and 20,000 lynx skins were harvested, valued at more than $16 million. Their current status is controversial: Some experts believe that they are common and have adapted well to habitat loss and human hunting and intrusion; others assert that they are endangered.

How to Observe

It is best to seek help from your local wildlife agency in locating lynx and bobcat habitat in the wild. Lynxes and bobcats are most likely to be seen in remote, rugged country

Bobcats are rarely seen but sometimes can be observed near wilderness trails.

during early morning or late afternoon feeding times. Because of their elusive nature and caution around humans, however, they are rarely seen.

Situations and Solutions

Bobcat Living on Property

WHY IT HAPPENS: Unlike mountain lions, bobcats have adapted to human settlement of wildlands. Even a woodlot in a farming area can sustain a pair of bobcats. Often people living on farms and in small towns are unaware of bobcats living nearby.

SUGGESTIONS: Bobcats avoid human contact as much as possible, and if you can share your land peacefully with a resident bobcat, it will help keep down rodent populations. State laws protect bobcats in many areas, so if the animal poses a serious threat to livestock or pets, call your local wildlife agency for assistance.

Ungulates

Ungulates are hoofed mammals that include wild as well as domestic species. They are usually classified into two categories: even-toed ungulates, such as deer, sheep, goats, wild boars, and peccaries; and odd-toed ungulates, including horses.

The main ungulate groups in North America are cervids (deer and their relatives), bovids, equines, suids, and peccaries. The cervid family includes all species of deer, as well as moose, elk, and caribou; only deer and moose are discussed below. The bovid classification includes the bighorn sheep and mountain goats, and bison; since contact with these is exceedingly limited except in a few wilderness parks, they are not covered here. Likewise for the North American equines: wild mustangs and wild burros. Suids include wild boars and feral pigs, and peccaries include javelinas. Both of these groups have a high incidence of interaction with humans and their gardens and crops.

The Deer Family

Members of the deer family (Cervidae) native to North America include the mule, or black-tailed, deer, the white-tailed deer, the reindeer (known as caribou in North America), the wapiti (better known as elk), and the moose (whose true name is actually elk). Their common North American names are used for description here.

[DEER]

There are 38 subspecies of white-tailed deer (*Odocoileus viginianus*). Those in the north tend to be large, some weighing up to 430 pounds, while the more southerly species are smaller. For example, Florida Key deer usually weigh less than 55 pounds. White-tailed deer coats are grayish brown in summer, turning to reddish brown in winter. The name comes from the white underside of its tail and the patch of white on its rump.

The mule (including black-tailed) deer (*O. hemionus*) is identified by its tail, completely black on top but whitish underneath, like the rest of the deer's underside. A buck (male) can be 3½ feet tall at the shoulder.

Bucks weigh from 250 to 500 pounds, while females (does) are considerably lighter. The name mule deer comes from the animal's large ears that move independently.

In both species, bucks begin to grow antlers in the spring, and their "rack" is fully developed by September. After the mating season in January or February, bucks shed their antlers and go without until a set of new velvet-covered stubs begins to sprout in May.

The first time they give birth, does usually produce a single fawn. From then on, they usually bear twins. Triplets are common, and even quintuplets are known.

Feeding by deer can eventually create a "browse line" on trees where other food sources are not sufficient.

Range and Habitat

White-tailed deer range in all habitats from southern Canada throughout the U.S. They prefer field and forest edges, frequenting patches of woodland as well as grassy openings. Their ranges average 500 acres but can be as large as 1,000 acres in mountainous areas. Key deer are found only on the islands (keys) off the Florida coast.

Mule deer range through western North America in a variety of habitats, including forests, deserts, chaparral, and grasslands with shrubs. Their home range is 90 to 600 acres, depending on the sex. While they enjoy well-forested areas, they do most of their feeding in open areas with a good deal of greenery.

As people have moved into deer habitat and planted vegetation, the deer have adapted to eating landscaped plantings, which has brought them into conflict with humans.

Other Characteristics

Like some other ungulates, deer are ruminants, meaning they have complex digestive systems divided into separate chambers containing microorganisms that break down the vegetable matter they eat. The food is at first quickly swallowed; then, after a period of digestion, it is regurgitated, thoroughly chewed (called chewing the cud), and swallowed again for further digestion. The whole process, which takes about 48 hours, is a survival adaptation for animals that often must snatch a few bites of forage and be on the move quickly to escape predators.

Most white-tailed and black-tailed deer are "browse" eaters, feeding on the shoots and leaves of woody plants, instead of grasses. Their most active browse times are early morning, from dusk into evening, and moonlit nights. They like young plant buds and shoots, leaves, succulent plants, shrubs, bark, berries, and other fruits. Black-tailed deer can survive for several days without water by getting moisture from succulent plants. They also help trim back poison oak.

In winter, the appetite of white-tailed deer literally decreases in relation to the food supply so that the animals do not expend excess energy looking for unavailable food. Fawns have been known to go a month without food and adults as long as two months. When hunger is severe, deer will eat browse up to the girth of a pencil (usually they prefer browse no thicker than a matchstick). In areas where deer have overpopulated for available food sources, a noticeable "browse line" appears at the bottom of trees where the deer have reached up to eat the low-hanging twigs and branches. When browse is no longer available, deer will start stripping bark from young trees. In such conditions, deer die of starvation—especially the young, which cannot reach as high as the older deer.

White-tailed deer occur singly or in small groups. While tending young, females remain solitary. In the fall, when the young are old enough, several females with young may band together for the winter. Bucks are solitary or gather in the winter in small bachelor groups. Large groups of white-tailed deer may join together for protection during harsh winters. The deer mark their territories with scent from glands on their hooves and faces, and with urine. They are capable of running 40 mph and jumping 8½ feet in the air.

Black-tailed deer have a more complex social organization. A female will aggressively defend an area 100 to 200 acres in diameter where her fawn lies, as long as it stays still. If the fawn moves, the territory only increases about another 16 feet. Wildlife experts are not sure whether the territory "moves" with the fawn or whether it remains a fixed location.

Black-tailed deer live in large clans, which the bucks defend against other mule deer. They follow definite trails and can run 35 miles per hour, leap 30 feet, and clear 8-foot fences.

Deer use ridges and hills during the day as heated air rises, carrying scents from below up to the alert deer. At night, they stay in the lowlands, because cooler air settles, again carrying scents to the deer for identification.

The yearly discarding and growing of antlers distinguishes deer from all other ungulates, which grow antlers or horns that stay with them throughout their lifetimes. In all North American deer species except caribou, only the males grow antlers, which they use for sexual display and to establish dominance within the herd. Sunlight stimulates antler growth. The antlers are formed by living tissue supplied with blood from vessels within the soft skin known as "velvet." After underlying tissue hardens, the velvet is scraped off, and the antlers become mineralized dead tissue. A yearling black-tailed buck usually has two points on each antler in the form of a Y, while an adult buck has an additional Y on each point, totaling four points on each antler. White-tailed antlers usually have one low, small prong with a larger branch containing four points on each antler.

Deer have a life span of 25 years in captivity and average 16 years in the wild.

Enemies and Defenses

Natural predators of black-tailed deer are mountain lions, occasionally coyotes, and, in Canada, wolves. However, like white-tailed deer and other large wildlife, their chief enemy is humans. Deer meat and rawhide fed and clothed many pioneers as they settled the West. The destruction of habitat through logging and clearing for farms played a large part in the decrease of deer. Today, hunters and automobiles destroy an estimated 400,000 deer annually. Also, domestic dog packs often kill deer.

Though bucks can use their antlers as weapons, their main defense is their hooves, powered by the strong forelegs. White-tailed deer use their tails to give warning signals. Black-tailed deer, when threatened, bounce stiff-legged with their small, ropelike tail down. All deer become more excitable during the mating season, and males can be particularly dangerous then. Does will go to great lengths to defend their young. *Never approach a deer at any time of the year, because humans are seen as a threat. Deer can attack, and serious injury or death can result.*

Conservation Notes

By the end of the nineteenth century, mule deer in western America had been reduced through overhunting to one-tenth of their former population, and white-tailed deer had become scarce. Conservation efforts and habitat restoration begun early in this century have replenished deer populations. Ironically, the movement of farmers to the cities, and of loggers from the Great Lakes to the Pacific Northwest, created opportunities in many areas for natural regeneration of wooded areas and grasslands.

Today the black-tailed deer population is fairly stable, although some subspecies are threatened because they cannot adapt to human development. The white-tailed deer population is still large overall, but, again, certain subspecies are endangered, including the trusting, gentle Key deer.

Deer are among the most coveted big game animals, and state wildlife agencies strictly regulate hunting of all deer species. Some wildlife enthusiasts oppose hunting, while other landowners choose to allow regulated hunting on their property in compliance with state laws.

In areas overpopulated by deer, many fish and wildlife departments advocate management of wildlife populations using techniques including regulated hunting, live-trapping and transfer of deer to other locations, using fencing and repellents to manage conflicts with humans, using fertility control agents to regulate reproduction, and reintroducing large predators to act as natural population controls. Supplemental feeding of deer is not recommended except in extreme winter weather emergencies, because it is quite expensive and makes the deer dependent upon nonnatural food sources.

How to Observe

The secret to observing deer is choosing the right time of day: dawn or dusk, because deer feed in the open around those times. Position yourself near a good browsing area where there is enough cover, and make sure you are downwind of the site so the deer cannot detect your smell. Deer in the wild will probably not stay around long once they have noticed you. Do not attempt direct contact (deer can be carriers of Lyme disease ticks), and let the animals leave on their own.

Situations and Solutions

Fawn Found Wandering and Crying

WHY IT HAPPENS: Fawns wander normally, but when they are crying as well, something is wrong. Usually the mother has been hurt and not returned.

SUGGESTIONS: If you are sure the mother has not returned for several hours and the fawn is so young it will let you pick it up, take it to a wildlife care agency, or keep it quiet and call such an agency. If the fawn is older and stays around the area, it may need help getting enough food and water. You may put out a clean container of water and set out its normal browse food (cuttings from blackberry bushes, roses, pyracantha, alfalfa, or apples). *Do not hand-feed deer.*

Fawn in the Yard

WHY IT HAPPENS: The mother may have left the fawn and will return for it soon, or the fawn may have wandered into the yard and not been able to find its way out.

SUGGESTIONS: Make sure the doe can get into the area. If this is not possible, find the hole in the fence through which the fawn got in, put the fawn outside of it, and close the hole. The mother will return for the fawn soon. If no humans are around when she returns, she will likely reclaim her fawn despite the human scent. Handle only fawns that are small enough to be carried. If the fawn is large and strong enough to run from you, don't chase it. Wait for the mother to return or call your local wildlife agency.

Apparently "Orphaned" Fawn

WHY IT HAPPENS: Fawns are often left alone for long periods of time while the mother forages for food.

SUGGESTIONS: Anyone who comes upon a fawn should leave it alone and go away so its mother can feel free to return. Only if the fawn is obviously emaciated or injured, or if there is a pack of dogs roaming the area, should it be touched. If a doe is found dead and the fawn orphaned, call your local wildlife care agency.

Fear that Deer May Attack Children or Pets

WHY IT HAPPENS: Though normally shy, deer may attack during the mating season, to defend fawns, or if they feel trapped or threatened.

SUGGESTIONS: *Never approach an adult deer for any reason.* If a deer appears to feel trapped in your yard, stay out of the way and let it take its time finding a way out. Your presence will only add to its frenzy. Deer will leap in any direction and have been known to leap through windows while attempting to escape.

Deer Eating Garden and Landscaping Plants

WHY IT HAPPENS: Deer are herbivores and must browse for their nourishment. During the dry summer and cold winter months, hilly terrain provides little if any forage for deer. They naturally spend their summers in valleys and canyons, where food is more plentiful, but these areas are increasingly filled with homes and the gardens that go with them.

SUGGESTIONS:

1. "Fence or share" is the general rule. Deer fencing should be 8 feet high if possible and made of high-tensile wire, mesh fencing, or electric wiring; placement may be angled to prevent the animal from jumping over. Consult local experts for effective materials and designs. If fencing the entire area is too expensive, fencing individual plants is effective. In constructing wood fences, be sure the slats are close to the ground. For wire mesh fences, extend the wire out along the ground and use rocks to hold it down, or bury it beneath ground level. This will prevent fawns from crawling underneath.

2. Black Dacron bird netting, purchased from a plant nursery, is effective when placed over planting beds or individual plants. The nets let new growth through, so they must be lifted and reset every few days to maintain protection. Netting can also be used as an extension above a fence that is too low.

3. Repellents are of two types: Some repel directly through bad taste and others indirectly by sight, smell, or sound. Direct repellents include commercial products containing the bittering agent thiram. Check with your local nursery for products recommended for your area. The following homemade concoction can be effective if sprayed directly on plants and reapplied weekly. Mix well two eggs, one glass of skim milk, one glass of water, and a spreader-thickener (a wetting agent purchased from plant nurseries). Apply. Any direct repellent should be applied in the fall, when plants first go dormant, and repeated per instructions.

   Hang indirect repellents, including nylon stockings containing small amounts of human hair; mirrors; strips of tinfoil; or commercial smell repellents. Or hang rags soaked in ammonia on branches; replenish with ammonia regularly to maintain the odor. Deer are adaptable, so it is important to vary the methods, or the animals will learn that the repellents are not harmful and will no longer be deterred by them.

4. Planting deer-resistant plants can be an alternative, although none is totally guaranteed, especially when drought conditions constrict food sources. Most plant nurseries carry lists of these plants. Publications with further information are listed in Appendix C.

5. Attempt live-trapping only with the assistance of trained, licensed wildlife agency personnel. Often, as with suburban deer populations, this solution is not effective due to lack of suitable habitat for relocation.

6. Many people choose to share their yards with deer and other wildlife, and purposely plant vegetation that will support wildlife. The National Wildlife Federation and other wildlife organizations sponsor backyard habitat programs; if you are interested in adopting this approach, see the list of related publications in Appendix C.

Deer with a Broken Leg or Other Injury

WHY IT HAPPENS: The deer may have been hit by a car or attacked by dogs, or it may have run into a fence.

SUGGESTIONS: Leave the animal alone unless it can't stand up. In this case, call your local wildlife care agency. If the animal is getting around with a broken leg, leave it on its own. Even though the injury may take a long time to heal, this is far preferable to the trauma of chase and capture.

[MOOSE]

The largest member of the deer family is known in the U.S. as the moose (*Alces americana*). Male moose (bulls) can stand 6 feet high at the shoulders and weigh up to 1,750 pounds. The moose has a long, drooping nose, a "bell" or dewlap under the chin, a hump on the shoulders, and long legs with splayed hooves. Only the bull moose have the characteristic huge, flattened, palm-shaped antlers that reach their full size at 10 to 12 years. Coat color varies from golden brown to almost black, depending upon the season and the animal's age. Adult males usually weigh 1,200 to 1,500 pounds, females 800 to 1,300 pounds.

Females give birth to one or two calves in mid-May to early June. Moose produce triplets only about once in every 1,000 births.

Range and Habitat

Moose are found in Alaska, Canada, and many parts of the northern U.S. from Idaho to Maine. They prefer open forestland that is accessible to rivers or lakes for water.

Other Characteristics

Moose feed on plants growing on the forest floor as well as on material stripped from trees. They may also eat aquatic plants, including horsetails and pondweed, and will wade into waterways up to the belly to feed for long periods, depending on water temperature. Their long noses let them feed on water plants while they keep their eyes above the water line, alert for predators. During fall and winter they eat large quantities of willow, birch, and aspen browse. In spring and summer, moose graze on grasses, weeds, and sedges while continuing to browse on twigs.

Moose tend to be solitary because of the limited food sources in the northern winter forests. It is estimated that half of all moose live alone, one-quarter live in pairs, and the other quarter in groups of three or more. Groups form only temporarily because of the moose's strong instinct to stay in its home territory.

Most moose migrate seasonally between calving, rutting, and wintering areas, ranging as far as 60 miles or as little as a few miles. Each moose's territory is 750 to 1,000 acres, and moose return to the same locations after migration each year. They maintain strict territorial boundaries through use of ritualized combat, even between females. Mature females tend to be aggressive toward all other moose, regardless of sex or age, especially when accompanied by their young. This behavior is explained as a defense against winter food shortages, the greatest threat to moose survival because of harsh living conditions in the north.

Enemies and Defenses

Moose have few natural predators other than large carnivores such as wolves and black and brown bears. Black bears take young moose in May and June, but grizzlies kill calves and adults throughout their hunting year. Wolves kill moose throughout the year. Moose meat is still an important staple food for native peoples in Alaska and Canada. Though some moose are lost to hunting, their primary natural enemy is other moose because of competition for scarce food in their northern habitats.

Conservation Notes

Human alteration of wildlands through timber logging and careless use of fire actually has benefited moose in some ways. In such areas, new stands of young timber have grown, providing great moose food sources. Where human development threatens moose habitat, management through controlled fires and predation will benefit future moose populations.

How to Observe

Moose are very big and very wild. Because they are solitary by nature, if a moose is encountered in the wild or happens to stray into a small town or other human area, it will likely leave of its own accord if it is left alone. Moose are a major tourist draw in Alaska, and many are visible and photographable from highways there. Do not attempt to approach moose, as they can be aggressive when defending their territory.

Situations and Solutions

Moose in Human-Settled Areas

WHY IT HAPPENS: Because of alteration of much moose habitat, it is not unusual for moose to eat crops, stand on airfields, eat young trees, wander city streets, or collide with cars and trains.

SUGGESTIONS: If you cannot wait for a moose to leave a settled area on its own, it can be easily frightened away with loud noises such as banging pans, sirens, fireworks (be careful of fire danger), or other noisy efforts.

The Pig Family

North American members of the pig family Suidae include the introduced wild boars and feral domestic pigs that were originally wild boars. All other members of the pig family are found in Europe, Africa, and Asia. Wild boars (*Sus scrofa*) are the largest members of the pig family, weighing up to 450 pounds. They can reach 6 feet in length and have brownish gray wiry coats, short tusks, and mobile, tasseled tails.

Females give birth to litters of up to 12 in nests constructed of branches, hay, and plants.

Range and Habitat

Wild boars are native to the grass- and woodlands of Eurasia and were introduced into the U.S. by settlers. Domestic pigs are direct descendants of wild boars, and many have escaped back into the wild, interbreeding with the wild stock. Wild boars and feral pigs are found in North America, primarily in the southeastern states, in dense forestland and swamp areas. Some are also found along the Pacific coast and on coastal islands. Wild boars and feral pigs can create problems for humans when they feed on cultivated crops.

Other Characteristics

Wild boars, the most omniverous of all hoofed mammals, eat a varied diet consisting of plant material as well as insects, worms, eggs, nestlings, frogs, and mice. They will also help themselves to the roots and tubers of cultivated crops like peanuts, corn, pineapple, grapes, pumpkins, and watermelon and occasionally have been known to take newborn sheep and goats. Small numbers of woodland boars are helpful to the environment because they keep down insect and rodent populations and spread seeds of woodland trees. They often take mud baths, wallowing in muddy pools to rid themselves of parasites.

Wild boars, like all pigs, have excellent senses of smell and hearing. They scent-mark their surroundings, though they are not strictly territorial. Female boars, usually related, and their young gather in small groups called *sounders*. When the sounder grows large, up to 100 animals, the members usually split up to form separate groups and occupy separate feeding territories. Males live alone or in bachelor herds and join the sounders only during breeding season.

While the females coexist peacefully, male boars fight often, usually over possible mates during breeding season. They fight shoulder to shoulder, raking each other with their tusks, and can inflict deep wounds even though their neck and shoulders have a protective layer of thickened skin. The position of their tasseled tails is used to communicate the boars' moods.

Enemies and Defenses

Wild boars have few enemies because of their large size. Large carnivores, like mountain lions, prey upon their young.

How to Observe

Wild boars are ordinarily found in wooded, moist areas, where they seek cover in dense vegetation and root for food. They can be aggressive and extremely dangerous, so do not attempt to approach one.

Situations and Solutions

Wild Boars Damaging Crops, Gardens, or Livestock

WHY IT HAPPENS: Boars are helping themselves to a ready food supply.

SUGGESTIONS: Many boars are intelligent and strong enough to dig under sturdy fencing to get at crops or livestock. Check with your local wildlife agency for the best techniques to aid in humane control of wild boars.

JAVELINAS

The peccary family (Tayassuidae) is made up of three species in two genera. The only species found in North America is the javelina, or collared peccary *(Tayassu tajacu).* Although javelinas bear a striking resemblance to wild boars, they are not in the "pig" family but are actually more closely related to even-toed ruminants such as deer. They are 2½ to 3 feet long, are about 1 foot tall at the shoulder, and weigh 38 to 55 pounds. They have grizzled gray coats, dark gray backs with a whitish band diagonally across the midback to the chest, and blackish limbs.

The female gives birth to one to four (usually two) young, who are up and around soon after birth.

Range and Habitat

Javelinas are found from the southwestern U.S. into northern Argentina. They prefer low and high dry tropical forests and chaparral and oak grasslands.

Other Characteristics

Javelinas are herd animals, depending on other family members within a strong social structure that provides for feeding, bedding, play, and predator protection. They live in herds of 14 to 50, divided into smaller family groups.

Javelinas are active during the day and prefer to sleep and rest in caves. They aggressively defend their 74- to 690-acre territories, which they mark using their scent glands. They have an 8- to 10-year life span in the wild. Normally they avoid human contact; however, as people have moved into their ranges, they have adapted to ready sources of food such as garbage, gardens, pet food, and bird feeders.

Enemies and Defenses

Humans are the main enemy, as javelinas are considered big game animals in some states, where they are governed by hunting laws. Most interaction between javelinas and humans occurs in neighborhoods that have been built adjacent to open land so that the animals have continued access to desirable yards.

Javelinas are not normally aggressive toward humans, but because of their poor eyesight, they can become frightened and attack if cornered. They have well-developed canine teeth and have been known to bite and charge.

How to Observe

Excursions into desert Southwest areas may result in javelina sightings. People who live in proximity to wild habitat often observe javelinas around their homes and yards.

Javelinas (collared peccaries) have adapted to the food source created by human garbage in recently developed arid regions.

Situations and Solutions

Javelinas Digging under a Mobile Home or Crawl Space

WHY IT HAPPENS: Javelinas' preference for caves and cool places in which to rest and sleep often leads them to dig around homes with hooves and snouts to obtain access to crawl spaces.

SUGGESTIONS: Securely close all entryways to spaces beneath buildings and mobile homes. Block access with wire-mesh fencing buried well below ground-surface level. Secure mobile home foundation skirts to the ground, or use masonry to protect foundation areas.

Javelinas Digging in Gardens and Flower Beds

WHY IT HAPPENS: In adaptating to human habitats, javelinas have learned that gardens and flower beds are good places to find natural food sources, such as insects and roots.

SUGGESTIONS: Sturdy fencing around garden and flower bed areas will help deter javelinas. Be sure to bury fencing at least 8 to 10 inches deep to protect against digging under it. Pick up fruit that falls from trees immediately.

Javelinas in Garbage Cans or Yard

WHY IT HAPPENS: Again, javelinas have learned that human dwellings may provide excellent food sources.

SUGGESTIONS:

1. *Do not feed javelinas.*
2. Do not discard edible garbage where javelinas have access to it. Secure garbage can lids and containers, and eliminate garbage odors.
3. Remove pet food from outside the home.
4. Eliminate availability of birdseed and water. Javelinas are attracted just as quickly as birds to these sources of nourishment. Keep all birdseed and water off the ground. It may be necessary to fence a small area around the bird feeder.
5. Trim and clear ground-level shrubbery that provides cover for rodents.
6. Actively discourage javelinas from visiting by throwing rocks, squirting with water, or making loud noises. Recruit your neighbors to join in similar efforts.
7. Fence around the entire yard, if affordable, to most effectively help keep javelinas out. One of the simplest and best forms of javelina fencing is two strands of wire strung close to the ground and powered by two D-cell batteries. This fence gives off a very low voltage shock, and javelinas quickly learn to avoid it.
8. If a javelina comes into the yard but cannot find its way out, open all possible means of exit and make noise or throw stones to edge it toward an exit. Do not get too close, because it might attack when cor-

nered. If these forms of persuasion do not succeed, leave the area and allow the javelina time to find its way out. If necessary, call your local wildlife agency for assistance.

9. Live-trapping and relocation is rarely successful and should only be undertaken with wildlife agency assistance. Relocated javelinas often find their way back (some have been known to return from 50 miles away). Also, because they are herd animals with definite territories, releasing them in a strange habitat almost guarantees nonacceptance by local herds and could lead to ultimate death from predation or starvation. Even if the trapped javelina does not return, others will likely move in.

Marine Mammals

Four separate types of animals are considered marine or ocean-dwelling mammals: the seal (order: Carnivora; suborder: Pinnipedia), the whale, the dolphin (order: Cetacea) and the manatee (order: Sirenia). The sea otter, a member of the mustelid family of land mammals, is also adapted to live in the ocean. The pinnipeds are broken into subgroups that include true (earless) seals, eared seals (Otariidae, including sea lions and fur seals), and walruses. The cetaceans are divided into toothed and baleen whales, dolphins (including killer whales), and porpoises. Because of the limited interaction between humans and whales and dolphins, only the seal family, sea otters, and manatees are treated in detail here. Many guidebooks about whales and dolphins are available for further study of these amazing marine mammals.

[SEA LIONS AND FUR SEALS]

Sea lions (*Zalophus californianus* and *Eumetopias jubatus*) and fur seals (*Callorhinus ursinus*), or eared seals, are the most commonly seen members of the Pinnipedia suborder along the Pacific coast. Fur seals are 6 to 8 feet in length. Males weigh between 400 and 800 pounds, females 100 to 200 pounds. Adult male sea lions may weigh over a ton and reach 12 feet in length. Both species have thick fur, which can be longer and denser around the neck and is brown in color (blackish when wet). They have small, pointed ears (external skin flaps) on small heads, and males sometimes have a high, crested forehead. Their bodies are tapered from the thick necks to the rear, with front and hind limbs that can support their bodies while they move across the ground.

Females give birth to one pup per year and mate within a week thereafter to produce the next year's young.

Range and Habitat

Sea lions are found on the Pacific coast from British Columbia, Canada, south to Mexico. Fur seals are widely distributed from the Alaskan islands south to South America. They are often seen on rocky beaches.

Sea lions are more agile on land than true seals because of the shape and position of their hind limbs.

Other Characteristics

Sea lions are carnivorous. They eat squid and fish, usually hunting after dark. Adults can consume 12 to 15 pounds of food daily and can swim very quickly while chasing prey. They spend much of their time swimming or sleeping on rocky islands. Gregarious and vocal animals, they usually congregate in groups of 30 or more with a definite dominance order, and their barking sounds are commonly heard. Sea lions can remain submerged for 20 minutes and can dive 450 feet below the surface. They have a life span of 20 to 25 years.

On land, the sea lion's thick neck acts as a counterweight to its heavy body when it rests on its front limbs. The hind limbs point forward and are always moved together. Sea lions and fur seals are much more agile on land than true seals because they support themselves with their limbs instead of wiggling on their stomachs. In the water, these species get most of their swimming power from their front flippers.

Fur seals are active during the night and spend much of the day resting along the shore. They eat a wide variety of fish, mollusks, and sea urchins.

Enemies and Defenses/Conservation Note

The sea lion's main enemies are killer whales and large sharks. Once threatened by overhunting, they are now fully protected by federal law. Their worldwide population, including both the northern (Steller's) subspecies and southern (California) subspecies, is estimated at 600,000.

Humans are the chief enemy of fur seals. For centuries, native peoples of the north relied on fur seals for food, oil, and clothing, but they took only as many as needed for their existence. But with the advent of a world market for blubber and fur, commercial hunting resulted in the slaughter of millions of animals. From a population of 4 million fur seals in the mid-1800s, there were only an estimated 200,000 left at the turn of the century. Until recently, the fur seal was threatened with extinction, but it is now protected and is making a comeback. World populations are now estimated at 1.5 million, with 500,000 pups born each year.

How to Observe

Sea lions can be observed off the coast of California, Oregon, Washington, and British Columbia. Some excellent locations from which to watch them are Point Lobos State Reserve near Carmel, California, and the Cliff House in San Francisco. Fur seals congregate in Arctic areas to breed, and some ecotourism companies offer special excursions to observe the herds. Check with local wildlife agencies for specific information about observation opportunities.

Situations and Solutions

Sea Lion or Fur Seal Appears Sick or Injured

WHY IT HAPPENS: Sea lions and fur seals do spend some time on land, resting and mating. They will also pull themselves onto land if they are sick or dying.

SUGGESTIONS: *Do not approach a sea lion or a fur seal.* Like any wild animal, when stressed by the close approach of humans, it can be dangerous. If you have reason to think such an animal is injured or sick, call your local wildlife agency for assistance.

[TRUE SEALS]

The North American members of the true (earless) seal family (Phocidae) include common or harbor seals *(Phoca vitulina)* and elephant seals *(Mirounga angustrirostris* and *M. leonina)*. These seals do have ears and hear well; they simply lack the external earflaps of sea lions and fur seals. They are streamlined with tapered bodies, small heads, pointed noses, and thick fur. Unlike sea lions and fur seals, these seals have hind limbs that permanently point backward like fishtails, so they are useless for moving on land.

Elephant seals are the largest of all seals, males measuring up to 20 feet long and over 5,300 pounds, females up to 11 feet and about 2,000 pounds. Their coloration is pale brown to grayish. Old males have large, trunklike snouts that are an extension of the nasal cavities—hence the name "elephant." This snout develops between ages five and seven and is used for mating displays and to trumpet warnings to other males.

Harbor seals are streamlined, with tapered bodies, small heads, and pointed muzzles. Should you have an opportunity to observe other species, they can be identified with a good guidebook.

Females give birth to one pup per year in their traditional breeding grounds from mid-November to mid-December.

Range and Habitat

Many species of true seals are found from the Arctic ice pack down into Alaska and parts of Canada. All except the monk and elephant seal require cold water temperatures and cannot tolerate summer ocean temperatures higher than 68 degrees F. During most of the year, true seals live at sea; they come ashore only to give birth, breed, and molt (shed their skin).

Elephant seals are found on sandy beaches from southeastern Alaska south along the Pacific coast to Baja California, Mexico.

Other Characteristics

True seals feed on fish, mollusks, and crustaceans; some eat larger forms of sea plankton, and some hunt marine birds. Seals are social, gregarious animals that swim or lie on shore together in large groups.

The seals' strong hind limbs provide their primary means of swimming. The forelimbs are not nearly as well developed and are rarely used, except for turning in the water. True seals move on shore by dragging their bodies, resting on the breastbone, over rocks and ice. While not as agile on land, true seals are better swimmers than sea lions and fur seals. They have been known to dive to ocean depths of up to 2,000 feet and to stay submerged for over an hour. After the sperm whale, they are the second–deepest-diving mammal.

All true seals have a thick layer of body fat (blubber) that insulates them from the cold waters in which they live. The oil from skin glands, along with their dense fur, keeps cold water from reaching the skin and prevents body heat loss. True seals have air-breathing lungs that cannot extract oxygen from water; however, they can spend long periods underwater without air. Seals also have well-developed senses of smell and eyesight and can navigate with echolocation for sensing prey, enemies, and land.

Enemies and Defenses/Conservation Note

The natural enemies of true seals are orcas (killer whales), sharks, polar bears, and, occasionally, walruses. Populations are also kept in check by a variety of internal parasites. True seals, like other marine mammals, defend themselves with fast swimming, agility, and keen senses. But humans kill many more seals. During the last century, elephant seals were slaughtered for the oil from their blubber. Numbering in the hundreds of thousands in 1800, by 1869 this species approached extinction. In 1922 it was granted protection, which continues today.

Hawaiian monk seals have returned from the brink of extinction through strict protection, increasing from 150 in 1956 to a total of 1,300 in 1991.

Northern true seals, especially the harp seal, are still favorite human prey. The white coats of harp seal pups are especially prized. Harp seal hunting is illegal in the U.S. but is still allowed in eastern Canada, although it is carefully researched and managed.

How to Observe

Many species of true seal are unlikely to be observed unless you are traveling in Arctic marine waters or on the ice. Harbor seals and elephant seals are fairly commonly seen along the coast of California and Baja California, Mexico. Elephant seals can be observed on Año Nuevo State Reserve, which is about 55 miles south of San Francisco; January through March are the best months to see them on shore. As with all animals in the wild, do not approach too closely.

Situations and Solutions

Seal Appears Sick or Injured

WHY IT HAPPENS: When seals are on shore to rest or molt, they can appear immobile or injured.

SUGGESTIONS: *Do not attempt to touch a seal.* It could be aggressive if threatened. If you think you have discovered an injured or sick animal, contact your local wildlife agency for assistance.

[SEA OTTERS]

The sea otter *(Enhydra lutis)* is the smallest aquatic sea mammal and a member of the Mustelidae (weasel) family—it is the only mustelid able to live in the ocean. It varies in length from 3 to 4 feet, with females averaging 70 pounds and males 100 pounds. Sea otters have thick, dark brown fur with long, silver guard hairs. Their forefeet are short, stubby, and clawed; the hind feet are webbed and flipperlike. The forelimbs are used not for swimming but for manipulating food.

In June, the mother bears one 3-pound cub, which it takes care of for 1½ years.

Range and Habitat

Sea otter range used to extend along 6,000 miles of the Pacific coast from the Aleutian Islands to Baja California, Mexico. The species is now limited to Alaskan waters and isolated colonies off the U.S. west coast. Sea otters sleep, feed, and breed in the ocean, usually staying within 200 yards of the shore.

Other Characteristics

Sea otters are meat eaters. Ninety-five percent of their diet is sea urchins, crabs, and mussels; they rarely eat fish. An otter eats 20 to 23 percent of its body weight each day. Adult otters dive to 150-foot depths in search of food, often staying submerged for 4 to 5 minutes. They live their entire lives (10 to 15 years) at sea, climbing out onto shore only during severe storms and to give birth.

The sea otter is one of the few tool-using animals other than primates. It brings abalones and sea urchins to the surface and uses its chest as a table when feeding. On its chest it also balances rocks on which to crack shells, and it uses rocks as tools to pry abalones and sea urchins from rocks.

Sea otters live in family groups called pods, made up of either adult males or of females with young. They are active during the day, spending most of their time feeding and resting among kelp beds. They use long strands of kelp to anchor themselves in one place while sleeping and eating. Sea otters must keep their fur clean and free from sludge to protect themselves from the cold; they give themselves a thorough grooming with their front claws several times a day.

Enemies and Defenses

Sea otters' enemies are humans and, on rare occasions, whales and sharks.

Conservation Notes

From the mid-eighteenth century to the end of the 1800s, sea otters were slaughtered for their pelts until almost extinct. In 1941, when effective protection first began, less than 100 remained on the California coast. The Marine Mammal Act of 1972 placed the sea otter under the jurisdiction of the U.S. government, so it is now fully protected, and by 1979 the California population had rebounded to about 2,000 and the Alaska population to about 125,000. A few colonies also returned to Oregon, Washington, and British Columbian coasts. Sea otters are still listed as an endangered species, though some fishers complain that they compete for food sources such as clams and abalones.

How to Observe

In California, sea otters are most often seen off the coast at Carmel (Point Lobos State Reserve). They can also be observed at the Monterey Bay Aquarium in Monterey, California, which started the first program to raise orphaned sea otter pups for release back to the wild. Check with local wildlife agencies for other possible observation areas.

Watching sea otters cavort in the ocean and use their food "tools" can be entertaining. Be prepared to use binoculars or a spotting scope, and do not attempt to approach too closely. Human presence can stress them and cause them to leave. If you encounter what appears to be an injured or orphaned sea otter, call your local wildlife agency for assistance.

Situations and Solutions

Sea Otters Orphaned

WHY IT HAPPENS: Because of a mother's death or injury, sea otter pups may be found orphaned on shore or along the coast.

SUGGESTIONS: For your safety, do not attempt to handle a sea otter pup. Cover it with a blanket to keep it calm, and call your local wildlife agency for assistance. The Monterey Bay Aquarium in Monterey, California, has pioneered an orphaned sea otter care program with excellent results in raising pups and releasing them back to the wild.

[WHALES AND DOLPHINS]

Whales and dolphins are cetaceans, mammals that have adapted to life in ocean waters. They are unable to survive on dry land because their own body weight would crush their lungs when not supported by water. Like all mammals, however, they breathe with lungs, are warm-blooded, and nurse their young with mother's milk. Cetacean species can generally be classed in two categories: The baleen whales include humpback, blue, fin, and gray whales; toothed whales include sperm, beaked, and white whales, as well as porpoises, dolphins, and orcas.

We will not describe in detail the whales and dolphins that occur in waters off the North American coasts. Opportunities do exist for observing them, on organized seasonal boat excursions off the West Coast and New England, as well as during the annual gray whale migration along the West Coast, which can be observed with binoculars from certain shore sites. There are a number of excellent guides to identifying cetaceans.

Occasionally, whales or dolphins may beach themselves on shore, if disoriented, stranded, sick, or injured. If you encounter a beached whale or dolphin, do not approach closely, as the animal might inflict injury due to its size and fear. Immediately call the responsible wildlife agency for assistance.

[MANATEES]

The West Indian manatee (*Trichechus manatus*), one of four members of an order called the sirenians, is a large, seal-shaped mammal with a flat, rounded tail. Adults average 9 feet long and weigh an average of 800 to 1,200 pounds; females tend to be longer and heavier than males. They continually shed their thin, grayish brownish, wrinkled skin, which covers a layer of blubber. Only sparse hair grows on the body, except for stiff face whiskers. Manatees have no hind limbs; their flipperlike front limbs are paddle shaped. They have small, wide-set eyes and nostrils on the upper surface of the snout. When the animal is submerged underwater, the nostrils shut tightly, and special membranes cover the eyes. The ear openings, located just behind the eyes, are small and lack external lobes. The flexible upper lip is used to manipulate food into the mouth.

Females usually bear one calf, occasionally twins, and care for them for up to two years.

Range and Habitat

Florida is essentially the northern end of manatees' winter range. During summer, they occasionally venture as far north as Virginia and the Carolinas and have been seen as far west as the Gulf coast in Texas. Manatees live in freshwater, brackish, and marine habitats and can move freely between extreme saline and freshwater conditions, and clear or muddy water. They prefer depths of 3 to 7 feet, avoiding shallows and flats unless adjacent to deeper water. They use high tide to reach otherwise inaccessible feeding grounds.

Other Characteristics

Manatees evolved from four-footed land mammals more than 60 million years ago. Their closest modern relative is the elephant. Manatees usually spend five hours a day feeding and consume large quantities of plant material (4 to 9 percent of their body weight), primarily sea grasses. Their digestive system, like those of other herbivores, is capable of processing large amounts of high-fiber cellulose food.

Manatees evolved in areas with relatively constant temperatures and abundant food supplies, so they had no need to develop complex feeding or protection behaviors, or social organization. This lack of species sophistication makes them more vulnerable to human intrusion than other creatures that are better adapted.

Manatees propel themselves through the water by undulating their

Manatees, aquatic relatives of the elephant, are endangered. Boaters in Florida should take care not to harm these remarkable creatures.

tails, and they steer with tail and flippers. They can move vertically by changing the volume of air in their lungs, thereby adjusting their buoyancy. Despite their large size, manatees are surprisingly agile; they can somersault, roll sideways, do head- and tailstands, and glide upside-down. They generally cruise at 2 to 6 mph but have been clocked at top speeds of 15 mph for short distances.

Manatees are essentially solitary creatures. Except for the relationship between mothers and calves, groups seem to form casually. They are not territorial or aggressive, nor do they use dominance behavior. Manatees rest daily for 2 to 12 hours at a time, floating near the surface or lying on the bottom. They come to the surface every 5 to 12 minutes for air. They have excellent eyesight and hearing and communicate vocally to maintain contact while traveling, playing, or feeding; when frightened; and during mating season.

Enemies and Defenses

Manatees have no natural enemies other than humans. Their only defense is to swim away. This was one of the first species ever protected by law: Since 1893, Florida law has protected manatees from killing and molestation through criminal penalties. Despite these long-standing efforts, many manatees are lost every year through collisions with boats and barges, in floodgates and canal locks, and by becoming entangled in or eating fishing gear. Although once a significant problem, poaching and manatee vandalism now account for few deaths annually.

Conservation Notes

The most serious threat to manatees continues to be habitat loss due to water pollution, herbicides, dredge-and-fill projects, and surface run-off—all created by coastal development. Some studies have shown that manatee tissues are accumulating high levels of herbicides. Manatees are also often harassed by skin divers, boaters, and fishers, and most often by noise pollution from boats. Manatees usually avoid all contact with humans, including divers; if they are too greatly harassed, they will move to less-preferred or marginal habitat, which subjects them to cold-related illnesses.

Manatees are susceptible to cold weather. At water temperatures below 60 degrees F, they become lethargic and stop eating. During unusually cold winters, they cannot produce enough metabolic heat to compensate for heat lost to the environment, so they use up stored fat reserves and basically die of malnutrition. Young in their first year are even more susceptible to cold-related deaths, possibly because their smaller bulk produces less body heat, and lack of experience in traditional migration routes strands them in cold waters. Many manatees take refuge during cold weather in warm-water discharges from power plants, which can kill them. Manatees are also susceptible to red tide conditions: toxic microorganisms—which infect animal matter—ingested while they feed on sea grasses.

How to Observe

Manatees are difficult to observe in the wild, as they spend most of their time below the water surface. Because of the difficulty in locating them, wildlife managers have had trouble getting an accurate count of the total population left, although it is small enough for manatees to be endangered. If you want to observe manatees in the wild, consult a local wildlife agency on the advisability of and locations for viewing. Do not attempt to approach manatees, which are susceptible to stress, and use extreme caution in operating boats and barges.

Situations and Solutions

Future Extinction of the Manatee

WHY IT HAPPENS: Because of continued mortality caused by humans, eventual extinction of the West Indian manatee is a distinct possibility.

SUGGESTIONS:

1. Protect and preserve manatee habitat and travelways by observing posted speed limits and boat exclusion areas.
2. Support efforts to preserve habitat for the endangered manatees. These include cooperative efforts between public and private groups such as Big Bend, 60 miles of coastline at the northeast corner of the Gulf of Mexico donated for manatee refuge waters. Preserving this area—some of the wildest land left in Florida—has also helped other species, including bald eagles, ospreys, and sea turtles.
3. As artificial sources of warm water (hydroelectric facilities) approach the end of their operating lives, support habitat management decisions that will help compensate for the losses of those warm-water areas.

Birds

Volumes have been written about the thousands of bird species found in North America. The scope of this book does not permit a comprehensive listing, so we discuss the most common species and families within five general categories: raptors (birds of prey), land birds (passerines and others), game birds, waterfowl (game birds that live mostly in freshwater habitats), and aquatic birds (either birds that are indigenous to salt water or fresh- or saltwater wading birds). (See Appendix C.)

More than 8,500 species of birds inhabit the world. Birds play an essential role in the natural order through pollination, the spreading of seeds, and insect population control. They also bring the priceless gifts of music, color, and the exhilaration of flight to our world. Our gifts to them can be a food chain free of toxins and a clean waterway system in which they can float and dive and from which they can feed and safely drink. These are gifts we all want and deserve for ourselves as well.

Some birds remain resident in their home areas year-round; others migrate over many miles. The ability to migrate gives a bird the great advantage of moving to where food sources are most abundant. When migrating, most birds fly below 3,000 feet; ducks and small, perching birds have been seen near 20,000 feet. In their everyday search for food, however, most songbirds fly at 150 feet or lower.

Flight

The shape of a bird's wings affects its style of flight. Vultures, for example, have broad wings with long primary feathers that stick out like fingers. Air flows past these surfaces with so little turbulence that the slightest forward motion of the wings gives them lifting power. These birds soar effortlessly on thermal air currents with little need to flap their wings. Designed differently, crows beat their wings about 3 times a second, chickadees 10 times that fast. The hummingbird ordinarily moves its wings about 50 to 70 times per second but in rapid flight may increase to 200 times per second. Most songbirds fly slower than many people think they do, averaging no more than 20 to 30 mph. Many waterfowl and shorebirds fly twice that fast, and the peregrine falcon diving after its prey can travel at 180 mph.

Feathers

A bird must keep its feathers in perfect condition. If it doesn't, insulation and waterproofing are compromised and flight is less efficient. The edges of feathers end in thousands of microscopic fringes called barbs and barbules, which must stay interlocked. This integrity is responsible for the feather's unique flexibility and strength as well as for its waterproofing properties. Air trapped between the barbs increases surface tension on the feather, causing water to run off. In water birds, air trapped in the plumage also increases buoyancy. Preening movements, in particular the gentle nibbling of each feather as it is drawn between the beak tips, are essential for proper maintenance. Male birds have brightly colored feathers, probably for mating display, while females, which most often tend the nest, usually wear subdued colors for camouflage and to protect the young from detection by predators.

Feeding

While some birds, such as owls and vultures, can go a day or two between meals, most must eat frequently, especially when raising young. Superb eyesight aids all birds in searching for food; birds have the keenest vision of all living things. A soaring eagle can spot its prey a mile below, and hawks and falcons can do almost as well. An owl can capture its prey in near darkness because of both its vision and its acute hearing. A chickadee, ever watchful of a distant hawk, can instantly focus on the tiniest insect in front of its bill.

While most birds have no sense of smell, this sense is well developed in some scavenger birds, like the turkey vulture, which use it to detect carrion while soaring far above ground.

Raptors

The types of birds ordinarily considered raptors (birds of prey) include hawks, eagles, ospreys, falcons, owls, and vultures. These birds prey on small mammals (mice, rats, squirrels), birds, snakes, and fish, as well as on the carrion of all animals. They swoop down suddenly and grab the prey in their talons, often without stopping flight. The vulture hunts only carrion (dead flesh), thus keeping our environment clear of dead animals while caring for itself.

Situations and Solutions for all raptors are grouped together and follow the section on Owls.

[HAWKS]

The hawks in North America comprise 26 species; of those, 17 species are called hawks, 4 are eagles, and 5 are kites. Hawks are symbols of fierce power and hunting ability in birds of prey. They are capable of incredible flight speed and can capture prey in midair. There are three different types of hawks: buteos, accipiters, and harriers. The buteo hawks have broad, rounded wings and a broad fanned tail. They soar very high while scouting for prey. Buteo hawks include, among others, rough-legged hawks, red-tailed hawks, broad-winged hawks, red-shouldered hawks, and Swainson's hawks. Accipiter species have long, narrow tails, but their wings are short and broad. Accipiter species include sharp-shinned hawks and Cooper's hawks. Harriers are slim, with somewhat rounded wings and long tails and bodies. They include the northern harrier, or marsh, hawk. Eagles and ospreys are also considered hawks but are covered in their own sections here.

Buteos, Accipiters, and Harrier Hawks

Red-tailed hawks (Buteo jamaicensis), sometimes known as chicken hawks, are among the largest North American hawks, measuring approximately 2 feet long and having wingspans of 4½ feet. The female is one-third larger than the male. Red-tailed hawks are broad winged, with a distinctive, rounded, red brown tail. Color varies from white to pure black, but most commonly the bird is dark brown with a white breast and a broad band of dark streaks on the white belly. Immature red-tails have brownish tails that may or may not show banding.

Rough-legged hawks (B. lagopus) can be mistaken for red-tailed hawks in their dark phase coloring. In their light phase they have a blackish belly, black patches at the "wrist" of the underwing, and a white tail with a broad black band near the tip. Their legs are feathered all the way to the toes, and their wings and tail are longer than those of the red-tailed hawks.

Swainson's hawks (B. swainsoni) are large hawks with variable plumage. Typically, adults are dark brown above with a dark breast and white belly. The tail is also dark above but with lighter, indistinct banding underneath. Young Swainson's hawks resemble white-breasted immature red-tails.

Red-shouldered hawks (B. lineatus) have thin, white bands crossing both sides of the black tail, rufous red shoulders, and pale, robin red underparts. Their wings are longer and slimmer than those of other buteos. They have white, almost translucent, spots near the wing tips.

Broad-winged hawks (B. platypterus) are small, crow-sized hawks, brown above with bar-striping of rust below. The adult's tail has white and black bands of nearly equal width.

Accipiter hawks (sharp-shinned hawk [Accipiter striatus], Cooper's hawk [A. cooperii], and goshawk [A. gentilis]) are long-tailed woodland hawks with short, rounded wings. Sharp-shins are small, bluejay-sized hawks, slate gray above with whitish and heavy barred rust beneath. Immature sharp-shins are brown above with darker streaked brown below. Sharp-shins are difficult to distinguish from Cooper's hawks except for their tails: the sharp-shin's is square, while the tip of the Cooper's is rounded. Cooper's hawks are crow sized with coloration identical to that of sharp-shins. Male Cooper's hawks and female sharp-shins may not be distinguishable in the field.

Northern harriers (Circus cyaneus), also known as marsh hawks, are slender, graceful birds. They are pale gray above and whitish below, with black wing tips, a distinctive white rump, and long, slim wings and tail.

Range and Habitat

Red-tailed hawks range throughout the U.S. and Canada. Typical habitat is open country, scrub woodlands, or wide, rocky canyons. They are migratory in the colder or snowier parts of their range. Red-tails have the widest ecological tolerance of any hawk in North America.

Rough-legged hawks range from northern tundra regions to southern winter grounds but are most commonly seen in the northern U.S.

Swainson's hawks are found primarily in the western plains and rarely seen in southern states. Like other hawks, they migrate from their northern spring and summer habitats to winter in warmer southern areas.

Red-shouldered hawks are more commonly found in wet bottomlands than red-tailed hawks are. Once numerous in southern parts of the U.S., their numbers have declined as a result of wetland clearing and drainage.

Broad-winged hawks summer in the southern U.S., from which they migrate in large flocks (up to several thousand) to Central and South America during winter. Unlike other buteos, they prefer forested areas to open fields.

Accipiter hawks are found in the northern U.S. but migrate south from

Hawks, among the most successful birds of prey, play a vital role in controlling rodent populations.

September to May.

Northern harriers are found throughout North America. They prefer open fields and wetland habitats.

Other Characteristics

Hawks are daytime hunters and have the best eyesight of all animals. Red-tailed hawks are readily observable because of their habit of circling high in the air, combined with their shrill, rasping cry. Red-tails are aerobatic technicians, especially during mating season, often touching their mates in midair or dropping 2,000 feet in a single dive. They are often found perching on trees, telephone poles, or fence posts. They fly level at 35 to 40 mph but can reach 120 mph during a dive. Their eyesight is estimated to be seven times better than that of humans.

Red-tails need a great amount of protein and calcium during their growth; therefore, they eat the whole bodies of prey, from insects to small mammals and birds. Small rodents make up 85 percent of their diet. Since the hawk cannot digest bones and fur, it will eject a pellet of these materials after eating. This behavior is triggered at dawn.

Rough-legged hawks are seen flying low like harriers over open fields, but they are larger and perch on small trees, unlike harriers. Rough-legged hawks hover, wings beating, while they search for small mammals.

Swainson's hawks feed on insects and are often seen chasing grasshoppers, crickets, and other insects on the ground. They hunt primarily from the air, cruising low over the ground like a harrier, or from high perches. Swainson's hawks also feed on small rodents like mice and ground squirrels; occasionally they will capture a frog or a small snake.

Both red-shouldered and broad-tailed hawks hunt from inconspicuous perches hidden in foliage to capture snakes, frogs, insects, mice, and other small mammals. Accipiter hawks hunt small birds with great swiftness. They are capable of flying through thick forests to capture prey. They also linger near home bird feeders during the winter to catch small birds.

Northern harriers hunt by flying close to the ground with their wings held in a shallow V as they search for rats, blackbirds, or other prey. They usually perch on the ground rather than in trees.

Enemies and Defenses

Humans are the chief enemy of hawks, which continue to be indiscriminately killed even though they are protected by state and federal laws. Ranchers and farmers, often not realizing their great benefit in controlling rodents, continue to shoot many hawks. Many are also hit by automobiles while feeding along highways or fly into power poles and lines. Cooper's hawks have suffered severe declines due to pesticide contamination that affects their reproductive ability.

How to Observe

In open country, most hawks can be observed soaring high in the air. Often they are far away, however, and therefore hard to identify. Check with your local wildlife agency to learn of good observation sites for hawks.

Eagles

The two most common eagles found in North America are the bald eagle (*Haliaeetus leucocephalus*) and the golden eagle (*Aquila chrysaetos*). Other than the nearly extinct California condor, bald eagles are the largest raptor, measuring 34 to 43 inches long and having a 6- to 7½-foot wingspan. Males weigh 7 to 10 pounds, females 10 to 14 pounds. Adults have snow white heads and tails. The bodies of eagles are brownish black; the eyes, feet, and bills yellow; the talons black. Immature bald eagles are grayish brown; they do not attain their distinctive adult coloration until they reach four to five years.

Golden eagles, also known as buzzard hawks, black eagles, war birds, or mountain eagles, are dark above and below, with a pale golden nape on the upper neck. Immature bald eagles are difficult to distinguish from golden eagles, because their coloration is so similar. Certain characteristics help identification: The golden eagle's legs are feathered all the way down to the toes; the bald eagle has 2 or 3 inches of bare, bright yellow leg. Immature golden eagles are dark with a white ring at the base of the tail and white patches in the flight feathers of the underwing; the immature bald eagle is dark with mottled white on the wing linings and never has a sharply ringed tail.

Bald eagles exhibit amazing power and flexibility while fishing for their dinner.

Range and Habitat

Bald eagles are found only in North America. Their populations are broken into two categories: the northern group is found primarily in Alaska and Canada but migrates and nests in the contiguous 48 states to fish in open waters between November and March each year. The greatest concentrations of wintering bald eagles from this northern population are in the western and midwestern states. The southern population ranges from southern California eastward through the southwestern states to the Southeast, and northward to Chesapeake Bay. The largest concentration of this population is in Florida. Bald eagles prefer large valleys, rivers, and lakes that provide ready sources of fish.

Golden eagles are not limited to North America but are found throughout the world. They inhabit mountains, foothills, and prairies throughout the U.S. and Canada, preferring arid mountain and grassland habitats.

Other Characteristics

Of the bald eagle's diet, 75 percent is fish. These eagles also feed on waterfowl, small and large mammals, and carrion of livestock and other animals. Golden eagles eat small mammals, such as rabbits, prairie dogs, and marmots, and carrion.

Bald eagles fly between 36 and 44 mph. Golden eagles have been clocked at 120 mph, but their average "cruising" speed is around 30 mph. While hunting, eagles will soar for miles with wings outstretched. They flap their wings when taking off and landing, but not usually in midair. Soaring on thermal currents conserves energy and allows them to travel many miles without fatigue. They swoop down to take their prey with strong talons and can lift up to 4 pounds. They use their beaks solely for tearing flesh to eat their prey and for feeding their young.

Enemies and Defenses

The main enemy of bald eagles is humans, who disturb nesting sites by cutting down trees, cause loss of waterside habitat through development, contaminate food sources (especially through pesticides in the water that impact eagles' health and reproduction), and intentionally or accidentally shoot, poison, and trap them. Adult bald eagles, more easily disturbed than juveniles, are forced to move when disturbed by humans. Frequent disturbance while feeding and forced movement to new feeding areas will threaten an eagle's survival. In addition, many golden eagles die every year while perching on or flying from high-voltage power lines. Many others are caught in traps set for—or poisoned by bait left for—coyotes and other animals.

Conservation Notes

When the bald eagle was adopted as the national emblem of the U.S. in 1782, an estimated 25,000 to 75,000 bald eagles nested in what is now the contiguous 48 states. The wolf-poisoning campaign of the late 1800s also killed many bald eagles, and the later use of DDT and other pesticides caused thinning of their eggshells and sharp declines in reproduction. Many eagles also have been killed by high lead levels in the fish they eat. Though eagles eat primarily fish and carrion, many have been shot by hunters, ranchers, and farmers wanting to "protect" livestock. By 1980, only 2,400 nesting bald eagles existed in the contiguous 48 states.

Captive-breeding programs have helped to restore bald eagle populations in the wild. In a remarkable comeback, by 1991 there were over 6,000 adults (over 3,000 active nests) and an unknown number of young and juvenile bald eagles in the wild. Currently classified as endangered in 43 states and threatened in 5 states, the bald eagle is protected by federal legislation, including the Endangered Species Act of 1973, the Bald Eagle Protection Act of 1940, and the Migratory Bird Treaty Act of 1918.

Despite great efforts to protect and restore the bald eagle, the demands of human development still impinge on the species' habitat needs. Some people also still shoot eagles, despite severe criminal penalties in state and federal courts.

Eagles are highly honored in Native American cultures, where they represent the power and vision of the Great Spirit; their feathers are sacred and used in ceremonial rituals. The U.S. Fish and Wildlife Service has developed a program to distribute carcasses and feathers of eagles and other raptors to Native Americans for use in their spiritual practices. The service's National Forensics Laboratory in Ashland, Oregon, maintains a list of Native American people who apply for receipt of these items. Anyone finding raptor remains in the wild (for example, a road kill) or wildlife rehabilitation centers coming into possession of such remains can directly contact the laboratory at 503-482-4191 to arrange for contributing them for the benefit of Native peoples.

How to Observe

Because eagles are easily displaced from their nesting and feeding areas, it is best not to attempt to observe them in the wild without the guidance of trained wildlife officials who can inform you of known nesting locations and observation techniques. Since 1979, the National Wildlife Federation has sponsored a multiagency cooperative winter bald eagle counting program, which gives volunteers an excellent opportunity to observe eagles in the wild while assisting local agencies in wildlife management. Check with your local wildlife agency about opportunities to participate in this rewarding program. If you attempt to observe bald or golden eagles, use binoculars or a spotting scope for long-distance contact, and remain as quiet as possible.

Ospreys

The osprey *(Pandion haliaetus)* is also known as the sea eagle or fish hawk. Adults are dark purplish brown above with a clear white breast below, sometimes spotted or streaked with brown. The head looks much like that of a bald eagle but with wide black marks on the cheeks and neck. The bills and claws are black, the legs and feet green white, and the eyes yellow. Ospreys have narrow wings with a black patch at the "wrist," and the long tail is narrowly barred in black. They average 21 to 24½ inches long and have a wingspan of 54 to 72 inches. Females are larger, weighing 2 to 12 pounds; males weigh 2 to 10 pounds.

Range and Habitat

During summer, ospreys are widely scattered near lakes, rivers, and seacoasts in Canada and the U.S. They migrate in winter to Central and South America.

Other Characteristics

Ospreys eat primarily fish but have been known to take frogs, snakes, small rodents, and sea- and shorebirds when fish are unavailable. They hunt by perching on snags or rocks near water and may fly 30 to 100 feet above the water looking for fish. When fish are found, ospreys dive straight into the water with tremendous force. They sometimes disappear completely below the surface, then reappear, gripping the fish in their talons, and become airborne again. Now and then, ospreys break wings by hitting the water too hard or drown because their talons become embedded in fish too large to lift out of the water. Eagles occasionally attack to make an osprey drop its captured fish; the eagle then catches the fish in midair and makes off with the prize.

Enemies and Defenses

Like most birds of prey, ospreys' primary enemy is humans. The birds are sometimes still shot, but most often they suffer the ill effects of pollution from pesticides and lead poisoning from lead sinkers swallowed by fish.

Conservation Notes

The development of shore recreation around lakes, rivers, and other wetlands has significantly reduced the number of available osprey nesting sites. Human activities in those areas have encouraged predators, such as raccoons, which raid osprey nests. But the most harmful human activity is littering, because the discarded plastic and other garbage that ospreys often gather as nesting material can choke and strangle their young.

How to Observe

Ospreys spend much time perched on tree snags or rocks near water.

[FALCONS]

Falcons are small, streamlined birds of prey with large heads; long, pointed wings; and long, narrow tails. In North America, there are seven native falcon species and one foreign visiting species (the Eurasian kestrel). The name *falcon* is Latin and refers to the hooked shape of the claws. The bills of birds in the falcon family are notched and toothed. The female is called the falcon and the male is called the tiercel.

Peregrine falcons *(Falco peregrinus)* are crow-sized birds with blue gray backs and streaked underparts. Their large heads have a dark "cap" and heavy black "sideburns." Young peregrines are brown above, streaked below. Male peregrines weigh a little over a pound; the larger female weighs up to 2 pounds. Adults have wingspans up to 4 feet.

Merlins *(F. columbarius)* resemble jay-sized peregrines with slate gray above and broad, black bands on the tail. Females and juveniles are dusky brown with banded tails. Both adults and young have streaked breasts and bellies.

American kestrels, or sparrow hawks *(F. sparverius)*, are the smallest and most common North American falcons. Males have blue gray wings, rufous red back and tail, light-colored chest and abdomen, and a multi-colored head with dark "whisker" marks on each side of the face. Females are duller in color and lack the bluish wings. Kestrels are 11 inches long with a wingspan of 1½ to 2 feet.

Range and Habitat

Most peregrines nest in Canada but migrate south. Kestrels are found from sea level to 12,000 feet from North America to Central America. They are common throughout the U.S. but do migrate from north to south for winter range. Their habitat is open country, prairies, desert, wooded streams, farmlands, and urban areas; they often perch along roads and near dwellings.

Other Characteristics

Peregrines dive faster than any other bird; it is estimated that they achieve speeds of 180 mph. Their speed aids them in catching prey and traveling long distances and protects them from other predators. Peregrines feed on other birds. They hunt by climbing to a high elevation and dropping toward their prey, building speed by quickly folding their wings against their body. The peregrine often hits its prey with its "fist" (folded talons), knocking the smaller bird out of control so the peregrine can catch it in its talons, often before it hits the ground. The peregrine can also seize a bird in midair and fly away with its catch.

Merlins fly low and fast with a steady wingbeat, somewhat like a pigeon.

Kestrels, like all birds of prey, are carnivorous, feeding mostly on insects and small rodents. They prefer grasshoppers and mice. They habitually hover when hunting and take their food by plunging from a hover or a perch. They rarely catch food in the air. The kestrel's flight speed has been clocked at 22 to 25 mph. It has an average life span of 1½ years in the wild and up to 14 years in captivity. Kestrels are solitary birds except when nesting.

Enemies and Defenses

Falcons' primary enemy is humans. Peregrines will aggressively defend their nests from any enemy, including humans, squawking loudly and diving at the intruder. They have been known to hit humans while protecting their nests. (Most other birds turn away at the last minute.)

Kestrels' primary enemy is humans, despite their protection under state and federal laws. Most banded American kestrels that are recovered have been shot.

Conservation Notes

Peregrine falcons have had great difficulty adjusting to the habitat destruction caused by humans. Their numbers have declined significantly worldwide because of the effect of pesticides on their ability to reproduce. The Arctic peregrine, which migrates to southern areas, is listed as an endangered species. Some captive breeding programs are starting to show success in releasing breeding pairs back to the wild. Amazingly, some peregrines have been reintroduced to highly urban areas, where they appear to be adapting, nesting on high-rise buildings and feeding on city-dwelling small birds. Their primary needs in all locations are clean water and nontoxic food sources.

How to Observe

Consult a local wildlife agency to determine safe and nonintrusive opportunities to observe falcons.

[OWLS]

Eighteen species of owls are found in North America. Some of the more common include barn owls, eastern and western screech owls, great horned owls, snowy owls, burrowing owls, northern saw-whet owls, and short-eared owls. Owls often overlap hawk and eagle territories, but because owls are night hunters, there is little or no conflict between these great raptors.

Owls are able to catch their prey unaware because of their noiseless flight feathers. Owls have extraordinary sight; unlike other birds, their eyes are positioned in the front of the head, which permits binocular vision even at close range. An owl's vision is 100 times more sensitive at night than a human's, and even better during the day. Owls cannot move their eyes, however, so must turn their heads to look in a different direction; owls have a 270-degree range of motion with their heads. They also have the largest eardrums of any bird, giving them sensitive hearing, and can move feathers on their heads to channel sounds to help them locate faint sounds of prey.

Historically, owls have been greatly misunderstood and feared. Because of their nocturnal hunting, night cries, and dark habitats, superstition has equated them with sinister deeds and darkness. In reality, owls are beneficial to humans because they keep down rodent and insect populations.

Great horned owls (Bubo virginianus) are 18 to 23 inches long with a wingspan up to 5 feet. Females are slightly larger than males. The basic body color is overall gray spotted with brown-and-white markings; these owls have a white throat collar above a dark-streaked breast. The beak is black, eyes deep yellow, and ear tufts 1½ to 2 inches long. Both males and females have distinctive "horns"—tufts of feathers—and four razor-sharp talons on each foot (only eagles have a stronger grip). Great horned owls give the characteristic owl cry of three to eight hoots: *Whooo, whooo, whooo.*

Barn owls (Tyto alba pratincola) are 15 to 20 inches high. They have white, heart-shaped faces and no ear tufts. Their bodies are pale yellow orange spotted with dark gray brown and white; the beak is pale yellow. They make a rasping cry and clicking sound.

Snowy owls (Nyctea scandiaca), as their name suggests, are mostly glistening white with black talons and beaks. Young "snowies" have dark bars and spots, but adults are primarily white. They are about 23 inches long and have round heads (with no ear tufts) and yellow eyes. Snowy owls are silent except during breeding season.

The *eastern screech owl (Otus asio)* is about the size of a small pheasant. This owl goes through three color phases—rufous red, gray, and brownish—and has a dark bill and yellow eyes. It is known for its mournful call: *Oh-o-o-o-o-o-o.* The *western screech owl (Otus kennicottii)* is one of the smallest owls, measuring only 8½ inches long. It is brownish and has prominent ear tufts, a dark bill, and yellow eyes. It has two common calls:

a series of accelerating whistles, and a short trill followed by a longer one.

The *northern saw-whet owl* (*Aegolius acadicus*) is also one of the smallest owls, no larger than a cardinal. It has long, broad wings, a short tail, and thick, downy feathers that can make it appear larger than it is. It is chocolate brown with large white spots above and white-streaked with brown underneath. The facial disk is whitish with a distinct dark edge, black bill, and white streaked forehead. Its call, often repeated up to 100 times a minute, is a raspy sound similar to a saw being sharpened, hence the name saw-whet.

The *short-eared owl* (*Asio flammeus*) is about 15 inches long, slightly smaller than a crow. It is streaked tawny brown with light facial disks, bright yellow eyes, a boldly streaked breast, and a paler, lightly streaked belly. It has more pointed wings than most owls, with light spots on the upper wing and dark spots near the "wrist" on the underwing. The short-eared owl does not hoot; it makes a high, raspy, barking sound.

The *burrowing owl* (*Athene cunicularia*) is 9 inches long, with a 21-inch wingspan. It is sandy brown spotted with white above and has a white chin stripe, barred underparts, yellow eyes, and unusually long legs.

Range and Habitat

The *great horned owl* ranges from the tree line in Alaska across most of Canada and all of the U.S. into Central America. It can inhabit almost any type of environment but is most common in timber and woodland regions. An individual's territory seldom exceeds half a mile from its roosting tree.

The *barn owl* may be found throughout the U.S. in woodlands, fields, and farmland. It often lives in the vicinity of people and occasionally nests in abandoned badger or coyote burrows or in a quiet corner of an unused building.

Snowy owls live primarily in the Arctic tundra regions of Alaska and Canada. About every four years, when the lemming population is small, they travel south into the contiguous 48 states in search of food.

Eastern screech owls are found in the eastern and southern U.S. They prefer open woodlands close to creeks, marshes, and fields.

Western screech owls range from southeastern Alaska through Canada into the western U.S. They prefer coniferous forests.

Northern saw-whet owls are usually found in dense tree stands. They are extremely shy and seldom seen but can be found throughout most of Canada and the U.S.

Short-eared owls, found throughout North America, are equally comfortable in open tundra and marshes.

Burrowing owls are found primarily in the western grasslands of the U.S. but also in southern locations such as Florida.

Other Characteristics

Great horned owls, like other raptors, are carnivorous. They hunt early in the evening, eating almost any kind of meat, including rabbits, mice, skunks, birds of all kinds, snakes, fish, and insects. Hunting techniques vary: on wing, wading in the water, or perching and then pouncing. These owls have powerful talons and have been known to attack coyotes, porcupines, dogs, cats, and skunks. Their eardrums are larger than those of any other bird. Great horned owls are protected by state and federal laws; they have a life span of 15 to 30 years.

Barn owls are more nocturnal than other owls and rely mostly on hearing to catch prey, which enables them to hunt in complete darkness. Their facial hairs are sound sensitive and aid them in detecting minute sounds. The leading edge of the wings has very soft feathers, permitting the owl to fly silently and surprise its prey. Barn owls are excellent rodent catchers, and a single hunting owl with nesting young may fly 10 to 15 miles a night, greatly helping farmers to control rodent populations. As in all owls, after food is digested in the stomach, a pellet formed of the undigested fur and bones is cast up from the stomach through the mouth and spit out. Barn owls live 15 to 30 years.

Snowy owls are unique in several respects. Their main food source is lemmings found in the Arctic north. Because lemmings experience regular population booms and declines, their predators—snowy owls, weasels, and Arctic foxes—are subject to alternating years of feast and famine. Because snowy owls can fly south to find other food, they are the only lemming predators that can escape the lean periods. Unlike other owls, they hunt during the day as well as at night. Small birds that attack or pester other sleepy owls during the day can become food for the snowy owl.

Eastern screech owls feed mainly on insects but also include crayfish, minnows, wasp larvae, rodents, birds, frogs, and spiders in their diets. Western screech owls feed on mice, voles, and songbirds found in the forests.

Northern saw-whet owls feed on mice, birds, and small squirrels. They are nocturnal feeders, with their busiest periods just before dawn and at dusk.

Short-eared owls prey on small mammals, shorebirds, and songbirds. They are often mistaken for northern harriers (hawks) because they fly low over fields in search of prey and because they lean forward on the ground in the manner of a hawk. In flight, their wings have a wavering, mothlike rhythm.

Burrowing owls feed at night on roaches, crickets, other insects, small lizards, frogs, snakes, and rodents. They live as single breeding pairs or loose colonies of two or more families and roost in nests underground. Usually the burrows extend 4 to 8 feet, with the nesting chamber at the end of the burrow, lined with grass, feathers, paper, and manure.

Enemies and Defenses

Crows, hawks, and smaller birds commonly harass great horned owls in territorial disputes. When threatened, a great horned owl will rapidly click its beak and fluff out its feathers to make it appear much larger. The chief enemy of these owls, however, is the automobile, which kills thousands every year. They are also still hunted by people who believe that owls damage game bird populations or livestock. Hunting of owls, as of all raptors, is illegal.

Barn owls' natural predators are great horned owls and prairie falcons. Their populations are threatened due to habitat loss. Because snowy owls nest on the ground, their eggs and young are especially vulnerable to Arctic fox predation.

The western screech owl, when startled, stretches tall and holds its wings close to its back, as if to look like a dead stub on a tree branch.

Burrowing owls, when threatened, will bob and bow in agitation and give out their chattering or clucking call, which has given them the nickname "howdy bird" in Florida. Although they have partly adapted to loss of habitat, burrowing owls are still subject to destruction by construction activities, malicious harassment by people, and flooding of burrows during heavy rains.

Humans have killed owls out of superstition and fear, or out of belief that owls prey on livestock. They do not. They have also been victims of habitat loss. The spotted owl and the burrowing owl have been declared endangered or threatened.

How to Observe

Visual encounters with owls in the wild are unusual because they are nocturnal, but often owls can be "observed" by their voices. Some wildlife agencies recommend recording on a simple cassette tape several minutes of the cries of several owl species, which are commercially available. Then head out on a dark, windless night into woodlots, creekside areas, wetlands, or forests, with binoculars, flashlights, and extra batteries. If owls are present, they will respond to the prerecorded calls right away. Screech owls will not call but may fly to perches near the tape recorder. If you remain quiet, you can sometimes spotlight the owls with your flashlight and observe them for several minutes. Do not play the tapes too long in one area, however, because doing so may force owls away from their nesting sites. Make every effort not to disturb owls during their spring nesting season, a critical time in their yearly cycle.

Burrowing owls can be observed on the ground or on fence posts during the day.

Situations and Solutions: Raptors

Raptors Taking Poultry

WHY IT HAPPENS: If natural food sources are greatly reduced, hawks, falcons, and sometimes owls may occasionally take young poultry.

SUGGESTIONS: Enclose poultry in pens with wire or solid tops that prevent entry by raptors from above. Remember, all raptors are protected by federal and state laws and are not to be shot. If the problem persists, contact your local wildlife agency.

Hawks or Falcons Nesting on Property or Homes

WHY IT HAPPENS: Although raptors rarely choose to live in urban environments, some, such as the peregrine falcon, have begun nesting in cities on apartment buildings in an attempt to survive by adapting to human habitat. In that habitat, they prey on songbirds as one available food source.

SUGGESTIONS:

1. Do not attempt to kill, trap, or disturb nests of eagles, hawks, falcons, or owls. All raptors are protected by law.
2. If raptors nesting in certain locations are troublesome, attempt to prevent nesting by using netting and other nesting guards described in detail in the section on Pigeons.
3. If these prevention techniques don't help, call your local wildlife agency for assistance.
4. Alternatively, encourage raptor nesting on your property, not only for rodent control, but also to help in the survival of the birds of prey.

Ospreys Nesting in Inappropriate Locations

WHY IT HAPPENS: Ospreys may build nests on buildings or other inappropriate platform areas because of unavailability of natural nesting sites.

SUGGESTIONS: If ospreys have built a nest on a building or platform that is hazardous to them or humans, call your local wildlife agency for assistance in relocating the birds.

Encouraging Osprey Nesting on Your Property

WHY IT HAPPENS: Humans can help counteract the loss of natural osprey nesting habitat.

SUGGESTIONS: If you want to encourage ospreys on your property and have few natural nest sites, consult a wildlife manager. Managers encourage the use of artificial nesting platforms and can provide instructions on how to construct such platforms.

Owls Needing Nesting Sites and Protection

WHY IT HAPPENS: Owls have lost a significant amount of habitat. Humans can help by erecting nesting boxes for different owl species.

You can encourage owls near your home by providing a suitable nesting box in wooded habitat.

SUGGESTIONS:

1. Contact your local wildlife agency for suggestions regarding owl nesting boxes for species in your area. Generally, place nesting boxes in locations similar to their natural habitat. For example, screech owl boxes should be placed in orchards, suburbs, and woodland edges along waterways; barn owl boxes in dark corners in barns, high up on silos, and in other locations

out of reach of predators. All nest boxes should have drain holes in the floor and some sawdust in the bottom to cushion the rolling of eggs when laid. It is best to use a natural building material, like rough cypress, which will last a long time and blend in with the surroundings.

2. Attract burrowing owls by removing a 1- to 2-foot circular plug from your sodded lawn, exposing sandy loose soil for the owls. You can even start the burrow a little and pile the loose soil near the entrance. Then construct T-shaped perches near burrow sites to give the owls an elevated view of the nesting area. The perches also mark the burrows to protect them from mowers and other machinery. Restrict use of pesticides, which can seriously harm burrowing owls that feed on insects.

3. Urge farmers, ranchers, and sportspeople to protect all owls and to avoid injuring them. Remind these people that owls are important in controlling rodents and insects.

4. See Appendix C for information on obtaining nest box plans.

Land Birds

For the purposes of this book, land birds include passerines (perching or songbirds) and other small land-based birds such as pigeons, hummingbirds, and swifts. These two groups will be treated separately below.

Information on Situations and Solutions for all land birds follows the Other Land Birds section.

[PASSERINES]

Passerines (perching and songbirds) constitute the largest category of birds. Almost three-fifths of the world's birds, approximately 5,100 species, belong to this group. The word *passerine* means "perching bird," the one characteristic all these species have in common. Each foot has four toes, three facing forward and one backward to give the birds a strong grip on branches, twigs, wires, and fences. Other similarities among these species are that their young are born virtually helpless and need intensive parental care; most seasonally migrate from North America into Central and South America; and most sing unique and beautiful songs. Great adaptability in their feeding habitats has enabled them to survive. The shape of different species' bills varies according to diet: Insect eaters usually have small beaks, and seed eaters have stout, cone-shaped bills for cracking open seeds.

Detailed discussion of all passerines found in North America is outside the scope of this book; instead, the more common passerine categories are described. Those interested in learning more about these birds that enrich human lives can turn to many field identification guides and other bird-watching publications; some of these are listed in Appendix C.

Of the many passerine families, those treated here include blackbirds, crows, finches, larks, mockingbirds, shrikes, starlings, swallows, tanagers, thrushes, titmice, tyrant flycatchers, warblers, waxwings, weaverbirds, and wrens.

Range and Habitat

Passerines are found in all habitats, including fields, forests, mountains, wetlands, tundras, and cities. Migration of passerines has been documented in separate groups: western and eastern. Western birds migrate from their summer grounds as far north as Alaska and western Canada to winter in Central America. Eastern birds migrate from summer grounds in eastern Canada and the U.S. into Central and northern South America. Migration is directly connected to the available food supply; because insect populations decline in the north during the winter, the birds fly south, where insects are more abundant.

Other Characteristics

The traits that distinguish passerines from each other are as plentiful as their similarities. Diets and food-gathering techniques vary greatly among species. Many songbirds eat worms and insects; some capture insects in midair; some prefer seeds; and many include berries and fruits in season. Poison oak berries are an important seasonal food for such birds as the mockingbird, jay, and crow. Nesting behavior also varies greatly. Cliff swallows, for example, make neat, pear-shaped nests out of mud plastered against walls; killdeers simply move a few twigs around on the ground; and robins build twig nests in trees.

See the individual groups for more details. Note that within each category, individual birds or smaller groups are described in summary fashion, with general descriptions and other characteristics combined rather than subdivided.

Blackbirds

This group contains blackbirds, orioles, meadowlarks, grackles, cowbirds, and bobolinks. These birds range in size from 6½ to 21 inches long and vary greatly in coloring. Members of the group include red-winged blackbirds *(Agelaius phaeniceus)*, the most numerous species, found throughout the U.S.; the orange Northern oriole *(Icterus galbula)*, found across the U.S.; eastern and western meadowlarks *(Sturnella magna* and *S. neglecta,* respectively)*, both brown above and yellow breasted; and brown-headed cowbirds *(Molothrus ater)*, found throughout most of the U.S. and southern Canada.

Members of this group also vary greatly in habits. American orioles are known for their bright coloring and for building the most complex nests of all birds. Cowbirds are social parasites; they lay their 10 to 12 eggs only in other birds' nests (one per nest) and dislodge (and sometimes eat) the eggs of the host bird so that foster parents incubate, hatch, and feed cowbird young until they fledge. Meadowlarks build their nests on dry ground in the West and on damp ground in the East.

This group feeds primarily on insects found on the ground, including crickets, ants, grasshoppers, and caterpillars, as well as worms, spiders, and snails. They also eat grains, such as corn and wild grasses. Other than the cowbird, blackbirds lay 3 to 7 eggs that incubate for 11 to 14 days; the young leave the nest at 10 days.

The Crow Family

Eighteen species make up the crow family (Corvidae) in North America. There are two subfamilies: the crows, which include crows, ravens, rooks, jackdaws, and nutcrackers; and the jays, which include jays, magpies, and choughs.

These birds are the largest of all passerines as well as the most aggressive and noisy. Males and females of each species appear the same, and some species (ravens and scrub jays) mate for life. The male feeds the female while she is nesting and helps to feed the young once they have hatched. Members of the crow family are thought to be the most intelligent of all birds. They have been taught to talk, solve puzzles, count up to four, and quickly associate symbols with food. They are excellent mimics of other bird calls as well as the human voice.

Ravens (Corvus corax), the largest passerines, are iridescent black, are 21½ to 27 inches long, and have a wingspan of 46 to 56 inches. They have heavy arched or curved black bills, shaggy throat feathers, large nostrils behind tufts of feathers, and long, rounded tails that become wedge shaped in flight. They alternate wing flapping and soaring and can hover like kestrels and circle like hawks. Ravens can be distinguished from crows in flight by the wedge-shaped tail and thicker-looking throat.

Ravens are found in the eastern and far western sections of the contiguous U.S., Canada, and Alaska; they disappeared from the central plains with the extermination of bison. Ravens are chiefly scavengers, competing with vultures and gulls for carrion. They gather in small groups, not large flocks, and will spend nights in communal roosts. When not disturbed by humans, ravens can become quite tame. They nest in trees or on rocky crevices, building large nests (2 to 3 feet across and 4 feet high) from dead branches lined with grasses, lichens, seaweed, and/or fur from carcasses.

Members of the crow family are thought to be the most intelligent of all birds. They are excellent mimics of the human voice and other birds' calls.

Common crows (C. brachyrhynchos) are smaller than ravens, measuring 17 to 21 inches long and having 33- to 40-inch wingspans. Both males and females weigh about 1 pound. Crows are among the most adaptable birds, living in open wooded areas throughout Canada and the U.S. Like ravens, they scavenge carrion for food, but they also eat insects, frogs, worms, spiders, snails, and cultivated crops such as corn on agricultural lands. Crows usually nest high up in trees but, if necessary, will even nest on the ground. Their nests are well built of twigs and branches lined with mosses, grasses, leaves, and animal hair.

There are eight species of *jays* in North America, the most common being blue jays *(Cyanocitta cristata)*, found mostly east of the Rocky Mountains; scrub jays *(Aphelocoma coerulescens)*, found in the western U.S. and Florida; and Steller's jays *(C. stelleri)*, found from Alaska to Mexico west of the Rockies. Jays range from 11 to 13 inches long, have 15- to 17½-inch wingspans, weigh 2¾ to 4½ ounces, and are known for their striking blue coloring. Other than these beautiful markings, the jay's best-known trait is its noisiness; it shrieks loudly and often. Blue jays were once birds of wilderness forests but have adapted well to living in towns and cities, especially in trees near gardens and in parks. Scrub jays live in dense shrubbery, and Steller's jays are common to western coniferous forests. Some jays migrate south in winter while others stay in their home range year-round.

Like crows, jays feed on much vegetable matter, such as corn, acorns, and beechnuts; they also eat insects, frogs, mice, snails, and fruit. Jays build nests, in trees and bushes, made of bark, mosses, grasses, paper, and string. Adults aggressively defend their nests by dive-bombing and pecking intruders, including humans.

Two species of *magpies,* the black-billed *(Pica pica)* and the yellow-billed *(P. nuttalli),* are found in western North America. Magpies are 16 to 22 inches long, have 9½- to 12-inch tails, weigh 5¾ to 7 ounces, and have 22- to 24-inch wingspans. Both species are black with white wing patches; they are distinguishable by the color of their bills. The black-billed magpie lives west of the Rocky Mountains and north of the deserts; yellow-bills are found only in California.

Magpies feed on the ground on grasshoppers, other insects, and carrion. They are found mostly along waterways, nesting in trees, and have adapted to living in urban parks. Nesting pairs join in loose colonies to build bulky nests high above the ground (40 to 60 feet).

Finches

Finches (Fringillidae) constitute the passerine family with the most species in North America. They include sparrows (except house or English sparrows, which are weaverbirds), bramblings, towhees, cardinals, goldfinches, rosy finches, crossbills, buntings, and grosbeaks, among others. (There is some disagreement about the classification of some species as finches.) The most common finch is the house finch *(Carpodacus mexicanus),* which inhabits all of North America, from arid lands to dense urban areas.

Finches are primarily small seed eaters with cone-shaped bills and notched tails, although some also eat insects. The bills of different finch species vary according to their primary diet. For example, crossbills, whose upper and lower beaks actually cross, force apart pinecones. The grosbeak has a strong, thick beak used for cracking into tough seeds.

A unique characteristic of some finches is their undulating flight patterns. Finches are also some of the finest singers among the songbirds; some even sing in flight, though most sing from their perches. Social birds, they tend to migrate and spend winters in flocks.

While many finches, like sparrows, are plain dusty brown, others are bold and conspicuous (males more so than females). House finches are brown with reddish markings. Most buntings are blue (although some are white), cardinals and crossbills are red, goldfinches range from solid yellow to yellow-marked grays, and grosbeaks come in all colors.

Larks

Only two species of "true" lark are found in North America: the native shore, or horned, lark (*Eremophila alpestris*) and the Eurasian skylark (*Alauda arvensis*) introduced by humans in the late 1800s. (Despite their name, meadowlarks actually belong to the blackbird subfamily.) Larks are small birds, usually about the size of sparrows, which live in open habitat with low, sparse vegetation. They nest and hunt for food on the ground, so they are seldom seen in shrubs or trees. Horned larks winter on the coast but in summer nest high on northern hills (such as in Idaho) and on the tundra. They feed on seeds but in summer take in insects, such as caterpillars, ants, and grasshoppers.

Horned larks are 6 to 7 inches long and have a wingspan of 12½ to 14 inches. They have brownish gray bodies above with paler undersides. Their primary identifiers are two tufts of dark feathers that resemble tiny horns on the head.

Mockingbirds

Eleven species of the mockingbird family (Mimidae), the mimics of the bird world, are found in North America. Members of the family include northern mockingbirds (*Mimus polyglottos*), brown thrashers (*Toxostoma rufum*), and gray catbirds (*Dumetella carolinensis*). These birds range from 8½ to 13 inches long and have 11- to 15-inch wingspans.

The true mockingbird has been known to mimic the calls of 32 other birds within a period of 10 minutes and is the state bird for five southern states. It is found throughout the U.S., especially across southern regions to California. Catbirds are common throughout most of the U.S. except in the Southwest and along the Pacific coast. Some thrashers are found throughout the U.S., while others are limited to the desert Southwest and California. Most members of the mockingbird family feed on insects and fruits, especially pyracantha and holly berries. All build heavy, cup-shaped nests in bushes or on the ground.

Old World Sparrows

Only two species, both introduced to the continent, are found in North America: the house sparrow and the European tree sparrow.

European tree sparrows *(Passer montanus)*, introduced in the U.S. in 1870, are now found mostly in east-central Missouri and west-central Illinois. They are approximately 6 inches long and are smoky gray to brown with a brown red crown and a black patch on white cheek. They feed primarily on seeds and grains and nest in tree cavities, woodpecker holes, and bird boxes.

The house sparrow *(P. domesticus)* is about the same size as the tree sparrow, grayish brown without the red, black, and white markings. Introduced in the mid-1800s, it is now found throughout the U.S. House sparrows feed primarily on insects, including beetles, grasshoppers, moths, and aphids. They also eat seeds and grains from cultivated fields as well as weeds and grasses. They nest in tree hollows, behind shutters, and in eaves and birdhouses.

Shrikes

Shrikes are the only true predatory songbirds. Like raptors, they prey on vertebrate animals. Only two species are found in North America: the northern (great gray) shrike *(Lanius excubitor)* and the loggerhead shrike *(L. ludovicianus)*. The great gray breeds in Canada and winters in the U.S. The loggerhead is found in southern Canada and most of the U.S. About 9 inches long, shrikes have strong, hooked bills; sharp, powerful claws; black face masks; black tails; pale undersides; and large, white wing patches that contrast with their dark wings. They are found in open country on high perches.

Shrikes have certain characteristics in common with birds of prey, especially their beaks and talons and their meat-eating diets. Formerly called "butcher birds," shrikes have the unique trait of impaling their prey, such as locusts, mice, other songbirds, and lizards, on the thorns of shrubs or trees or on barbed-wire fence prongs. They strip pieces off the carcass for ease in eating and actually hang their food (as butchers hang their wares) to store it for times when food is not as abundant. Shrikes' calls are harsh shrieks, although they can mimic more melodic songs to lure unsuspecting birds for capture.

Humans have at times persecuted shrikes for their apparent brutality to other small birds. But shrikes play an important role in helping to balance natural population levels. Without shrikes, some small bird populations can increase to such an extent that they cannot be controlled and can become health hazards.

Starlings

Starlings (Sturnidae family) are not native to North America. Three species, the European starling *(Sturnus vulgaris)*, crested myna, or Chinese starling *(Acridotheres cristatellus)*, and hill myna *(Gracula religiosa)*, were introduced into North America by humans. All are 7½ inches long, "chunky" but active songbirds, and dark colored with a black metallic sheen. They have short, square tails, pointed wings, and strong legs and bills. The European starling is the most widespread starling, now found throughout the entire U.S. It has become a serious competitor with native species for food and nesting sites.

European starlings are noisy, chattering most of the time while they fly or perch. They do not have their own song—they mostly whistle—but are capable of mimicking calls of other birds. They usually prefer open country to densely forested lands. Highly social, starlings migrate and roost in huge flocks that are capable of amazing aerial acrobatics, such as twisting and turning in unison (with no apparent leader), to escape preying hawks.

Starlings feed on insects hunted at ground level but also eat worms, snails, berries and other fruits, seeds and grains, and even garbage. They nest in natural tree cavities, bird boxes, building crevices, and even woodpecker holes.

Swallows

There are eight species of swallows in North America. Some swallows are also known as martins. The most numerous species is the common, or "barn," swallow *(Hirundo rustica)*. Others include the bank swallow, tree swallow, purple martin, and cliff swallow. Members of the swallow family range from 5 to 8¼ inches long, with wingspans of 12 to 16¾ inches.

Swallows are usually seen flying in large flocks. Of all passerines, swallows probably spend the most time in the air during daylight hours. They are adept flyers and catch many insects in midair by holding their small mouths open in flight. The weather affects the level at which insects fly and therefore the flight level at which swallows fly.

Swallows are often mistaken for swifts because of their slender bodies and long, pointed wings, but the two families are not related. Swallows have broad, sometimes forked tails; their plumage is often dark above and paler below with an iridescent gloss. They have short legs used more for clinging than for walking, and they land on the ground only to collect mud from puddles for nest building.

Swallows often nest near houses. Most nest in single pairs, but some species, such as cliff swallows, nest in large colonies. Each bird applies many beakfuls of mud to build a cup-shaped nest attached to a wall; then the nest is lined with grass and feathers.

Swallows have adapted well to living alongside humans, often nesting in tunnels, outhouses, roof spaces, and eaves. The barn swallow gets its name from nesting in outhouses and barns. Farms once provided the birds with a ready source of insects, but since the growth of mechanized agriculture, barn swallows are declining due to lack of nesting sites and the use of pesticides, which limits available insects.

Species such as tree swallows and purple martins often must compete with starlings and sparrows for nesting sites. Many wildlife agencies can supply information about assisting swallow nesting and controlling competition with other birds. Swallows, like most small birds, are vulnerable to predator attack, especially from hawks. For this reason, they often build their nests under rocky outcroppings or in areas protected from raptor attack.

Swallows migrate to the tropics every winter. They are usually the first passerines to begin migration, often gathering in large groups on telephone wires and other perches before departing. Their return migration is seen as the renewal of spring each year.

Tanagers

Five species of tanagers (Thraupidae family) are found in North America, including the blue gray tanager of south Florida, the scarlet tanager of the eastern U.S. and Canada, and the western tanager, found only rarely in Louisiana. Tanagers are the most varied and brilliantly colored of the songbirds. They range in size from 3½ to 12 inches, with 11- to 12-inch wingspans.

Some tanagers have weak or no voices and songs, while others, like the scarlet tanager, are beautiful singers. Some nest in deciduous forests, building shallow, saucer-shaped nests on limbs of trees. The nests are made of twigs, grass, and weeds. Tanagers feed on insects found well above ground and forage for nuts, fruits, and other foods in the trees and bushes.

Thrushes

This group contains a large number of different but well-known species. Nineteen thrush species are found in North America, including bluebirds (*Sialia* spp.) and the American robin (*Turdus migratorius*), hermit thrush, gray-cheeked thrush, and Swainson's thrush. Some of these, such as the hermit thrush, are known as the finest singers of all birds. Others, like bluebirds and robins, have taken significant places in American folklore.

Thrushes primarily eat insects and fruits. Some even are known to get intoxicated on fermented fruit in the fall. Thrushes range from 4½ to 13 inches in length. Their bills are narrow and notched. Plumage varies widely among species, though males and females of each species have similar plumage.

Some thrushes, such as the American robin, build their own mud and twig nests; others, like the eastern bluebird, nest in tree cavities or birdhouses.

Titmice

The species that relate to the titmouse family (Paridae) in North America include chickadees, bushtits, titmice, and the verdin. They are small birds, ranging from 3¾ to 6 inches long, and weigh only about ½ ounce. Their colors range from grays to browns, and they have soft, thick plumage. Some members of the titmouse family migrate south in winter, although some remain in regular territories. For example, the black-capped chickadee is capable of withstanding severe cold winters.

Different species of chickadees (*Parus* spp.) are found throughout North America. Bushtits (*Psaltriparus minimus*), among the smallest American birds, are found only in the western deserts and mountains and along the Pacific coast. Titmice (*Parus inornatus*) are found across the U.S., and verdin (*Auriparus flaviceps*) are found only in the desert Southwest.

Nests of members of the titmouse family range from the hanging gourd or ball-shaped nests of bushtits and the verdin to woodpecker holes, natural tree cavities, dugout knotholes, or bird boxes for chickadees and titmice. All members of the titmouse family feed primarily on insects.

Tyrant Flycatchers

Thirty-five species of the migratory tyrant flycatcher family (Tyrannidae) are found in North America. Tree-dwelling birds, they live mostly in forest habitats and range from the edge of the tree line near the Arctic Circle into South America. They feed primarily on insects captured in flight, hence the name *flycatcher.* If they cannot consume the whole insect at once, they hold it under their feet and bite it off in pieces. Flycatchers vary in length from 2 to 20 inches, excluding the tail. Most are plain olive green, yellow, brown, or gray. They have large heads with flattened, hooked bills. They are long winged and fork tailed and perch in an erect position as they watch for prey.

Some of the North American tyrant flycatchers include the vermilion (bright red) flycatcher in the southwest U.S., the great-crested flycatcher of the eastern U.S., and the scissor-tailed flycatcher, found in the southern states. One of the most common and far-ranging species is the aggressive, 9-inch-long eastern kingbird. Kingbirds are known to attack any other birds, including large crows and hawks, which fly over their territories. They have a dark gray back, black tail with white tip, and white underparts.

Flycatcher nesting locations vary from areas near the ground, such as upturned tree roots, to woodpecker holes and natural tree cavities, to high and far out on tree limbs.

Warblers

Wood warblers (Parulidae family) are the second largest group of songbirds in North America (next to finches), with 56 species. Their colors vary from gray to olive to green; many are brightly patterned in black, white, blue, red, yellow, and orange. Some of the many species are the wood warbler, bay-breasted warbler, Nashville warbler, hooded warbler, black-and-white warbler, blue-winged warbler, and Audubon's (yellow-rumped) warbler. Besides those birds called "warblers," this group also includes the yellow-throats, ground chats, redstarts, ovenbirds, and waterthrushes. The largest warbler is the yellow-breasted chat.

Wood warblers are among the most popular songbirds because of their beautiful songs. They often have bright yellow plumage that is more brilliantly colored on the males than on the females. They are small, active birds with slender, straight-pointed bills. The common yellowthroat is one of the most numerous wood warblers in North America.

Warblers have short, slender, sharp-pointed bills, slender legs, and long toes for perching. They are active, flitting from ground to trees to bushes. Most eat insects, but some add fruits to their diets. Most warblers build nests in trees, vines, or shrubs, although some nest in tree cavities or hanging moss.

Waxwings

The two waxwing species found in North America include the Bohemian waxwing (*Bombycilla garrulus*) and the cedar waxwing (*B. cedrorum*). The long-tailed silky flycatcher and the phainopepla also appear to be related to the waxwing family. Waxwings are found in forests, dry scrubland, and even desert regions. They are plump, 7- to 9½-inch birds with long, triangular wings and slightly rounded tails. Their plumage is usually a dull fawn, gray, or chestnut color with white patches. The tip of the black tail is usually barred in red or yellow. Waxwings have a top crest on their heads, and their wings have drop-shaped, waxy-looking appendages at the tips of their secondary flight feathers—hence the name *waxwing*.

Waxwings eat mainly fruits but also partake of flower petals and insects. They are gregarious and form closely knit, sometimes large flocks when migrating and throughout the winter. They usually nest in trees up to 20 feet above ground. Their nests are made of twigs, moss, and lichens woven together to form a bowl, lined with down and animal hair.

Wrens

Wrens (Troglodytidae family) are among the smallest birds, most species ranging from 3 to 5 inches long. These brownish gray chunky birds are streaked, striped, or spotted with black, brown, white, or gray. They have uptilted, barred tails; slender, slightly down-curved bills; and short, rounded wings. They utter loud, persistent songs and are known for aggressively defending their territories. They are usually solitary except when paired for nesting.

An excellent nest builder, the male wren often builds several nests within its territory. Wrens will nest in almost any cavity but are known for nesting on rocky crevices or stone buildings. Rock wrens get their names from their paving the nest entrance with small stones. Wrens spend much time near the ground and feed mainly on insects.

Species include the brown-throated wren, found only in Arizona; the cactus wren, found from Utah to Mexico and Texas to the Pacific coast;

the Carolina wren, common in the southeastern states; and the house wren and long-billed marsh wren, found throughout the U.S. and Canada. The life span of the wren in the wild ranges from four to seven years, depending on the species.

[OTHER LAND BIRDS]

Hummingbirds

John James Audubon described the hummingbird as "a glittering fragment of the rainbow," a fitting tribute to the tiniest jewel of the bird world. The colors of this bird are extremely varied but are almost always of an iridescent hue. Hummingbirds get their names from the drone of their wings beating up to 78 times per second. Worldwide, hummingbirds (Trochilidae family) are the largest nonpasserine bird family.

Hummingbirds are found only in the Western Hemisphere. Fourteen species live in the U.S., though only eight ever get much farther north than the Mexican border. The four species that nest as far north as Canada are the ruby-throated, rufous, calliope, and black-chinned hummingbirds. Anna's hummingbird is the only species that nests in just one state: California.

Hummingbirds range from 2¾ to 5¼ inches in length, with up to a 5-inch wingspan. They have slender, pointed bills for feeding on flower nectar and the unique ability to hover while feeding. They also eat small insects and spiders for protein. They must eat every 10 to 15 minutes to maintain their metabolism. Hummingbirds are integral to the survival and reproduction of many flowering plants because, by feeding on the nectar, they cross-pollinate plants.

Hummingbirds are found in most habitats except aquatic or marshy habitats or sage and grasslands. Some prefer dense forested areas, while others prefer low vines or bushes. They are capable of flying at great speeds (the ruby-throated has been clocked at 50 to 60 mph), darting backward and sideways and flying straight up and down. Their great speed and maneuverability helps them elude predators like hawks and bats. Most hummingbirds also migrate great distances (the ruby-throated migrates completely across the Gulf of Mexico each year). To prepare for migration, hummingbirds gain an additional half their normal weight before starting south.

Hummingbird nests are tiny, 1½-inch-wide cups, which they fashion

Hummingbirds must feed every 10 to 15 minutes to maintain their extremely fast metabolism, and help pollinate plants in the garden.

from lichens and plant down and fasten to trees or bushes with spider webbing.

Some hummingbirds, like the ruby-throated, have adapted to feeding on garden or shrub flowers in urban and suburban areas. But others, especially the long-billed species, are specialized, depending on a limited range of particular flowers. As their natural habitat is destroyed or altered by humans, their survival is increasingly threatened.

Pigeons

Doves and pigeons are members of the pigeon order (Columbiformes), in which there are 17 reported species in North America. They include the mourning dove, or turtle dove *(Zenaida macroura)*, found in all 48 contiguous states and classified as a game bird in 31 of them; the rock dove, or common domestic pigeon *(Columba livia)*, introduced into the U.S. in the 1600s; and the band-tailed pigeon *(C. fasciata)*, found only in far western states. Another indigenous species, the passenger pigeon, was the most numerous bird (estimated at 3 to 5 billion) in North America in the 1600s but became extinct in the late 1800s due to hunting and deforestation for agriculture.

Doves are usually distinguished by their smaller size and pointed tails; pigeons are larger and tend to have square or rounded tails. Doves and pigeons range from 6 to 15½ inches long. With 17- to 19-inch wingspans, they are strong flyers. They are plump birds with small heads and thick gray, brown, or bluish plumage, usually varied in color with some iridescent feathers. They have many color variations due to inbreeding. Some species migrate annually, but others, especially the rock dove, stay in their home territories. Doves and pigeons are known for their low, cooing voices.

Rock doves (also known as homing pigeons) have become domesticated birds; however, they ordinarily are not kept as pets but are bred for racing, exhibition, laboratory work, and meat. During wartime, doves have served many nations as message carriers. Pigeons have developed bad reputations in cities as disease carriers and general nuisances. While they can pose a public health hazard, their role as disease carriers has been exaggerated. There are 12 dove-borne diseases; however, doves do not play a significant role in communicating infections to humans.

Doves and pigeons feed mainly on seeds, grasses, roots, berries, and grains. Rock doves also eat a few insects and are excellent scavengers. Members of the pigeon family share an unusual characteristic: They submerge their beaks in water to drink (much like a horse), while most birds take a small amount of water in their beaks and tilt their heads back to swallow.

Pigeons build flimsy platform nests of twigs and grasses just about anywhere they can find a flat surface, including building ledges, rafters, beams, cliffs, the ground, and caves. They produce a unique substance called "crop milk," with which they feed their young.

Rock doves are occasionally taken by birds of prey, but their primary enemy is humans. They are heavily hunted in certain areas of the U.S. They have a life span of 5 to 15 years in the wild.

Swifts

Swifts (Apodidae family) are the fastest flyers of all birds in level flight. They seldom land, having legs so small and weak that they sometimes cannot take off again. They do have strong feet, though, which allows them to cling to vertical surfaces such as rock walls and cliffs. Swifts resemble swallows but are classified with hummingbirds rather than as passerines. They are 4 to 7½ inches long with a 12- to 15-inch wingspan and have streamlined pale gray or brown bodies with long pointed wings that curve backward. Their wings beat rapidly in shallow strokes, followed by short glides.

Only four species of swifts are regularly found in North America: the black swift, white-throated swift, chimney swift, and Vaux's swift. Most swifts migrate great distances every year. One 9-year-old banded chimney swift was estimated to have flown 1.35 million miles in its lifetime migrations between North and South America. Because swifts seldom land, they perform all bodily functions, including feeding on insects, bathing, drinking, and mating, in midair.

Swifts build cup-shaped nests of mud and grasses usually located in dark, protected areas such as barns, silos, chimneys, mountain ledges, or tree cavities.

Woodpeckers

The woodpecker family (Picidae) is made up of flickers, sapsuckers, and woodpeckers. There are approximately 23 species in North America, including the ivory-billed woodpecker (the largest North American woodpecker, which may be extinct), the yellow-bellied sapsucker, and the common flicker. Woodpeckers, sapsuckers, and flickers are found throughout most of Canada and the U.S.

True woodpeckers spend most of their lives on tree trunks, head up and tail down, feeding on insects. They are unique among birds because of their strong, straight, chisellike bills and strong neck and skull muscles, with which they pound holes in trees to feed and create nesting sites. They have short legs and strong feet for grasping tree trunks and use their short tails to prop themselves when climbing. Different species vary in coloration, including red, yellow, white, black, and brown. They are 7 to 20 inches long and have a 11- to 17-inch wingspan.

Woodpeckers use their strong, flexible tongues to extract insects and larvae from between bark and tree flesh in live, dead, or dying trees. They usually locate insects with their excellent hearing. Flickers are woodpeckers that feed on the ground by probing their tongues into anthills. Sapsuckers feed on tree sap that oozes from holes they drill in tree limbs; they also eat insects attracted to the sap. Other birds, such as warblers, also feed on the sap thus made accessible.

In addition to their "hammering," a sound used to mark territory, members of the woodpecker family have raspy, harsh calls and sharp cries. Woodpeckers' nests are built in holes they excavate in tree limbs or trunks. They usually tunnel down 6 to 18 inches to create the nesting cavity, which is lined only with a few wood chips at the bottom.

Situations and Solutions: Land Birds

Swallows Nesting on Buildings

WHY IT HAPPENS: Many swallows, including cliff and barn swallows, migrate all the way from their wintering areas in South America to nest in North America, returning to the same area each year. The nests you see under eaves of buildings are built by cliff swallows out of mud plugs. These industrious birds may carry and mold over 1,200 plugs for one nest.

SUGGESTIONS: Besides causing great distress to the birds, removing a completed nest of any species is illegal. If you don't want to allow the nest on your building, the best solution is in prevention. When you see birds attempting to start a nest, knock it down with a long pole or a strong hose spray. If you do this for several days, the birds will move elsewhere, sooner or later finding a site acceptable to both you and them. They can still raise their young, and you can still enjoy watching them and the benefits of their feeding on thousands of mosquitoes, flies, wasps, and other insects.

Feeding Hummingbirds

WHY IT HAPPENS: Hummingbirds are attracted to brightly colored flowers, especially those that are red, orange, blue, and purple. Bell- or tube-shaped flowers, such as fuchsias, are very attractive to them. These birds are favored visitors to gardens and yards, and it is easy to supplement their natural food.

SUGGESTIONS:

1. Put out feeders by early April and take them in late in November, depending on location and climate. Presence of food in feeders will not deter migration and may assist early or late migrators when food supplies are limited.
2. Hummingbird feeders should be of clear glass so you can see when they are empty and detect any harmful substances such as mold. Place them away from windows so the birds cannot inadvertently injure themselves.
3. Most commercially available hummingbird feeders have red coloring on some part of them, so it is not necessary to put red dye in the solution to attract the hummingbirds. *Do not use honey* in the solution; it is

thought to cause a fungal infection on the bird's tongue. *Do not use synthetic sugar substitutes.* To make feeder solution, combine one part cane or beet sugar with four parts water. Bring water to a full boil and add sugar. Once the solution has cooled, add it to the feeder. Refrigerate extra quantities.

4. Thoroughly clean feeders with soap and hot water once a week. Be sure to remove all mold and rinse thoroughly.

5. If you live in a part of the country where hummingbirds remain over winter, be sure to keep feeders thawed out during unexpected freezes. Because hummingbirds must eat often to maintain their metabolism, frozen feeders in otherwise temperate climates can result in significant winter destruction of hummingbird populations.

6. If you install a feeder that hummingbirds come to depend on, it is important not to interrupt the feeding for any reason. Take seriously the responsibility you have assumed in providing them food.

7. Plant tubular red flowers such as impatiens, salvia, trumpet vine, cardinal flower, columbine, mimosa, penstemon, phlox, butterfly bush, hollyhock, petunia, nasturtium, verbena, and red honeysuckle to attract hummingbirds to your yard. Choose plants that are native to your locale.

Injured Hummingbirds

WHY IT HAPPENS: The hummingbird is an inquisitive and territorial species that will fly up to or into a window for a closer look or even attack its own reflection, defending its territory or feeder from intruders.

SUGGESTIONS: If you find an injured hummingbird, take it to a wildlife care agency immediately. Hummingbirds need to eat so often that to survive they need trained round-the-clock care.

Swifts Nesting in Chimney

WHY IT HAPPENS: Chimney swifts sometimes build their nests of twigs and saliva on the interior surface of chimneys. Most chimney roosting occurs during their annual migration. Swifts spend all day flying and roost in chimneys at twilight.

SUGGESTIONS:

1. Swifts are an extremely beneficial species because they ingest large amounts of flying insects. They actually cause few, if any, problems

for homeowners, so try to tolerate them unless you must use the chimney.

2. If you must evict the birds from a chimney, do so only outside breeding season—May through August—when you are sure all the young have left their nests. Wait until all birds are out feeding during the day and then screen the top of the chimney so they cannot get back in.

A simple wire mesh cap can protect a chimney from nesting swifts.

Woodpeckers Damaging Siding on Buildings

WHY IT HAPPENS: Woodpeckers hunt for insects and store acorns in old wood and rotting trees. Sometimes they target houses or other wood-sided buildings, even when the siding is new. Especially in the spring, they may be heard hammering away, not just on wood but also on metal objects like gutters, chimney caps, and television antennas. This drumming activity serves to establish territory and attract or signal potential mates.

SUGGESTIONS:

1. Take action quickly, before woodpeckers establish their territory. You can entice them away from the house by providing ample quantities of suet (hard beef or mutton fat) away from their pecking area. Keep suet in the shade or it will become rancid.

2. A coat or two of clear wood preservative to the affected area effectively discourages woodpeckers because they do not like the taste. If the bird moves to another part of the building, treat that area as well. Repair damaged areas with metal rather than wood.

3. Techniques to frighten woodpeckers away include hanging strips of colored cloth or aluminum foil (several inches wide and 3 feet long) or strung-together tin can lids near the pecking sites.

4. Make sure that any foods attractive to woodpeckers, such as insects or suet at bird feeders, are moved far away from the pecking site. If insects in siding or shingles are a problem, use nontoxic pest control methods whenever possible.

Droppings from Roosting Birds

WHY IT HAPPENS: Birds such as pigeons, starlings, or sparrows often roost in protected areas, such as entryways or trees, where their droppings become an unsightly and potentially unhealthy problem.

SUGGESTIONS:

Woodpeckers will seek insects found in unprotected house siding.

1. Frequently hose droppings away with a strong spray of water.
2. Products that discourage pigeons are available to place on ledges. Some give the birds a burning sensation on their feet but do not harm them.
3. Place flexible mesh netting or rolled chicken wire on the ledge to create an unstable and uncomfortable surface on which to perch. The wire or netting can be fastened under eaves if this is the roost area. To keep birds off window ledges, attach netting to the roof and lower it to drape across the front of the building; then tightly secure it at the base. Or use it under beams, supports, or girders to create a "false ceiling," blocking birds' access to roosting areas. If access through open doorways such as loading docks is a problem, hang netting in loose panels that allow people to pass through but keep the birds out.
4. Block openings to lofts and vents with netting, wire screen, metal, or glass.
5. Pigeons prefer to roost on flat surfaces. Install metal, wood, or stone sheathing at a 60-degree or greater angle, to make it difficult for the birds to obtain secure footing. Or install a product known as "porcupine wire" in parallel rows to create a grid of upreaching barbs on which the birds cannot stand. Despite its appearance, this product

evidently does not harm birds. Some people also have tried placing a board with rows of nails (½ inch apart) pounded upward on the surface where the birds like to roost. *This method is discouraged,* however, because the nails can seriously injure the birds' feet.

6. Use flexible mesh netting to protect trees and garden vegetables from droppings.

7. Exclude pigeons from level roosting areas such as awnings, roofs, and ledges by installing a taut, fencelike barrier (stainless steel wire or monofilament line) stretched with support posts every 6 to 18 inches. Electrify such fencing for greater effectiveness, if necessary.

8. Habitat modification can be effective. For example, thin tree branches where starlings tend to gather. This decreases both wind protection and roosting sites. These birds tend to roost in large groups and will move to another location, if there is not enough space.

9. *Do not feed roosting birds, especially pigeons.* The free handouts birds have become accustomed to in cities, parks, and yards are largely responsible for the abundance of roosting birds, especially pigeons. If feeding is eliminated, chances are good that the birds will move elsewhere.

10. Many forms of repellents are also effective. Noise making, with fire-crackers, wind chimes, or radios, is effective so long as the noise is loud and sudden. Noise repellents must be used frequently to be effective. Visual repellents include balloons, bright, revolving lights, and reflecting surfaces. (Other visual repellents, such as replicas of hawks, owls, and snakes, have had limited success, depending on the type of "predator" used, placement, and type of roosting birds being repelled. Some birds become habituated to the replicas quickly so are no longer deterred by them.) Using audio and visual repellents together is most effective.

11. Ornitrol is the only registered reproductive control agent approved for use with pigeons. When properly used, it can control pigeon reproduction, but it can also cause debilitating illness and death to some birds. It should be used only by government agencies as a last alternative to poisoning.

Birds Dive-bombing People or Pets

WHY IT HAPPENS: Parent birds use this method to keep predators, including humans, away from a nearby nest.

SUGGESTIONS: Although such attacks can seem frightening or intimidating, few birds ever actually strike the target of their attack. Try to stay away from this area until the young are raised (three weeks or so) and ask others to do the same. If you must walk there, wave your arms slowly overhead to keep the birds at a distance. If you are frightened, wear a hat. If the birds have nested near your home, turn a hose on the dive-bombing bird only.

Birds Flying into Windows

WHY IT HAPPENS: Some birds (such as cardinals or robins) fly into windows because they see their reflection and, thinking it is another bird, attack to defend their territory. These thumps on windows usually do not harm the birds but can disturb humans in the house. Birds also may hit windows (usually large picture windows) where they can see large potted houseplants or see through part of the building to a yard beyond. Collisions so caused can be harmful or fatal to the flying bird.

SUGGESTIONS:

1. Draw the drapes or blinds or place a bright light inside the window to cut down on the reflection. If this is insufficient, hang strips of yarn or colored plastic outside the window, place strips of masking tape on the glass, or temporarily cover the outside with screen, paper, or cloth.
2. Purchase a silhouette of a hawk (a bird predator) from a wildlife care agency or nature store and affix it to the window.
3. Place or hang a plastic owl, available at nurseries, outside the window. Move it weekly to maintain its realism.
4. Place wind chimes or plastic bags that create noise outside.

Single Bird in Chimney

WHY IT HAPPENS: The bird is probably trying to find a place to nest.

SUGGESTIONS: With the fire screen closed to keep the bird from entering the room on its own, open the fireplace damper and wait. The bird eventually will come to the bottom; then you can toss a towel or net over it. For future protection, place a special ember screen over the top of the chimney to prevent bird access.

Bird Singing Loudly Day and Night

WHY IT HAPPENS: The lusty singer is probably a mockingbird, which sings most intensely in the spring when courting a mate or defending territory and food sources, and especially its nesting young. Its song warns other birds to stay out of the territory.

SUGGESTIONS:

1. This behavior will last until the young are born and raised, usually a few months. If the bird sings from the same perch repeatedly, try a gentle spray of water to get it to move on. You will need to repeat any scare-away tactic such as this often to be successful.
2. If the bird seems to be defending a food source, such as berry bushes, try plucking all the berries to remove the food. This can be time-consuming with no guarantee of success.
3. If the singing interferes with sleep and all else fails, try using earplugs (available at pharmacies) to block out the sound.

Birds Feeding on Garden Plants

WHY IT HAPPENS: Many birds visit garden areas in search of insects and seeds. They actually harm plants in three ways: by unearthing and eating newly planted seeds, eating buds and flowers (thereby reducing the amount of fruit produced), and feeding on maturing fruits. Some of the most common garden-feeding birds include blackbirds, scrub jays, magpies, finches, larks, sparrows, and starlings.

SUGGESTIONS:

1. To effectively address garden damage problems, first identify the birds causing the damage. These species commonly cause the following types of damage:

   - *Blackbirds:* These species take vegetables (lettuce, peppers, tomatoes, sweet corn) and nuts (almonds, sunflower seeds).
   - *Crow Family:* Crows love maturing sweet corn. Scrub jays eat orchard fruits and nuts. Magpies feed on fruits, nuts, grains, and garbage.
   - *Finches:* Goldfinches debud almond and apricot trees and feed on flower and vegetable seeds, strawberries, and sunflowers. House finches debud and deflower nut and fruit trees. They attack all kinds of seed crops and eat fruits and berries in gardens and orchards.
   - *Horned Larks:* These birds feed primarily during seeding stage on vegetables, including broccoli, carrots, and lettuce. They also like melons and flowers.
   - *Sparrows:* Crowned sparrows debud fruit and nut trees and damage

young seedlings in fall and winter. They eat vegetables and fruit crops, including lettuce, grapes, melons, almonds, and strawberries. House sparrows damage newly seeded lawns and flowers and eat young seedlings, buds, and fruits.

- *Starlings:* Starlings actually pull small seedlings from the ground. They damage fruits, including grapes, cherries, and strawberries.

2. Next, observe bird activity in your garden. If you see fruit-eating birds in your area before fruits have started to ripen, take early action to protect the fruits. Bird damage is often sudden and can wipe out entire crops because birds opportunistically feed when crops are ripe. Sometimes the birds seem to have a sixth sense, feasting the day before you are ready to harvest.

3. Modify the habitat to make it less desirable. Because many birds feed on weed seeds, keep weeds in and near gardens down, and especially do not let them go to seed. Brush piles can become protective cover for many birds, and clotheslines or other perches provide opportunities for the birds to "shop" for their favorite foods. Try to remove as many of these opportunities as possible.

4. The best method for protecting your garden is to exclude the birds altogether. Flexible mesh netting is ideal for covering seedbeds, vines, berries, and small trees. Netting used on trees can be suspended from a trellis to avoid interfering with plant growth or can be placed just before ripening, the most likely time for bird damage. If you hang netting over an entire tree, make sure to secure it at the base (so no birds can get underneath) and to pull it tight to avoid entangling and injuring birds.

5. Some audio and visual repellents can be effective for a limited time. Loud, booming noises, recordings of alarmed birds, and high-pitched sounds help to frighten birds away. Visual repellents such as scarecrows, reflecting surfaces, and owl or snake replicas are rarely effective in gardens subject to migratory bird feeding; their impact decreases as the birds become accustomed to them.

6. Migratory nongame birds are subject to federal protection laws. Any form of toxic control can be undertaken only with a permit issued by the U.S. Fish and Wildlife Service. Exceptions include starlings, house sparrows, and pigeons, which are all nonnative, introduced species. Live-trapping is allowed only for these species, and each requires a specific method. Check with your local wildlife agency for assistance

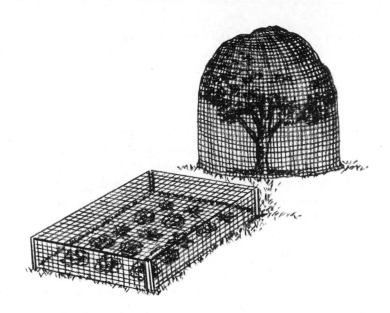

Netting protects gardens and fruit trees from raiding birds and other animals.

in the design and placement of such traps. Note that live-trapping is of limited success with migratory birds because so many usually appear around the same time that it is impossible to trap them all. And once released, the birds are likely to return.

Injured Birds

WHY IT HAPPENS: Birds are injured in a variety of ways, many due to coexistence with humans. They may be found suffering from concussions or broken limbs from hitting windows, from injury from domestic pets, or from internal injuries from pesticides, herbicides, oil spills, or other forms of environmental degradation. The increasing number of birds injured by cats reflects the increasing popularity of house cats. Most injuries require the kind of care that only a wildlife care agency can provide.

SUGGESTIONS:

1. If you find an injured bird, you can provide the most essential immediate needs of warmth, quiet, and protection (a covered box). Use a minimum of handling to avoid as much stress as possible. *Do not feed the bird.* Arrange to take it to a wildlife care agency or call for assistance.
2. If it is a small bird, pick it up with your hands and place it in a well-

ventilated, covered box or paper bag, padded with paper towels. (Do not use unwoven cotton in balls or rolls because it gets tangled in birds' feet.) The box should be small enough to keep the bird from thrashing around in an attempt to fly.

3. Maintaining body heat is essential, as many birds go into shock when injured and their temperature drops. Place the box on a towel-covered heating pad set low, or fill a plastic container with warm water, cap it tightly, wrap it in a cloth, and place it in the box. To avoid overheating or burning the bird, try to maintain the water at 80–85 degrees F. A limp chick with a continuously open beak is too warm.

4. For larger birds (ducks, owls, hawks, crows, egrets, gulls, and so on), throw a large cloth over the entire bird and then gently take hold of the body and head. Be careful of sharp beaks and toenails. Place the bird in a sturdy, vented, padded box. Follow the same procedure for birds contaminated by oil. Place on a heating pad or use a warm water bottle as described in number 3, and get medical assistance for the bird as soon as possible. If you feel insecure about carrying out this procedure yourself, place a box over the animal, weight it down with a rock, and call a wildlife care agency for transport.

5. If you cannot keep your cat inside during the day (especially spring and summer), put a bell on its break-away collar.

Baby Birds Out of the Nest

WHY IT HAPPENS: Infant birds and fledglings (newly feathered birds) often fall out of their nests. Contrary to popular belief, it is quite all right to pick up baby birds and put them back in their nest. Songbirds have no sense of smell, so human scent will not cause parents to reject them.

SUGGESTIONS:

1. When you are sure you have located all of the young, warm each in your cupped hands and return it to the nest. Do this at the site where you found the birds so the parents can keep an eye on the babies and will not fly away.

2. If the nest is destroyed or inaccessible, make a new nest using a plastic berry basket from the grocery store. Add dry leaves and dry grass. *Do not use unwoven cotton,* because it gets caught in the birds' feet. Attach the new nest to a high branch of a tree or shrub as close as possible to where the nest or birds were found. Be sure there are branches above

the nest to shelter the chicks from direct sunlight and to keep the nest out of easy view of predators. Secure it well with wire, strong string, netting, or hosiery.

3. Place the young in the nest. Observe the nest closely to make sure the parents return, and listen for sounds. Chicks are noisy when being fed (feeding may last only a minute or even less) and quiet when parents are absent, protecting them from predator detection. If you are not certain of the parents' return, call your local wildlife care agency for further information. (Hummingbirds are the exception. Normally silent, they make a high-pitched sound only when in stress. You might hear this if the mother has not returned to feed the birds as usual. Hummingbirds must be fed frequently. Call your wildlife care agency for instructions.)

4. Some birds, such as quails, raise their young on the ground in poorly defined nests. If you see quail parents coming to feed, the chicks are probably in their proper home.

Fledgling (Newly Feathered Bird) Out of the Nest

WHY IT HAPPENS: The bird may have fallen out of the nest, or it may be beginning to fly and not stay in the nest.

SUGGESTIONS: If the nest is nearby, try putting the bird back into it. If it will not stay there, put it inside shrubbery near the nest or near where the bird was found. Parents still care for their young at this stage and will return. If you have observed continuously for several hours and no parents have returned, something may have happened to them. Take the baby to your wildlife care agency.

Bird in the House

WHY IT HAPPENS: Doors or windows have been left open, or there are holes in the attic.

SUGGESTIONS:

1. If you can, darken all windows with sheets and then leave one door or window open. The bird will likely fly toward the light and escape unharmed.

2. Gently try to keep the bird flying. As it tires, it will lower and have to land. Have a towel ready to toss over it to help catch it. Do not toss

a bird into the air to release it as it may be hurt or temporarily disoriented. Place it on a ledge safe from predators (like house cats) and observe it until it takes off. If it still does not fly, take it to a wildlife care agency to be checked.

Birds and Pyracantha Berries

WHY IT HAPPENS: Normally, birds have to work fairly hard to find enough food. When pyracantha berries appear, the birds are overwhelmed with abundance and overindulge, not unlike many of us at the Thanksgiving Day dinner table. They simply overload themselves and cannot fly properly until the food is digested.

SUGGESTIONS: If a bird is trying to leave the feeding site and cannot, put it in a ventilated box where it can feel protected while you observe it for a few hours. When it is alert, release it.

Game Birds

Any birds that may be hunted legally under state or federal law can be classified as game birds. Those covered in this section are the land-based varieties pheasants, turkeys, and quails. Others that are hunted in some states, such as mourning doves (Other Land Birds), ducks (Waterfowl), and woodcocks (Aquatic Birds), are listed in the sections noted according to their appropriate classification. Situations and Solutions for game birds are grouped together following the section on Turkeys.

[THE PHEASANT FAMILY]

Species of pheasant, partridge, quail, and turkey are North American members of the pheasant family. The six quail species are indigenous to North America, while the ring-necked pheasant and the two partridge species were introduced from Eurasia.

Partridges

Partridges (Oerdicinae subfamily) are 12 to 13 inches long and have wingspans of 18 to 22 inches. They are gray brown with no bright markings.

Range and Habitat

Two species of partridges were introduced into the U.S. from Eurasia in the late 1800s and early 1900s. Now found in separate populations throughout the northern U.S. and southern Canada, they prefer cool, moderately dry climates, with gently rolling pastures, hayfields, and grainfields. Like pheasants and quails, partridges nest in shallow ground depressions.

Other Characteristics

Like quails, partridges tend to join coveys that seldom range more than one-quarter mile. Unlike pheasants, they prefer open, stubbly grainfields even in severe winter weather. They feed on cultivated grains like barley, wheat, corn, and oats, as well as on seeds of wild weeds and grasses. They also eat insects for protein.

Enemies and Defenses

Like all game birds, partridges' natural enemies are large mammal predators, birds of prey, and reptiles that feed on their eggs. Their main enemy is humans. Each year many are lost to mowing machines in hayfields; by flying into utility poles, wires, and barbed and electrical fences; and by being hit by automobiles.

Quails

New World quails (Odontophorinae subfamily) have mottled blue gray, brown, black, and white feathers. They are smaller than pheasants, measuring 10 to 12 inches long and weighing only about 6 ounces. The females tend to be duller in color.

Range and Habitat

Various species of quail are found in different locations throughout the U.S. and southern Canada. Some of the subspecies include the bobwhite (eastern states), blue quail and desert quail (arid Southwest), mountain quail (Pacific Coast mountains), and California quail (western woodland foothills and valleys). Within the quarter-mile extent of their territory, quails need grass in the spring and summer for nesting, croplands for fall and winter feeding, and brushy woodlands for escape and roosting cover. California quails feed on grasses, insects, and seeds of wild plants.

Other Characteristics

Quails require food in the form of insects, grains, and wild seeds. They also need adequate protective cover and water. They are social birds, forming large coveys of 30 or more birds for roosting, sometimes shoulder to shoulder for warmth during winter.

Enemies and Defenses

Quails' natural predators are coyotes, foxes, raccoons, and raptors. Many are also lost to weather in years of severe winters. Quails' primary enemy is humans, who still hunt them in great numbers. Although they tend to stay immobile even when approached closely by a hunter, hunting dogs are successful in flushing them into the air. When disturbed, quail coveys "explode" into the air, upward and outward, leaving them vulnerable to gunshots.

Ring-necked Pheasants

Ring-necked pheasants (*Phasianus colchicus*) are large birds, weighing up to 5 pounds and reaching up to 36 inches. Males are larger than females. These pheasants have short, rounded wings that allow quick flight but for only short distances. The male ringneck is brightly colored with a greenish blue head and white ring around the neck, rust-colored breast, yellow sides, and a bluish green rump. The hen is drab in comparison, an adaptation that permits her to blend in with her environment to protect her young. Pheasants have long, slender brown tail feathers cross-barred with black markings.

Range and Habitat

The ringed-neck pheasant, a native of Asia and the Orient, was introduced into the U.S. at different times from 1857 to 1945 and has become well established in most of the northern states and southern Canada. Ideal pheasant habitat combines fertile grainfields and croplands with fallow, weedy areas, pastures, small wetlands, and some woody patches with thick underbrush of berry shrubs, thorny hedges, and fencerows. Protective cover is important because of the generally severe winters in the pheasants' home ranges. If caught in open land during blizzards, the birds do not fare well.

Other Characteristics

Ringnecks feed primarily on waste grains (those dropped on the ground during harvest), weed seeds, and insects found at ground level. If food supplies are limited during the winter, they may eat buds, fruits, and berries in shrubs and trees. Pheasants, like most game birds, do not migrate but overwinter in their established territories. Nesting broods break up by late summer to reform with others in small winter groups.

Enemies and Defenses

Pheasants' natural predators are skunks, ground squirrels, crows, and magpies, all of which take unhatched eggs. Foxes, coyotes, raptors, and even cats and dogs prey on pheasant chicks. But the pheasant's main enemy is humans, who hunt them in huge numbers annually. For example, an estimated 800,000 pheasants are killed by 110,000 hunters in Nebraska each year. Pheasants are most bountiful in grain-producing states of the plains and the Midwest, where they are hunted regularly. The ring-necked pheasant is the state bird of South Dakota and a major source of hunting revenue. In some states where they have been introduced, however, natural reproduction cannot keep pace with hunting demands, so states like Connecticut annually restock large pheasant populations. Ringnecks have excellent survival techniques (the main one being running instead of flying) and are often able to elude human hunters. Nesting females can be killed or injured by mowing machines. Many are killed by cars or trains or die when they fly into utility wires.

[GROUSE]

Members of the grouse family (Tetraoninae), five species of grouse, three species of ptarmigans, and two species of prairie chickens, are native to North America. Members of the family vary greatly in size: The smallest is the white-tailed ptarmigan (12 to 13 inches long and ¾ pound); the largest is the 6- to 7-pound, 30-inch-long sage grouse. Grouse are chickenlike birds with fan-shaped tails; short, curved, strong bills; and short, rounded wings. They occur in a range of colors, including gray, reddish, and white.

Range and Habitat

Some of the grouse include the ruffed grouse (in open forests across the U.S.), blue grouse (of the western mountains), sage grouse (in dry sage foothills and warm deserts), white-tailed ptarmigan (above timberline in western states), willow ptarmigan (in the Arctic tundra), and prairie chicken (of the plains grasslands). Generally, grouse are ground nesters.

Other Characteristics

Grouse feed on grasses, sorrels, and other plants in spring; insects and fruits in summer and fall; and acorns, berries, and seeds in winter. Some grouse migrate; others stay close to their home territories. Although they spend a great deal of time on the ground, grouse are strong flyers and, like quails, "explode" from the ground when disturbed. Grouse and ptarmigans roost together in groups.

Enemies and Defenses

Natural predators include egg-stealing skunks, crows, snakes, and ground squirrels. Foxes, raccoons, and raptors take adults and chicks only occasionally. Humans are the chief enemy of all grouse, which are subject to hunting as well as harm caused by habitat destruction. One species of prairie chicken is listed as endangered, mainly due to the plowing under of prairie grasslands.

[WILD TURKEYS]

The only species of turkey found in North America is the wild turkey (*Meleagris gallopavo*). The ancestor of the domestic turkey but generally smaller, this bird is 36 to 48 inches long, has a wingspan of 42 to 48 inches, can stand 3 to 4 feet tall, and weighs 7 to 24 pounds. Males are larger than females. Feathers are drab brown with an iridescent gold, green, and red sheen; females are a lighter, buff color. Wild turkeys have naked heads and necks that are red, blue, purple, or white. They have a fleshy outgrowth called a *leader* that grows from their heads and hangs to the side. Males have large, fan-shaped tails and distinctive, tasseled "beards" dangling from their breasts.

Range and Habitat

Wild turkeys are found throughout the U.S. They live on the ground and roost in trees in wooded areas interspersed with open land. Wild turkeys nest in shallow depressions on the ground near openings in woods, at edges of grainfields, in greenbrier thickets, and under fallen branches.

Other Characteristics

Wild turkeys feed twice a day, at dawn and dusk, foraging on the ground for seeds, acorns, and nuts produced in mature forests. They also eat berries and other fruits, insects, frogs, snakes, and grasses. A large wild turkey is capable of eating up to a pound of food per feeding. Although they spend much time on the ground, wild turkeys are strong flyers that have been clocked at speeds of 32 to 42 mph. They fly to reach trees, where they roost in flocks, and may range over an area of several square miles.

Conservation Note

The wild turkey's main enemy is humans. Native to North America, this bird was once so abundant that Benjamin Franklin proposed it as the national bird, but thereafter it disappeared from large sections of range because of overhunting and destruction of forest habitat. From an estimated population of 10 million birds, as few as 300,000 were left by the early 1950s. Since then the bird has made a comeback through conservation efforts, altered land-use practices, and reintroduction programs, though it is still hunted in many states.

Situations and Solutions

Enhancing Game Bird Habitat and Survival

WHY IT HAPPENS: Some people make efforts to improve game bird habitat to increase populations for hunting, while others just want to encourage the presence of these beautiful birds.

SUGGESTIONS:

1. Adopt agricultural practices that improve winter food, winter cover, and nesting cover to provide the greatest benefits to pheasants.

   * To enhance winter food supplies, plant cereal grains such as buckwheat, oats, millet, or sorghum. Leave a portion of existing crops (such as corn) unharvested near field edges. Plant native fruiting shrubs such as autumn olive, barberry, juniper, winterberry, grape vines, and multiflora rose.

   * To enhance winter cover, leave brushy fencerows, roadsides, windbreaks, travel lanes, or other uncultivated areas. Plant evergreens in small groups.

- To enhance nesting cover, delay mowing until after nesting season. To prevent livestock grazing, establish buffer zones around drainage ditches, farm ponds, and wetland areas that are fenced.
2. To encourage wild turkeys, leave stands of mature, mast-producing trees such as oaks, beeches, ashes, and hickories. Create small 1- to 3-acre openings in the woods that are isolated from homes and roads.

Waterfowl

Waterfowl is a general category of game birds that live mostly in freshwater habitats. All waterfowl are members of the duck family (Anatidae), which includes ducks, geese, and swans, and share characteristic webbed feet and flattened bills. All are migratory birds and are hunted (except for trumpeter and mute swans) subject to regulations of the U.S. Fish and Wildlife Service. They migrate from northern Canada to Central America annually along four documented flyways.

Waterfowl were among the first animals to be domesticated and have had a long and close association with humans. There is probably more written literature available about waterfowl than about any other bird group. The major types of waterfowl are described briefly in this section. Information on Enemies and Defenses, Conservation Notes, How to Observe, and Situations and Solutions is grouped together at the end of the Waterfowl section. For more detailed descriptions, consult the sources listed in Appendix C.

[DUCKS]

Of the five general categories of ducks (dabbling ducks, diving ducks, perching ducks, stiff-tailed ducks, and mergansers), the dabblers and diving ducks are by far the most common.

Fourteen species of dabbling (surface-feeding) ducks occur in North America, including the mallard, teal, pintail, and shoveler. Male dabblers have brightly colored, patterned plumage and large wings. For example, all mallards have blue purple iridescent wing patches; males are identified by their glossy green head and white neck ring, while the smaller females are a more nondescript brown. Both sexes have yellow bills and orange feet. Dabbling ducks range from 11 to 29 inches long and weigh up to 3 pounds.

The most common perching duck is the wood duck *(Aix sponsa)*, 17 to 20 inches long and having a wingspan of 28 to 30 inches. Males are green, purple, bronze, and white with distinctive red eyes. Females are mostly gray with a light brown crest and a white teardrop-shaped eye ring.

Among the diving ducks in North America are the canvasback, scaup, eider, and ring-necked ducks. Although similar in appearance to dabbling ducks, diving ducks are smaller, measuring 13 to 28 inches long; they have smaller, more pointed wings; and their large feet and short legs are set farther back on their bodies.

Range and Habitat

Dabbling ducks are the most common ducks on western flyways. Their habitat includes freshwater marshes, irrigated land, grainfields, ponds, rivers, lakes, and bays. They are often seen on lakes in city parks and sometimes in brackish or saltwater marshes. Diving ducks are found in fresh- and saltwater habitats, depending on the time of year; they as well as dabblers migrate from summer locations in Canada to the southern U.S. and Central and South America each fall. The most important wetlands for adult duck populations are shallowly flooded areas with dense cover, such as forested swamps and marshes surrounded by cattails, bur reeds, and rushes. Wood ducks prefer open woodlands around forested lakes.

Mallards build ground nests near waterways. They dig shallow depressions in the earth and line them with grasses and feathers plucked from their own breasts. Wood ducks nest in tree cavities or nesting boxes high above the ground (from 6 to 50 feet), lined with wood chips and sawdust, and return to the same nesting site year after year. Diving ducks nest near water, usually among reeds and cattails, but some species, like the scaup, actually nest in open land.

Due to conservation efforts, wood ducks have made an extraordinary recovery from near extinction to become the most common duck in North America.

Other Characteristics

All ducks have a unique foot structure that allows blood to flow through the arteries to keep their feet from freezing in cold water. Dabbling ducks are omnivorous, eating grain, corn, mosses, and aquatic plants as the bulk of their diet. They usually feed on or near the water's surface and seldom submerge themselves, finding food with their sensitive bills, which they use as sieves to filter food from the water. Because of their large wing size, dabbling ducks are able to take off directly out of the water instead of needing a "running" start on the surface. All but two species of dabbling ducks are migratory. Mallards usually fly in a V formation with up to 40 to 60 members. They can fly at altitudes up to 9,000 feet at 40 to 55 mph; one mallard has been recorded as covering 322 miles per day. In the wild, duck life span generally ranges from 10 to 15 years.

The special wing configuration of diving ducks makes for fast flight but compels the birds to scoot across the water for a distance before taking off. Diving ducks feed mostly underwater, propelling themselves with their large, powerful feet. Because of their feet placement, they seldom feed in cropfields.

Wood ducks eat wild rice, aquatic plants, and insects.

[GEESE]

Geese are smaller than swans but larger than ducks. Eight species are found within North America, including the Canada goose, snow goose, and white-fronted goose; the Canada goose (*Branta canadensis*) is the most common. These gray brown birds have pale gray breasts; black heads, bills, and necks; and white cheek patches. A narrow band of white separates their black tail feathers. They have strong legs and webbed feet that are placed more forward on their bodies than those of swans or ducks. They range from 21 to 43 inches long (including the tail) and 6 to 13 pounds, with an average wing length of 20 inches.

Range and Habitat

Canada geese migratory ranges, or flyways, stretch from northern Canada south to the southern U.S. Some geese do not migrate, however, but remain in their home locations year-round. Canada geese, like all waterfowl, need wetland areas for nesting and feeding, but they have also adapted well to agricultural lands. They nest in diverse locations, such as muskrat houses, dikes, cliffs, creekbanks, and artificial nesting platforms.

Other Characteristics

Canada geese feed on cultivated grain crops such as buckwheat, oats, millet, corn, alfalfa, sorghum, soybeans, wheat, clover, and rye, as well as on many grasses and aquatic marsh plants.

Flocks of geese, like mallards, travel in long, V-shaped formations. These formations allow each bird to travel in the wind draft of the bird ahead, requiring less expenditure of energy in flight; the birds take turns breaking the wind by leading the V. The distinctive honking cries of Canada geese can be heard for miles.

[SWANS]

Swans range from 47 to 72 inches long, with 6- to 8-foot wingspans. They have short legs, long wings, and very long, curved necks that give them their characteristic grace in the water. Four species are found in North America: the trumpeter swan, mute swan, tundra swan, and extremely rare whooper swan. All are white. Trumpeter swans (*Cygnus buccinator*), the largest, have black bills and the longest necks, producing a deep, resonant, buglelike sound. Tundra swans (*C. columbianus*) also have black bills but are distinguishable by yellow marks in front of their eyes. They make a high-pitched cooing call. Mute swans (*C. olor*) have orange bills that they hold pointed downward. They are usually silent, producing only weak barks and hisses.

Range and Habitat

Like other waterfowl, all swans require wetland habitat. Formerly ranging over most of the north-central and northwestern U.S., and southern to southwestern Canada and Alaska, trumpeter swans are now found only in limited numbers in nesting colonies in southwestern Montana (Red Rocks Lake), in Yellowstone National Park, and along the South Dakota–Nebraska border (LaCreek National Wildlife Refuge) in the U.S. and in west-central Alberta (Grande Prairie) and southern Alberta and Saskatchewan in Canada. Tundra swans, the most abundant North American swans, breed in remote Arctic regions. Mute swans were introduced into the U.S.; their limited populations are concentrated on the northeast coast, in Michigan, and in Washington's Puget Sound.

Swans build their nests, using marsh grasses and reeds lined with down, in shallow pools, on muskrat or beaver lodges, along shorelines, or on islands.

Other Characteristics

Adult swans feed exclusively on aquatic grasses and other plants found in their marshland habitat. For the first month, their young require protein-rich diets for quick development, so they feed primarily on insects and crustaceans found in the same marshlands.

Because their legs are short compared to the length of their wings, swans must build up speed across the surface of the water before they can take off. They are territorial, often driving other nesting swan pairs away but sharing space with other waterfowl species. Territories range in size from ½ mile of shoreline to entire lakes and ponds.

Enemies and Defenses

Waterfowls' main enemy is humans. Mallards are the most sought after game duck in America. Each year they make up a third of the total of North American ducks killed by hunters. Dogs, foxes, snakes, snapping turtles, and birds of prey also hunt waterfowl eggs and young. Waterfowl are safest on water where they can readily escape by diving and swimming underwater.

Conservation Notes

The largest threat to waterfowl by far is the loss of critical wetland habitat, without which they cannot survive to make their yearly migrations. The Canada goose is a prime example of the impact on waterfowl from loss of wetlands. In 1946, as few as 53,000 Canada geese were in the area called the Mississippi Flyway. Due to conservation efforts, by 1977 that population had rebounded to 920,000.

Besides suffering from the drastic loss of wetlands, both trumpeter swans and tundra swans were almost shot into extinction in the nineteenth century for feathers, food, and skins. Again through conservation practices, by 1979 trumpeter swan populations had increased to approximately 4,000 birds in Alaska, 750 in the contiguous 48 states, and only 150 in western Canada.

The feral mute swan population exceeds 4,000 birds and continues to grow quickly. The success of this belligerent outsider is cause for some concern because it tends to drive native waterfowl from nesting and feeding areas. Development of remote Arctic lands, however, and continued wetland drainage, stream channelization, pollution, and development in migratory corridors still threaten the future for all waterfowl.

Trumpeter swans can be very aggressive when defending nest and chick.

How to Observe

Migrating ducks and geese are most commonly observable during spring and fall months when en route to the target end of their migratory journey. Often large flocks of ducks and geese can be observed in wetland areas. Because of their limited populations and locations, swans are more difficult to observe in the wild. Check with your local wildlife agency for the best waterfowl observation sites.

Situations and Solutions

Waterfowl Nuisance and Damage

WHY IT HAPPENS: The Canada goose has made such a strong comeback that in some locations, such as Connecticut, nuisance and damage problems caused by the geese have increased dramatically. Ironically, mostly resident geese are responsible—geese that were released into certain areas in the 1930s when it became illegal to hunt with live decoys. Other resident geese have been released by private individuals or groups to help the resurgence of the species.

Geese can damage golf courses, lawns, ponds, and swimming pools by dropping molted feathers and fouling waters with their droppings. Waters overfertilized with geese droppings can suffer algae bloom (loss of oxygen in water that can eventually kill a lake or pond). The presence of resident geese often attracts migrating geese, greatly swelling the local ranks at certain times of the year. By feeding in large numbers, geese can damage winter cover crops, pastures, and cranberry bogs. Noisy honking can also irritate human residents.

Even though still of limited populations, mute swans are belligerent and can become a nuisance if they become dependent on a human-provided food supply.

SUGGESTIONS:

1. *Do not feed waterfowl.* Feeding can result in overpopulation and dependency on human-supplied food. Also, nutritionally deficient food such as bread can weaken the animals, making them more susceptible to diseases, which are then spread among the visiting wild populations. Some species (mute swans, for one) can become belligerent if food sources are cut off.

2. Use plastic netting or wire mesh over garden beds and other small-enough areas to exclude some waterfowl. Another effective method is to plant trees or tall shrubs in the line of flight between a pond and adjacent property.

3. Some repellent techniques have proven effective in controlling nuisance problems. As with most repellents, they are usually most successful when used in combination. Consider trying the following:

   * Place scarecrows every 10 to 15 acres to control damage to crops, lawns, and gardens. Some part of the scarecrow must blow in the wind, and scarecrows must be moved every two to three days to be effective.

   * Install plastic flag systems, an effective repellent if in place before waterfowl establish feeding and roosting patterns. Staple a 2-by-3-foot black plastic flag with a V-shaped slot to a 4-foot wood stake. Place the flags at a density of one to five per acre.

   * Use free-ranging dogs trained to chase landing birds. These can be effective but must be controlled to ensure that they do not form packs and hunt domestic fowl or livestock.

   * Suspend helium-filled balloons (2 feet in diameter) 50 to 75 feet off the ground with 50-pound (or stronger) test monofilament line. These are effective because waterfowl are leery of moving objects over their heads. "Eyespot" balloons (marked with a bull's-eye pattern) have been successful in frightening geese away from shorelines. Be sure such balloons are well secured so that they do not escape into the atmosphere. Lost balloons, whether rubber or metallic, can pollute lands and waterways and injure wildlife that may mistake them for food.

   * You can try using strobe lights (aircraft or other emergency lights),

but these have had only limited success. If used, the flash should occur at one- to two-minute intervals. Like scarecrows, the lights should be moved every two to three days so the birds do not become accustomed to them.

- Use radio-controlled model boats (somewhat successful) to harass waterfowl until they leave a pond or lake.
- In areas where human hearing will not be affected, use automatic exploders (propane, gas, or acetylene powered) to make noises louder than shotgun blasts. These devices allow the operator to adjust blast timing, intensity, and length. Again, like most repellents, they should be moved every two to three days.
- Fire special bird-control shotgun shells (cracker shells) to scare off waterfowl as you move from field to field. Always handle firearms with extreme caution to avoid injury to humans or wildlife.

4. Live-trapping (by wildlife agency personnel) during flightless molting periods has been used with limited success and is a short-term solution at best. Although some geese may be relocated, many more will just take their place.

Ducks Landing in Pools

WHY IT HAPPENS: Ducks are used to landing in water and have no understanding of private property—except their own when they are nesting.

SUGGESTIONS: Keep a pool covered to prevent duck access as much as possible. Once the birds are there, shouting and waving arms will usually frighten them off. If that does not work, squirt them gently with a garden hose.

Aquatic Birds

Aquatic birds are a general unrelated group of water birds that either are indigenous to salt water or are fresh- and saltwater shoreline wading birds. The aquatic bird groups treated here include cormorants, cranes, grebes, gulls and terns, the heron family, loons, pelicans, and woodcocks. There are many other groups of aquatic birds, such as auks, avocets, gannets, murres, plovers, sandpipers, and storks. For information about species not described here, consult sources listed in Appendix C. Information on

Situations and Solutions is grouped at the end of the section.

Aquatic birds feed on aquatic life, chiefly fish. The pelican hunts only fish, spotting them from upward of 100 feet in the air, then diving and scooping them up in its gaping pouch. Standing in water on their stiltlike legs, herons and egrets watch and wait for their prey to swim by and then, with lightning swiftness, spear it with their sharp bills. Shorebirds such as the killdeer, avocet, and sandpiper spend much of their time poking through coastal sand in search of tiny crustaceans.

While some species lay their eggs without benefit of a nest (for example, murres nest on cliff ledges), aquatic birds are among the world's most skillful nest builders. Egrets and herons create 5-foot-wide, heavy nests out of twigs. They and other large aquatic birds produce young that do not leave the nest for 8 to 12 weeks, keeping both parents busy in a constant search for food. Young birds cannot take large pieces of food, so the parent often swallows and predigests the food and then regurgitates it into the baby's ever-gaping mouth.

[CORMORANTS]

Six species of cormorants are found in North America, the most common of which are the double-crested and Brandt's cormorants. Cormorants range in size from that of a duck to that of a large goose. They are long legged and long necked with stout bodies; short, rounded wings; and long, stiff tails. They have fully webbed feet and long, thin bills sharply hooked at the tip.

The double-crested cormorant (*Phalacrocorax auritas*) is 29 to 36 inches long and has a 54-inch wingspan. It has an orange throat pouch, a year-round identification feature. Birds under one year old are brown above and paler on the underside. Adults are dark overall with a greenish gloss. As their name indicates, they have a double head crest of feathers worn during their short breeding season.

Brandt's cormorant (*P. penicillatus*) is 35 inches long and has a 49-inch wingspan. It is black and in breeding season has a blue throat patch but no head crest. The great cormorant (*P. carbo*), the largest species found in North America, is 32 to 40 inches long with a wingspan of more than 5 feet. It is uniformly blackish with a distinctive white patch at the base of the bill.

Range and Habitat

Double-crested and Brandt's cormorants range along the Pacific coast from Alaska to Baja California, Mexico. They live on rocky coasts, bays, and sloughs and can also be found in lake, river, and swamp areas. Double-crested cormorants also inhabit the Atlantic coast from Newfoundland to Florida. The great cormorant is found only along the North Atlantic coast from Canada into New England. Cormorants nest in large colonies on rocky isles, ledges of cliffs, or trees.

Other Characteristics

The cormorant's diet consists mainly of fish and aquatic invertebrates. It eats mostly fish that are not of interest to commercial fishers, such as saltwater eel, rock cod, smelt, surf fish, and sculpins, and freshwater bull-heads, crappies, sunfish, and carp. Cormorants are excellent divers with eyes adapted for underwater as well as aerial vision. They dive from the surface to find food and sometimes swim at great depths (70 to 100 feet). They usually stay submerged for less than 30 seconds but have been known to dive up to 70 seconds. When fishing, they spread their wings slightly and use their webbed feet for propulsion, returning to the surface to swallow their catch.

After fishing, cormorants go to land to dry their feathers, which are not as waterproof as those of ducks; these birds are often seen with wings spread. Although scientists once thought that the wing-spreading behavior was solely to dry feathers, they now believe that this position may regulate body temperature, maintain balance, and initiate parasite movement, making removal easier. Cormorants are not vocal birds.

Enemies and Defenses

Cormorants' primary enemies are human pollution, especially oil spills, and fishing nets. They have few natural predators other than some large fish that may take them while they are submerged in search of food.

How to Observe

Cormorants can be observed in their nesting grounds and migrating in large groups (from 200 up to 10,000) following coastlines, river valleys, and other waterways.

[CRANES]

The crane family (Gruidae) is one of the oldest known bird families still existing; fossils of these species have been dated back as far as 40 to 60 million years. Two species, the sandhill and the whooping cranes, are native to North America. The common, or gray, crane of Scandinavia is an occasional vistor. Sandhill crane subspecies and their estimated populations include the greater (22,000 to 30,000), the lesser and Canadian (290,000), the Mississippi (30 to 45 and endangered), and the Florida (4,000 to 6,000) sandhill cranes. Only 155 endangered whooping cranes remain in the wild.

Cranes are long necked and long legged and have four sharp-clawed toes on each foot with a hind toe greatly elevated above the others. Their bills are long and straight. Sandhill cranes *(Grus canadensis)* are slate gray to brownish gray with gray black legs and beak. Their feathers are often rust colored from minerals in their breeding range waters. They have ostrichlike ruffs of feathers over their rumps and dark red bald patches on their heads. Greater sandhills are lighter gray, stand 4 feet tall and have a 7-foot wingspan, and weigh up to 14 pounds. Lesser sandhills tend to be darker gray, stand 3 feet tall and have a 5- to 6-foot wingspan, and weigh 8 to 10 pounds. Sandhill cranes are often mistaken for whooping cranes or great blue herons but can be distinguished from the former by color and from the latter by their black head tuft and neck shape (herons have crooked S-shaped necks).

Adult whooping cranes *(G. americana)* are white with black wing tips, while yearlings are rusty red and white with black wing tips. Adults have red foreheads and pates and are larger than sandhill cranes, standing 5 feet tall with a wingspan of 7½ feet.

Range and Habitat

The lesser sandhill crane nests in the Alaskan and Canadian Arctic but migrates through the center of the U.S. to its winter range in Oklahoma, Texas, New Mexico, and Mexico. Greater sandhills both nest and summer in the contiguous 48 states. Several different greater sandhill populations are found in restricted ranges, such as the Rocky Mountain (Idaho and Montana to New Mexico) and the eastern (Manitoba and Ontario to Texas and Florida) populations. The Mississippi and Florida subspecies are nonmigratory.

Once found in large summer ranges from Illinois to Canada and winter ranges from the Carolinas to Mexico, whooping cranes are now isolated in tiny populations in central and western North America. The main flock ranges from Wood Buffalo National Park in northern Canada to Arkansas National Wildlife Refuge in Texas.

Crane habitat is marshes and wetland meadows. Sandhill cranes get their name from their preference for roosting on slightly submerged sandbars in the middle of rivers, which offer them good protection from predators. Whooping cranes favor nesting among cattails, bulrushes, and sedges for similar reasons. Cranes build their 4- to 5-foot nests of marsh plants, grasses, and weeds pulled up by their roots, mounding them until they are above the waterline.

Other Characteristics

Sandhill cranes feed by using their beaks to dig out roots and, as clippers, to cut up tender green browse. They also feed on insects, seeds, berries, and spiders, as well as on mice, small birds, and crayfish. In summer and early fall they particularly like grasshoppers, but during winter they shift to grains and roots, as well as other insects. They pulverize larger prey by beating it on the ground until it is reduced to bite-sized pieces, which they then toss into the air, catch, and swallow. Whooping cranes eat crabs, crayfish, frogs, and other aquatic animals, but seldom fish.

Cranes are known for their spectacular dances involving awkward bows, stiff-legged hops, strutting and wing flapping, and slow-motion leaps into the air. They perform most of these rituals in springtime courtship but can display them at any time for various reasons, such as the arrival of new cranes, a change in the weather, or any disturbance requiring defense of their territory.

During migration, sandhill cranes fly in V or diagonal-line formations as high as 8,000 to 12,000 feet and from 25 to 35 mph. They like to soar in flocks of 10 to 1,000 on thermal air currents, often spiraling until they are out of sight from the ground.

Greater sandhills begin their northward migration in February, arriving at their nesting sites in April. Lesser sandhills start north in late March and arrive in May. The lesser sandhills "stage"—that is, gather to rest along their northern migration—for up to six weeks on the Platte River in central Nebraska, while greater sandhills stage at different locations, depending upon the population. The southerly winter migration starts in August for lesser sandhills and in October for greater sandhills.

Enemies and Defenses

The primary enemy of cranes is loss of wetland habitat to agriculture and other development. Many cranes are lost each year from flying into power lines or other obstacles, and to avian diseases. The whooping crane, although still endangered, had recovered from a population of only 20 birds in 1941 to 155 birds in 1989. A captive-breeding program, combined with techniques such as placing whooping crane eggs in sandhill crane nests, is responsible for the success achieved so far.

How to Observe

Check with local wildlife agencies to determine the best crane-viewing times and locations. Anyone who observes a rare whooping crane during the April–May and September–November migration periods should notify a local wildlife agency or the U.S. Fish and Wildlife Service.

[GREBES]

Six members of the grebe family (Podicipedidae) are found in North America. They are small aquatic birds that resemble ducks but have pointed (not flat) bills with toothlike edges and lobed toes with partial webbing that make them one of the most perfectly adapted of all water birds. Grebes have soft, thick, dark plumage with scarlet, green, white, and other brilliant markings around the head and eyes; their breast feathers were once used to decorate women's hats. They have small tails with no stiff feathers and, when flying, keep a small dip in their necks.

Range and Habitat

Grebes are found throughout North America, with certain species located in specific areas. For example, the eared grebe lives in the southwestern and western U.S.; the horned grebe is found mostly in the Pacific Northwest; the least grebe (smallest species) is found in southern Texas and as an occasional visitor in Arizona and California; the pied-bill grebe (the most widespread species) nests across Canada and ranges south through the entire U.S.; the red-necked grebe is found in Alaska, Canada, and the northern U.S.; and the western grebe is in the western U.S. as far east as Minnesota. Some prefer inland ponds and freshwater waterways, while others prefer saltwater habitat. Grebes that nest in the far north migrate southward by flying overland; those that nest farther south fly from inland lakes and ponds to winter on salt water. Nesting sites range from marshy shallows to open waterways, depending on the species.

Other Characteristics

Grebes are strong swimmers and divers, although they do not usually dive as deep as loons. They dive and swim rapidly below the water surface in search of aquatic insects and small fish. They usually do not stay underwater for long but, depending on the species, can stay submerged from 30 seconds to 3 minutes. Besides feeding, grebes court and sleep on the water. They require a running start to take off, are relatively weak flyers, and move clumsily on land.

Enemies and Defenses

Grebes have few natural enemies except the usual mammals and reptiles that might take their eggs and young. Their primary enemies are human-caused factors such as loss of habitat and pollution.

How to Observe

Grebes are best observed in marsh and wetland areas where they nest and feed.

[GULLS AND TERNS]

There are 25 gull species and 18 tern species found in North America; all belong to the family Laridae and are similar in appearance. Gulls are long-winged birds with slightly hooked bills, typically white. Some have gray backs, some black wing tips, some dark heads or crests. There is no size or coloration distinction between males and females. Young gulls are usually all brown and do not reach adult plumage for an average of three to five years.

The related terns are often mistaken for gulls. Their coloration is similar, but terns tend to be smaller and more slender and graceful. They have sharply pointed bills that are not hooked at the tip like those of gulls; long, pointed wings; and sharply forked tails. During flight, the swallow-shaped terns carry their heads and bills pointed downward; gulls carry theirs pointed forward. Terns have webbed feet but seldom swim.

Range and Habitat

Gulls are found mostly along coastal saltwater bays and inland freshwater lakes, rivers, and marshes. Their typical habitat is harbor, beach, and garbage dump. Terns also are found along seacoasts and interior waterways but, because of their more selective diet, seldom around garbage dumps.

Gulls nest on sea cliffs, sandy islands, marshes, and prairies in small groups or large colonies, usually building a poor nest on the ground. Terns are also colonial nesters but always nest separately from other species.

Other Characteristics

Gulls are omnivorous scavengers and consume almost anything, including insects, worms, fish, and garbage. They pick up food from the surface of water and from land, seldom diving or reaching underwater for food as terns do. Gulls benefit people and the environment by cleaning up dead fish and other waste products. They have the unique habit of dropping edible mussels and clams from great heights to break them open. Gulls' heavy and slightly hooked bills help them tear up dead fish; they are also known to eat eggs of other seabirds and to steal food from other birds. They can drink either fresh or salt water and eliminate excess salt through two special glands on the top of their skull. Gregarious, noisy birds, they live an average of eight years in the wild.

Like most seabirds, gulls have long and slender wings, naturally adapted for long periods of soaring on ocean air currents, alongside and behind ships, and over cliffs. Terns tend to use their strong wings to fly more than to soar.

Enemies and Defenses

The main enemy of gulls and terns is human pollution, especially oil spills and toxic substances in garbage dumps. Gulls have few natural predators, but foxes, raccoons, weasels, rats, gulls, and other seabirds prey

Gulls help keep coastlines clear of natural debris because they are scavengers. The same behavior also subjects them to injury and death from toxic litter.

on terns. Some tern species were nearly annihilated in the late 1800s by plume hunters but have made a good recovery since such plumes went out of fashion. Like all birds, the primary defense is flight.

How to Observe

Gulls and terns are most often found along ocean beaches, inland waterways, and even coastal garbage dumps.

[THE HERON FAMILY]

Long-legged wading birds, members of the heron family (Ardeidae) include herons, bitterns, and egrets. Some of the more commonly known species are the great blue, green-backed, and night herons, the great and snowy egrets, and bitterns.

Herons have long necks that are permanently S curved, even in flight; broad, rounded wings; a short tail; and a long bill adapted for either grasping or impaling prey. The best-known heron is the great blue, which reaches 4 feet in height and has a 6-foot wingspan. The green-backed heron is much smaller (15 to 22 inches tall) and chunkier. The night heron, also shorter than the great blue (23 to 26 inches), has a squat appearance, red eyes, black-and-white body, and yellow legs. Adult night herons have a black plume extending backward from the top of the head.

Bitterns (also known as "thunder pumpers" or "stake drivers" because of their unusual pumping-sound calls) are 17 to 23 inches tall. Their striped coloring camouflages them in marsh reeds and grasses.

Great egrets stand 37 to 41 inches tall and have a wingspan up to 55 inches; snowy egrets are smaller (22 to 26 inches long with a 38- to 45-inch wingspan). Both are white feathered with black legs and yellow feet. Great egrets have yellow bills, while snowy egret beaks are black. Egrets are known for their soft, lace-feathered head plumes.

Range and Habitat

Members of the heron family are at home in both salt and fresh water. They are found throughout North America, except in the northernmost areas. Another member of the heron family, the cattle egret, is native to Africa but recently spread to South America and then into Florida in the 1950s. Since then, it has extended its range north and westward as far as Oregon. Herons nest in colonies or alone, in a wide variety of locations, depending on the species.

Other Characteristics

The great blue heron's diet includes fish, frogs, snakes, and mice and other mammals; though it eats mainly aquatic animals, it is also known to feed in farm fields and meadows. The green-backed heron prefers secluded areas in which to stalk its aquatic prey (fish and frogs) in shallow marsh waters. Night herons, as their name implies, are most active during evening and night hours. Egrets also feed in shallow marsh waters, shuffling their feet to stir up minnows and frogs and darting quickly to capture prey. Cattle egrets feed in open fields near cattle and horses, where they eat insects at ground level as well as from the backs of the livestock.

The great egret may have a wingspread of 55 inches. Efforts to save it formed the basis of the nationwide migratory bird refuge system.

Enemies and Defenses/Conservation Note

The heron family's primary enemy is humans. Many of the larger wading birds, especially great blue herons and egrets, were nearly hunted to extinction at the end of the last century because of the fashion for using their plumes on women's hats. Within only a short decade, egrets had disappeared from all but a few nesting islands in North America. State and federal laws passed in the early 1900s created refuges for their preservation, which formed the foundation for the present nationwide migratory bird refuge system. Since that time, heron and egret numbers have rebounded so that they are no longer endangered.

How to Observe

Herons, egrets, and bitterns can be found almost anywhere there is sufficient surface water to provide a food source. Hikers often follow small creeks in deep, secluded ravines to locate and observe members of the heron family.

[LOONS]

Four species of loons (Gaviidae family) are found in North America: the common, Arctic, yellow-billed, and red-throated species. Loons are large birds, ranging from 23 to 36½ inches long and having 43- to 58-inch wingspans. They have thick necks, sharply pointed bills, well-developed but short tails, and small, pointed wings. Their three front toes are webbed. Coloration tends to be dark, with markings such as stripes and throat markings particular to each species.

Range and Habitat

Loons are migratory birds that nest in northern lakes during summer and overwinter along coastal waters. Arctic loons are found in Arctic tundra in the summer and along the Pacific coast in the winter. The common loon is found from Canada and Alaska along both the Atlantic and Pacific coasts and inland along the northern tier of states such as Maine, New Hampshire, and Michigan. The yellow-billed loon is found mostly in Alaska and western Canada and winters along the California coast. The red-throated loon is found mostly in Alaska and down the Pacific coast. Loons are solitary nesters.

Other Characteristics

Loons are strong divers, able to submerge in search of food for up to one minute. In fresh water, they feed mainly on suckers, minnows, sunfish, and other small freshwater fish; in salt water, they eat cod, gunnels, sculpins, and other ocean fish. They swim using their strong webbed feet to propel themselves. Because their legs are set so far back on their bodies, they have difficulty walking and cannot take off on land. They also require a great deal of open water to take off. Loons can be caught in quickly frozen lakes because of insufficient open water for takeoff. Once in the air, however, loons are strong flyers, reaching up to 60 mph. They fly with neck thrust forward and down, making them appear humpbacked.

Enemies and Defenses

Loons' primary enemies are pollution, especially from acid rain, and other human-caused harm.

How to Observe

To see loons, quietly approach marsh, wetland, and lagoon nesting and feeding areas. Check with your local wildlife agencies for locations.

[PELICANS]

Only two species of pelicans are native to North America: the endangered brown pelican *(Pelecanus occidentalis)* and the white pelican *(P. erythrorynchos)*. Both are large water birds with long, flat bills and large throat pouches. Brown pelicans are dark in color with much white around their heads and necks. White pelicans are among the largest living birds, measuring from 4 to 6 feet long, with 6½ to 9-foot wingspans and weighing 10 to 17 pounds. Pelicans often perch on posts, rocks, and boats.

Range and Habitat

Brown pelicans range from the central California coast south to Mexico and South America on the west coast and are also found along southeastern U.S. coastal waters. Their typical habitat is rocky shoreline, swamp, or harbor. The largest concentration of brown pelicans is found along the Sea of Cortés in Baja California, Mexico. White pelicans are found mainly on inland lakes from central Canada throughout the central U.S., south to Texas and east to Florida. Pelicans are colonial ground nesters.

Other Characteristics

Both species of pelicans eat mainly fish and crustaceans, although their feeding habits are very different. When a brown pelican spots prey over salt water, it plunges from as high as 100 feet into the water. Except when feeding, it flies low, almost touching the water with its wing tips. White pelicans, after spotting a fish, actually land on the freshwater surface feetfirst, then plunge only their heads under to capture the fish. White pelicans often fish cooperatively by gliding in a semicircle and then, with much wing flapping and splashing, driving fish ahead of them into shallow water for capture. When fishing, the pelican scoops water into its large pouch along with the fish and then strains the water out the corners of its mouth so it can swallow the fish. Fish are not carried in the pouch but may be carried in the gullet or esophogus. Because of their size, pelicans must consume large quantities of food every day—up to 4 pounds of fish per adult. Their preferred diet—mullet, menhaden, carp, and catfish— does not conflict with the needs of commercial or sport fishers.

Brown pelicans are still endangered and are protected by federal and state laws.

Pelicans are generally not vocal birds but are gregarious and live in large flocks. They are strong swimmers, using their fully webbed feet for propulsion, but awkward waddlers on land. Pelicans are often seen in a wings-spread posture thought to aid in drying feathers and regulating body temperature. The brown pelican is on federal and state endangered species lists, mandating serious penalties for killing, harming, or harassing them.

Enemies and Defenses

Brown pelicans' primary enemies are pollution and pesticides. The pelican population has been greatly reduced by the indirect ingestion of DDT and other pesticides used for agricultural pest control. Now banned, DDT causes the thinning of eggshells, which then break before the young are ready to be hatched.

How to Observe

Pelicans are found only along ocean coastlines.

[WOODCOCKS]

Woodcocks, members of the sandpiper family (Scolopacidae), also known as timberdoodles, wood snipes, and bogsuckers, are short, stocky birds with a long bill (hinged at the very tip) and large eyes set far back in the head to enhance peripheral vision. Only one species, the American woodcock *(Philohela minor)*, inhabits North America. The female is bigger and has a longer bill than the male. Their mixed colors of brown, buff, gray, and black resemble a "dead leaf" pattern in their feathers, while the head is usually gray with dark bars across the crown. Their wings are wide but short and rounded to ease flight in dense cover. They weigh 5 to 8 ounces, are 10 to 12 inches long, and have an 18-inch wingspan.

Range and Habitat

Woodcocks range in summer from eastern Canada and the U.S. to the south and southeastern U.S. in winter. Although classified in the sandpiper family, they are migratory shorebirds that prefer wooded areas along wetlands. They need moderate shrubs and seedlings interspersed with weedy or grassy openings, all on moist soils. Woodcocks are most commonly found feeding in young, fertile, moist-soiled second-growth hardwood forests, but they also need open areas such as old fields, forest clearings, and bogs for courtship and roosting; open hardwood forests for nesting and raising their young; and dense hardwood forests for feeding and resting. Woodcocks nest between March and June by creating cuplike depressions on the ground, usually surrounded by 12-foot-high trees.

Other Characteristics

Woodcocks feed mostly at dawn and dusk. They prefer earthworms, insect larvae, slugs, snails, insects, and some seeds such as blackberry, raspberry, dogwood, smartweed, alder, and sedge. They find their food chiefly through poking their long bills into moist soils. The hinged tip of the bill is particularly sensitive to movement and can open even underground to capture prey.

Enemies and Defenses

The primary enemy faced by woodcocks is loss of habitat due to urbanization, maturation of forestlands, and drainage of wetlands, along with hunting in some states. In the northeastern U.S., some farms that are reverting to forests contain the diverse habitat needed to support woodcock populations, but generally their preferred habitat is declining.

How to Observe

Woodcocks tend to be secretive and do not flush easily from their ground habitat. Determine the best locations for viewing by contacting your local wildlife agency.

Situations and Solutions: Aquatic Birds

Injured Aquatic Bird Found in the Wild

WHY IT HAPPENS: An aquatic bird may be injured from flying into a power line, contacting foreign objects (especially plastics and other pollution), or coming into contact with predators.

SUGGESTIONS: Consult your local wildlife agency immediately. Be wary of approaching an injured aquatic bird too closely. Because of their size, the larger species, such as cranes and loons, can be dangerous when injured. If necessary, attempt to cover the bird with a blanket to calm it and wait for trained wildlife care assistance. With smaller birds, cover with a blanket or cloth, keep warm, and transport in a covered box to the nearest wildlife rehabilitation location, if trained wildlife assistance cannot come to the site.

Seaside Scavenging by Gulls

WHY IT HAPPENS: Gulls eat garbage or pet food at seaside homes, grabbing bites of meals served outdoors on decks or raiding beach picnics.

SUGGESTIONS:

1. Keep garbage picked up. Be prepared to pack out whatever you pack in to the beach.
2. If gulls become assertive in efforts to steal food, scare them away with loud noises, arm waving, and other antics.

Herptiles

The term *herptiles* is used to refer to reptiles and amphibians. One reason these species have survived so long in harsh environments may be that they are cold-blooded—they absorb heat from their surroundings instead of manufacturing body heat by burning energy taken in the form of food.

The key difference between reptiles and amphibians is that amphibian skin loses body moisture through evaporation, which requires these species to live in or near water (or wet vegetation) and to lay their eggs in water or wet spots. Reptiles, however, have waterproof skin composed of tough scales, which retains their body moisture and allows them to live and lay their eggs away from water.

Reptiles

Reptiles addressed here include snakes, alligators and crocodiles, turtles, and lizards.

[SNAKES]

There are two general types of snakes: nonvenomous and venomous (most of which are pit vipers). More than 250 species of snakes are found in North America; most are nonvenomous and are extremely important and beneficial to the natural environment because they control rodent populations. Some of the common nonvenomous species are the black snake, gopher snake, rat snake, king snake, hognose snake, garter and ribbon snakes, water snake, milk snake, ring-necked snake, and other little snakes, some of which are briefly described here. (For additional information, consult Appendix C and your local wildlife agency.)

Venomous snakes found in North America are limited to rattlesnakes, water moccasins (also called cottonmouths), copperheads, and coral snakes. The venom of the pit vipers (Viperidae family)—rattlesnakes, cottonmouths, and copperheads—is hemotoxic: It destroys its victim's red blood cells and blood vessel walls. That of the coral snake, the only venomous snake that is not a pit viper, is neurotoxic: It attacks the nervous system, causing paralysis in the victim.

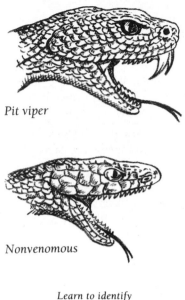

Pit viper

Nonvenomous

Learn to identify poisonous from nonpoisonous snakes so that the latter are not sacrificed to fear or ignorance.

Body characteristics that distinguish pit vipers from non-venomous snakes are (1) heat sensory pits that appear as tiny holes on each side of the snake's face between its eye and nostril; (2) elliptical (not round) and vertically positioned eye pupils; (3) a triangular-shaped head that is broader than the neck (most nonvenomous snakes have heads that blend in size with their bodies); and (4) a single row pattern of scales on the underside of the tail (coral snakes and non-venomous snakes have two rows of scales). *If you would rather not get close enough to distinguish these characteristics, just wait for the snake to leave. If you choose to interact with the snake, always use caution in case it is venomous.*

Situations and Solutions are grouped together at the end of the Snakes section.

Range and Habitat

Depending on the species, snakes can be found in all types of habitats, from grasslands, to forests, to lakes and rivers, to deserts.

Other Characteristics

Snakes are quiet creatures, relatively inactive except when looking for a spot in the sun or while hunting. They are important to the natural order in controlling rodents and insects. Though a mouse or rat may seem too large for a snake to swallow, snakes have extremely stretchable skin and a loosely connected jaw that opens wide to swallow prey whole. Snakes always swallow their prey headfirst to make sure that fur or feathers lie flat and cannot get stuck in the throat. Often a meal can last the snake a week or longer.

Snakes generally have poor eyesight and hearing but do have a unique sense of smell. They stick out their forked tongues to lick gaseous particles out of the air that are then conveyed to a sensing organ (called Jacobsen's organ) in the roof of the mouth.

Depending upon species, some snakes give birth to live young, while others lay eggs.

Enemies

Snakes have many enemies in the natural world, such as livestock (chickens, ducks, geese, turkeys), other snakes, raptors, cranes, herons, opossums, skunks, bears, badgers, and raccoons. Their worst enemy, however, is humans because of habitat destruction and human fear.

Few snakes pose any danger to or conflict with humans, and most are quite beneficial. Habitat destruction, such as mowing meadows and field borders and burning woods, fields, and brush piles, kills many snakes every year. Automobiles account for more snake deaths than any other cause because the cold-blooded snakes are drawn to the warm pavement to sun themselves. It has been estimated that cars kill over 10,000 snakes each year in one southern California county alone.

Humans kill many snakes each year solely out of fear and ignorance; most of the snakes are later identified as harmless species. Humans must understand that the chances of dying from the bite of a venomous snake are less than 1 in 34 million for people who are not snake handlers and 1 in 24 million for snake handlers. Humans have a greater likelihood of dying by lightning strike, in a hunting accident, or by drowning than by snakebite. Venomous snakes are definitely dangerous, but there are few areas where their abundance would prevent humans from enjoying nature. Precautions for safely coexisting with snakes are listed in Situations and Solutions.

How to Observe

Observation of snakes in the wild depends upon species and habitat. Consult your local wildlife agency for suggestions regarding local species.

Rattlesnakes

Of the more than one dozen species of rattlesnakes (*Crotalus* spp.) found throughout North America, the most common include the eastern diamondback (*C. adamanteus*), western diamondback (*C. atrax*), western pygmy (*Sistrunus miliarius*), timber (*C. horridus horridus*), and prairie (*C. viridis*). Adult rattlesnakes are stocky and range from 1½ to 5 feet long, depending on the subspecies. The largest is the eastern diamondback, which can reach 8 feet in length; the smallest is the pygmy rattler, which rarely exceeds 24 inches. Rattlesnakes are usually colored gray, tan, or green, with dark, evenly spaced triangular patches along the back and sides. However, patterns are highly variable, and subspecies are generally identified by location and color.

Like all pit vipers, rattlesnakes have elliptical pupils and a triangular head that is wider than their bodies. Rattlesnakes get their name from the blunt tail ridged with brittle, button-shaped segments that form the rattle. Occasionally rattles may be missing, perhaps due to injury.

Range and Habitat

Rattlesnakes are among the most widespread venomous snakes in the world, found in North America from coast to coast and from Canada through Mexico. Depending on the subspecies, they occupy a wide variety of habitats, including grassland, brushland, woodland, forests, and even deserts. For example, western diamondbacks are found in dry areas (especially pine flatwoods), wooded hillsides, bluffs along rivers, and sparsely vegetated rocky foothills. Pygmy rattlesnakes are found in pine flatwoods, cedar glades, mixed pine-hardwood forests, cypress lakes, and mountain stream borders. Timber rattlesnakes favor wooded hillsides, rock outcroppings, river lowlands, and canebrake thickets.

Other Characteristics

Rattlesnakes are active at dawn and dusk and also, during warm summer months, at night. They prefer warm-blooded prey such as small mammals—-mostly mice and rats—-but also feed on insects, lizards, birds, and eggs. They generally feed once a week. Their rattles are made of a skinlike substance, much like the horns of mammals. Like most snake species, rattlesnakes shed their skin three to five times per year. Following each skin shedding, a new segment is added to the rattle.

Because of their cold-blooded systems, rattlesnakes are extremely sensitive to external temperatures. During cold winter months, they hibernate in large groups in rocky crevices, holes under tree stumps, animal burrows, and other protective locations, emerging in spring to sun themselves and look for food. Because of this temperature sensitivity, those that live in desert environments tend to be mostly nocturnal to avoid the extreme heat of the day, which can kill them.

Enemies and Defenses

See information on enemies in the introductory section on snakes. Rattlesnakes are seldom aggressive but will aggressively defend themselves from predators. In addition to using their rattles for warning, they will also crawl away and coil into a protective position. They bite as a last resort.

A rattlesnake's strike is directed by heat and sense organs located in the tongue and head (these organs are also used in food gathering). The hemotoxic venom, used primarily to disable prey, is injected into the victim by a pair of hollow, folding fangs in the upper jaw. The snake does not have to be coiled but can strike from any position and in any direction. Striking distance is usually one-third to one-half the snake's body length, and it can strike and return to its original position so quickly that humans see the movement only as a blur. The bite of a rattlesnake can be fatal to humans, but the chance of death usually depends on the size of the snake: The smaller the snake or species, the less chance of fatality. (See Situations and Solutions for steps to take if bitten by a venomous snake.)

Water Moccasins

The water moccasin (*Agkistrodon piscivorus*), also known as the cottonmouth, is a large, heavy-bodied, water-living pit viper with color patterns varying from olive brown to black. Cottonmouth heads are much broader than their necks; a dark band extends from the eye to the rear of the jaw; the mouth line appears to droop; protective shields overhang the eyes; and the tail tapers abruptly. The name *cottonmouth* comes from the snake's white mouth lining.

Range and Habitat

Cottonmouths are found throughout the southern U.S. Preferred habitat is streambanks, swamps, lakeshores, and tree-bordered marshes. These snakes like to sun themselves on low-hanging tree limbs over the water.

Other Characteristics

Cottonmouths are primarily nocturnal hunters. They feed on fish, frogs, lizards, small mammals, and other snakes.

Defenses

In defense, the cottonmouth pulls itself into a loose coil, cocks its head up, and opens its mouth wide to show the white lining. Cotton-

Water moccasins like to sun on low branches overhanging streams. It is not uncommon for them to fall into fishing boats.

mouths do not need to be coiled to strike. They lunge and keep hold of the victim, chewing to drive their fangs deeper. Cottonmouth bites cause great pain and severe swelling but are only occasionally fatal to humans. (See Situations and Solutions for information on snakebite treatment.)

Copperheads

Copperheads (*Agkistrodon contortrix*) are pit vipers colored pinkish tan with reddish brown crossbands that run wide along the sides and narrow across the back, forming a sort of hourglass shape. They get their name from the brassy brown color of their heads. Copperheads average about 30 inches and seldom exceed 3 feet in length.

Range and Habitat

Copperheads are found in the U.S. south of the Great Lakes region from the plains states eastward, in terrain that varies from lowland swamps to rocky mountain ridges. In their range, they are found almost anywhere rodents live, including barns, berry thickets, rock ledges, edges of fields and haystacks, and piles of lumber, junk, and sawdust.

Other Characteristics

Copperheads feed primarily on small rodents but also eat frogs, lizards, insects, and other snakes. They hibernate in winter in large groups, especially in the north, sometimes even sharing hibernation space with rattlesnakes. The adaptable copperheads can live 20 years in the wild.

Defenses

Copperheads usually remain coiled and quiet unless too closely approached or touched. When disturbed, they vibrate their tails but often seem reluctant to strike. A large percentage of snakebites in some southern states, however, are attributable to copperheads. Because their coloring blends in with leaves on the forest floor, they are easy to step on and are more likely to interact with children and pets than other vipers. Fatalities from copperhead bites are almost unknown, however, because the venom is only mildly toxic. (See Situations and Solutions.)

Coral Snakes

The two coral snakes (Micrurus and Micruroides) are the only venomous snakes in North America that are not pit vipers. The only coral snakes found in the U.S. are the eastern coral snake *(Micrurus fulvius)* and the much smaller Arizona coral snake *(Micruroides euryxanthus)*. Related to the Asian and African cobras, they are small, slender bodied, and brightly colored in bands of red, black, and yellow, which makes them easily confused with the harmless king snake. Coral snakes have black heads, and their red rings are bounded on each side by yellow; king snakes have red heads and red rings bounded by black on both sides. An easy way to remember the difference is to think of a traffic light: Red means "stop" and yellow means "caution." If the red and yellow rings touch each other, it is a coral snake and should be avoided. Coral snakes average about 24 inches long but can reach up to 4 feet.

Distinguishing it from the pit viper, the coral snake's head is not larger than its neck; the fangs do not fold back under the roof of the mouth; and there are no external pits between eyes and nose. The eye pupils are round, not elliptical.

Range and Habitat

Coral snakes are found in the southern U.S. in rocky hillsides and valleys, pine flatwoods, and densely vegetated hardwood forests. They are usually secretive, hiding in leaves, logs, stumps, and debris, but they also frequent rock crevices, including those on patios and around suburban swimming pools.

Other Characteristics

Coral snakes feed primarily on lizards, snakes, frogs, and small mammals.

Defenses

Coral snakes are usually shy and secretive and are seldom aggressive unless startled, tormented, or hurt. Their short fangs and small mouth prevent them from striking like a pit viper; rather they bite and chew their victim to inject the poison. Their venom is more toxic than that of any other North American venomous snake because it is neurotoxic (attacks the nervous system for the sole purpose of killing) instead of hemotoxic (attacking the blood cells and vessels to start the prey-digestion process).

Garter Snakes

There are more than two dozen species of garter snakes (*Thamnophis* spp.) ranging from Canada to Central America. This snake is the most common reptile encountered by people. It is slender and 2 to 4 feet long, and though its coloration is highly variable, the back and side stripes (coral or yellow) are usually well defined. Red blotches or a double row of black checks are present between stripes.

Range and Habitat

Garter snakes can live in many environments from the Pacific to the Atlantic coast and are found farther north than any other reptile in the Western Hemisphere. They are excellent swimmers and are normally found near water.

Other Characteristics

Garter snakes are carnivorous, eating small fish, frogs, earthworms, snails, slugs, tadpoles, salamanders, and small mammals. They have a life span of 6 to 10 years.

Defenses

The garter snake's first defense is to escape. If grasped, though, this energetic snake defends itself uniquely by coiling around its predator and rubbing fecal matter and foul-smelling liquid from the anal scent glands on its enemies.

Gopher Snakes

The nonvenomous gopher snake *(Pituophis melanoleucus)*, also known as the bull snake, is often mistaken for a rattlesnake because, when threatened, it hisses loudly and shakes its tail against the ground. Its tail has no rattles, however, and is tapered to a point. Its head is not enlarged and triangular like the rattlesnake's but small and thumblike. It may also have a dark horizontal line in front of the eyes. Gopher snakes occasionally puff out their cheeks to change their normal appearance. They have round pupils and average 3 to 5 feet in length, though they occasionally reach 8 feet. Body coloration is cream or yellowish with blotches on the back that can be black, brown, yellow, or reddish brown.

Range and Habitat

Gopher snakes are found in all of the western U.S., southwestern Canada, and Mexico, from sea level to 10,000 feet. They prefer cultivated land, rocky areas, or bushy deserts that support large rodent populations. Western forms prefer grasslands and open bushlands.

Other Characteristics

Gopher snakes are active at dusk and at night, eating rats, mice, ground squirrels, and birds. They kill their prey by constriction. Snakes are one of nature's most efficient rodent controls. According to herpetologists, gopher snakes got their name because they use their coils to clear away dirt from gopher mounds and then pursue the gophers in their burrows. They seek refuge in rodent burrows and under objects such as stones, logs, and boards. They are capable of digging, loosening the earth with their snout, and then withdrawing the soil by catching it in a loop in the neck and hooking it backward. They are also good climbers.

Defenses

Because of their unusual size and rattlesnakelike coloration, gopher snakes are often mistaken for rattlesnakes and killed by humans. Natural predators are primarily hawks and eagles. The gopher snake's defensive behavior is distinctive: It makes a loud, raspy *hiss* while shaking and coiling its tail, mimicking a rattlesnake. Gopher snakes are nonvenomous, but their bite can be painful.

Hognose Snakes

Hognose snakes (*Heterodon* spp.) are stout bodied and usually have alternating brown and tan or yellow blotches, although some are black above. Depending on the subspecies, they reach 24 to 45 inches in length. Their name comes from their peculiar upturned nose, used for digging out toads (their major prey).

Range and Habitat

Hognose snakes, including western, eastern, and southern forms, are found in North America primarily in the U.S. They prefer upland habitats, especially sandy woods and fields.

Other Characteristics

Hognose snakes feed chiefly on toads and some insects.

Defenses

When alarmed, hognose snakes hiss, puff, and jerk about; raise their heads; and flatten their necks into a cobralike hood. They may even strike but do not open their mouths. If these defenses do not work, they thrash around, release foul-smelling musk, roll over on their backs, and play dead, often with mouth open and tongue dragging on the ground. Despite these dramatics, their defenses often backfire with people, and unknowing humans kill the harmless snakes.

King Snakes

King snakes (*Lompropeltis* spp.) average 3 to 5 feet long (though some can reach 7 feet) and have variable back and belly patterns. The most common is dark black or brown with narrow crossbands of white or yellow, similar to a zebra's stripes.

Range and Habitat

King snakes are found throughout North America from southern Canada through Mexico. They can be found in many different types of habitats, often near water.

Other Characteristics

The king is a constrictor snake that eats other snakes (including rattlesnakes), lizards, birds, and rodents. It is active at night during the summer.

Its reputation as the "king of snakes" probably comes from its preference for eating other snakes, including pit vipers, whose venom does not harm it. These are good snakes to encourage on one's property to keep other snake species away.

Rat Snakes

The red rat snake, also known as the corn snake (*Elaphe obsoleta*), is one of several rat snakes. This snake varies in color from yellowish tan to orange with a row of large, dark-edged red or rusty blotches down the center of the back. It has a black and white belly that resembles a piano keyboard. Because of its color, the red rat snake is often mistaken for a copperhead.

Another subspecies is the yellow rat, or "chicken," snake (*E. obsoleta quadravittata*), also known as the gray rat, or white oak, snake, depending on coloring. The most common is the yellow variety, which is orangish with four narrow brown stripes running the length of its body. The gray rat snake is gray with irregular darker blotches on the back. Rat snakes grow from 30 to 84 inches in length.

Range and Habitat

Rat snakes are found in North America east of the Mississippi River. Their preferred habitat is in trees, under brush and mulch piles, or inside old buildings or structures.

Other Characteristics

Rat snakes are among the strongest climbers of all snake species. They have powerful constricting muscles and specially edged belly scales that they press into tiny surface irregularities to climb vertically up tree trunks and other structures. They feed mostly on rodents and birds but also on lizards and frogs. They kill by constriction and are considered useful in controlling rodent populations.

Defenses

Rat snakes tame easily but will defend themselves aggressively if threatened. When cornered, they may vibrate their tails rapidly.

Ring-necked Snakes

There are 12 subspecies of ring-necked snakes (*Diadophis punctatus*) found in North America. They are slender snakes 10 to 30 inches long, with a yellow, cream, or orange neck ring and bright yellow, orange, or red belly. The back is gray, olive, brown, or shiny black. Ringnecks are constrictors that eat earthworms, slugs, lizards, and newborn snakes.

Range and Habitat

Ringnecks are found throughout much of the eastern and south-central U.S. One subspecies, the San Diego ringneck, is found only in southern California and Baja California, Mexico. Ringnecks are secretive and prefer protective habitat under mulch or leaf litter and are commonly found in gardens and backyards.

Other Characteristics

Ringnecks are weak constrictors that feed on small lizards, earthworms, slugs, and salamanders.

Defenses

Ringnecks are among the most nonaggressive of all snakes and rarely attempt to bite humans. Even if one tries, the mouth and teeth are too small to cause a wound. When threatened, ringnecks defend themselves by thrashing around and expelling musky scent.

Water Snakes

Water snakes (*Natrix* spp.) include, among others, the plainbelly, banded, brown, and Florida green snakes. They are often mistaken for cotton-mouths because both can be thick bodied, dark with rough scales, and more than 4 feet long. Harmless water snakes can be distinguished from cottonmouths by their faces and their behavior. The cottonmouth has an angular, chiseled head with a dark brown band running from eye to jaw and a scale that protrudes over the top of the eye. Water snakes lack any protruding scales, so they look more bug-eyed and have more rounded heads. Cottonmouths tend to stay put, often coiled, when encountered; if sufficiently threatened, they will display their open, white-lined mouths. Harmless water snakes usually escape immediately into the water when encountered. Cottonmouths swim with their entire bodies on top of the water, while water snakes are more likely to escape underwater or swim with only their head on the surface.

Range and Habitat

Water snakes are found in eastern North America. They prefer habitat along the banks of rivers, lakes, and ponds and like to bask stretched out on tree branches over water.

Other Characteristics

Water snakes are excellent hunters, living on fish, frogs, and other aquatic animals. They have long teeth adapted for holding slippery prey.

Defenses

Water snakes, though harmless, are known for aggressively defending themselves. They will bite and draw blood when captured. Although non-poisonous, such bites, like all animal bites, should be washed thoroughly to avoid infection.

Situations and Solutions: Snakes

Snake in the Yard or on a Concrete Walkway

WHY IT HAPPENS: Snakes like to hide and hunt in protected areas such as under wood and rocks, in high grass, or in shrubbery. Since they are cold-blooded (unable to raise their own body temperature), they are attracted to rocks, concrete walkways, and foundation walls that have warmed with the sunshine. They do not damage property in yards, because they are unable to dig; they use mouse holes and other natural openings to obtain cover.

SUGGESTIONS:

1. To prevent snakes from appearing near your home,
   * Keep grass and fields mowed and do not pile the clippings high. Keep such potential snake cover back from the house.
   * Do not leave pet food outside.
2. If you observe a snake,
   * Stand back and watch it. Snakes do not purposely position themselves to frighten people. They would much rather avoid encounters and will usually flee. Try to identify whether it is a poisonous or nonpoisonous species.
   * *Do not kill any snake unless it poses an immediate danger to persons or pets.* Snakes usually bite only if molested; biting is their only means

of self-defense. Even a poisonous snake in the woods or crossing the road poses no threat and should be left alone. Most large snakes range over large areas, so one seen in your yard today will likely be far away tomorrow.

* If the snake is nonvenomous and you do not want it around, wait a few hours for it to move on its own, or spray it with a hose or push it with a broom.
* If the snake is venomous, *do not attempt to handle or move it.* If you cannot wait for the snake to leave on its own, call your local wildlife agency for assistance in relocating it. See Avoiding Snakebite, following.

Snake in the House

WHY IT HAPPENS: Snakes may be inside a house either because they have accidentally entered to escape an unsuitable habitat or because they have taken up residence with a good source of rodent food. Accidental visitors are usually small snakes like young garter snakes and ring-necked snakes. Those that tend to take up residence include rat snakes, king snakes, black snakes, and other rodent-eating species. Sometimes snakes will hibernate in older homes with leaky cellars or crawl spaces with dirt floors. The presence of shed skins indicates that a snake has been in residence for some time.

SUGGESTIONS:

1. Make your home unattractive as a snake residence by using the following techniques:

   * Close even the smallest holes in walls, foundations, steps, and porches. Check the corners of doors and spaces around water pipes and electrical service entrances. Snakes can climb low fences and borders. Openings near the ground are vulnerable, especially if the snake is following mice under a house.
   * Snakeproof fences (made of ¼-inch mesh hardware cloth 3 feet high, buried 2 inches deep at the base, and angled outward 30 degrees) will keep snakes out, so long as gates are sealed tightly. Usually, however, the expense of such a fence is not justifiable.

2. If you find a snake in the house, stay calm and do nothing that will disturb the snake and send it into hiding. If circumstances permit, carefully open a nearby door and use a broom to gently herd it outside. Otherwise, carefully place a pail or wastebasket over a small coiled snake, then weight the covering to trap the snake until an experienced snake handler can be called. If you cannot cover the snake, you may be able to confine it in a limited area by using boards or boxes as barriers, again until an experienced wildlife handler arrives.

3. Resident snakes, their presence identified only by shed skin or droppings (similar to white and black bird droppings), may be difficult to locate because they can retreat into walls and crevices for long periods without food. If you have reason to believe a snake is living in your home, carefully inspect the dwelling inside and out, looking for the snake as well as for possible entrances.

- Look for interior openings like unsealed pipe and wire channels or unfinished closets. Check under and behind all furniture, boxes, appliances, and piles of clothing. Keep a list of all such openings for use in the final sealing process.

- Check for possible entrances near ground level outside the house, and for climbable surfaces such as chimneys or trellises that may have allowed the snake higher-level access through openings in the roof or eaves. Also carefully check behind concrete porches or steps and where decks attach to the house.

- Once you complete the entire inspection, try to identify the likely opening being used, judging by the estimated size of the snake and the opening, ease of access, and direct connection between the opening and the area where the sign of a resident snake was found.

- Seal all openings except the one you identify as the main entrance. Then install a one-way door that allows snakes to exit but not to re-enter. (See the section on Skunks for designing such doors.) Leave it in place for at least one month to allow time for the snake to leave; if the door is installed in the fall, be sure to leave it until spring, when snakes come out from hibernation.

- Old houses with a significant rodent population may be difficult to snakeproof because of elaborate rodent tunneling systems.

Avoiding Snakebite

1. Learn how to identify poisonous snakes, and keep a healthy distance when possible.
2. Never handle venomous snakes. Over 30 percent of all snakebites in the U.S. are made by captive snakes.
3. Teach kids to leave all snakes alone. Children aged 5 to 15 are more susceptible to snakebite than any other age group.
4. Be attentive in snake country. All poisonous snakes except the coral snake are naturally camouflaged.
5. Do not put your hands and feet where you cannot see, and look carefully before sitting down outdoors.
6. Camp in a floored tent with a zippered door.
7. Keep in mind when boating that cottonmouths are attracted to overhanging limbs, shady cover around boats, and stringers of fish.
8. Do not gather firewood after dark when some snakes are most active.
9. Do not crawl under fences in high grass or uncleared areas.
10. Watch for snakes on roads when jogging at night. Carry a flashlight and wear shoes after dark.
11. Be especially careful around stacks of building materials, woodpiles, or brush around your camp and home.
12. If a poisonous snake is found away from human habitation, *leave it alone*. Serious and even fatal bites occur when people try to kill venomous snakes.

Human or Pet Bitten by a Venomous Snake

WHY IT HAPPENS: A person or pet has ventured into an area of snake habitat and has threatened the snake in such a way that it is forced to use its last-resort defense. Deaths from snakebites are rare—only about 10 deaths result from some 8,000 snakebites in the U.S. each year. However, these injuries can be painful, crippling, or even fatal if not properly treated.

SUGGESTIONS:

1. Seek medical assistance immediately. If the victim does not die within the first 10 to 30 minutes, you have in excess of 12 hours to get proper medical attention, but it is important not to delay.

2. Treat the victim for shock, which is responsible for more snakebite deaths than the actual venom. Keep the victim quiet. Maintain body temperature; when cold, wrap the victim in a blanket; when hot, cool off by fanning. If the victim's face looks pale, elevate the feet. If the face looks red and flushed, elevate the head.

3. Most important:

   • *Do not cut and suck the wound.*

   • *Do not apply ice or cold packs to the wound.*

   • *Never use a tourniquet.*

   Do nothing but treat for shock and temperature extremes, and get to a doctor right away.

4. Dr. Maynard Cox, director, founder, and associate pathologist of the World Poison Bite Information Center in Orange Park, Florida, is considered one of the world's foremost snakebite experts. Make sure the doctor who treats the victim knows how to treat snakebites and, if not, ask the doctor to call Dr. Cox at 904-272-6398.

[CROCODILIANS]

Only two species of crocodilians—the largest of all reptiles—are native to North America. They are the American alligator (*Alligator mississippiensis*) and the American crocodile (*Crocodylus acutus*). Because the crocodile is much rarer (endangered, in fact), we will focus mainly on the alligator in this section.

The alligator is a large, lizard-shaped reptile with four short legs. The young are black above with bright yellow stripes and blotches that disappear so that adults are uniformly black on top. Both young and adult have light-colored undersides. Alligator feet have widespread toes: five on the front feet, four on the back. The three inner toes on each foot are clawed, and the hind toes are webbed. The hide is covered with smooth, horny scales in rows connected by heavy, wrinkled skin. Large, strong scales form ridges along the back, and the long, muscular tail is ridged on the last third of the upper side.

Alligators have large, flat, elongated heads with large, hinged jaws that can open extremely wide. Their eyes are positioned on the side rather than on the front of the face and have protective, transparent membranes that cover them underwater. Alligators have no external ears; their eardrums, covered by protective flaps of skin, are located just behind the eyes. The nostrils at the tip of the snout can be closed when submerged. The location of the eyes, ears, and nostrils allows the alligator to remain submerged with only the top of its head exposed so that it can still see, hear, and breathe.

The growth rate of alligators and crocodiles is determined by food availability and temperature. Alligators grow about 1 foot each year until they reach about 8 feet, then begin to broaden as length slowly increases. Males reach an average of 11 to 12 feet, though specimens as large as 17½ feet have been found. Females grow to about 8 feet long. Large individuals can weigh up to 500 pounds, with their tails totaling half their length.

Although extremely similar in appearance, American crocodiles can be distinguished from alligators by their more tapered snout, lighter grayish green color, and visible fourth tooth on both sides of the lower jaw when the mouth is closed.

Range and Habitat

Alligators are found in the southeastern U.S. from Georgia, Florida, and the Carolinas west to Mississippi, Louisiana, and Texas, in both fresh and brackish marine areas. They live in rivers, ponds, swamps, marshy lowlands, and even human-made canals and water impoundment ponds. Their northern range is limited by temperature because they cannot survive cold. Females build nests made of vegetation that mounds above high-water levels.

American crocodiles are found only in extreme southern Florida, in quiet coastal mangrove swamps protected from onshore winds rather than in open bays. They build nests in well-drained soil adjacent to deep water.

Other Characteristics

American crocodiles are extremely shy, reclusive, and less vocal than alligators. They are easily disturbed by human activity, which is why they

During the rainy season, alligators dig dens ("gator holes"), which hold vital water for fish and other wildlife during dry times.

are an endangered species. Alligators have more readily adapted to the human environment and tend to be more aggressive, or at least not as shy of humans.

Alligators and crocodiles eat anything that flies, walks, swims, or crawls and is small enough for them to kill. Their powerful jaws can crush shell and bone, so fish, turtles, mammals, snakes, birds, and crabs are frequent prey. Alligators hunt by lying in wait and catching whatever comes within range of their jaws. They swallow food by raising the head and gulping. If a large meal is eaten, it may take up to a week to be digested by strong stomach acids. Digestion is directly affected by external temperature, so feeding habits can be traced to weather conditions. For example, alligators are most likely to eat on calm days when the water is at least 73 degrees F. They are least likely to eat when the water temperature is below 68 degrees F.

Alligators swim by folding their legs against the body, propelling themselves with a sweeping motion of the tail from side to side. On land, they may lumber along dragging their tails, but they can hold their body and most of their tail off the ground and move on their toes with surprising speed. Individual alligator territories can be as large as 12,000 acres, and males can travel over 5 miles a day. Females tend to stay in much smaller territories (6 to 40 acres) and move into open water only for courtship and breeding. Alligators have a loose dominance hierarchy that is more pronounced during breeding season. Young alligators grunt or bark; adults bellow and hiss. They produce scent from four prominent musk glands during courtship.

Cold-blooded like all reptiles, alligators cannot tolerate temperature extremes. Temperatures over 100 degrees F can be lethal, and in cold weather, metabolism slows and they do not eat. They do not actually hibernate but spend the cold months of October through March in dens. In extreme cold conditions, if ice is present and temperatures are below 41 degrees F, alligators will lie underwater for long periods with just the tip of the snout exposed and the rest of the head and body angled downward; this ensures an air supply if the water freezes when exposed to freezing air temperatures. Some alligators found with their snouts completely surrounded by ice fully recover, even if they have been exposed to water temperatures as low as 36 degrees F. American crocodiles are much more sensitive to cold than alligators, which is why their range is limited so far south.

Both males and females dig dens or holes, used year after year, by digging or tearing earth and roots loose with their mouths and claws; they sweep away the loosened material with the tail. Dens are usually holes in the bottom of large ponds or openings dug in a mudbank. They are built with a slide or ramp leading from the water to a basking site on the bank. The depression stays full of water during the wet season and holds the water after the rains stop. During the dry season, and especially during extended droughts, "gator holes" provide vital water for fish, insects, crustaceans, snakes, turtles, birds, and other animals, thus preserving the vital food chain of the wetlands.

Enemies and Defenses

Alligator eggs, hatchlings, and small juveniles are subject to danger from many predators, such as raccoons, otters, wild hogs, skunks, bears, wading birds, large fish, and other alligators. The alligator's primary defenses are biting, striking with its strong tail, and escaping into the water. The sole enemy of adult alligators and crocodiles is humans.

Conservation Notes

From 1855 through the early 1970s, alligator hunting (and poaching) was a profitable business due to the demand for alligator skin for boots and shoes. Alligators were hunted almost to the point of extinction and were listed as an endangered species in 1967. In the 1970s, hunting and shipment of skins were finally controlled to the point where poaching was mostly eliminated. Since the control of hunting and poaching, alligator populations have successfully rebounded. Although alligators once again may be hunted for skins, the trade in alligator skins is closely regulated by the U.S. Fish and Wildlife Service to protect the endangered crocodile, whose skin looks similar. Only an estimated 400 to 500 crocodiles remain in the wild.

The chief threat to alligators now is the devastating loss of wetland habitat due to development of swamplands and coastal areas as well as "active water management." Draining wetlands removes habitat for gator holes and nesting sites. Flooding caused by seasonal release of water in management programs results in serious loss of nesting sites each year.

How to Observe

The best way to observe alligators in the wild is to seek out wildlife preserves where alligators are protected from hunting, such as Ding Darling Wildlife Preserve on Sanibel Island, Florida. Any alligators encountered in the wild should be left alone.

Situations and Solutions

Encountering Alligators in the Wild

WHY IT HAPPENS: Wetland areas, natural habitat for alligators and crocodiles, have become attractive areas for humans for water-related activities such as swimming, skiing, fishing, and hunting. Human-alligator interactions rarely result in attacks, but precautions should be taken to reduce potential conflicts.

SUGGESTIONS:

1. Do not swim outside posted swimming areas or in waters that may contain large alligators. Always swim with a partner within marked swimming areas, which are specially situated and designed to reduce the potential of alligator-human conflict. Do not swim at night or dusk when alligators most actively feed.

2. Use common sense. Avoid areas with thick vegetation along shorelines, which provide good natural habitat for large alligators.

3. Do not feed or entice alligators. They overcome their natural shyness and become accustomed or attracted to humans when fed. The most dangerous alligators are large individuals that have lost their fear of people. Inform other people that feeding alligators is against the law and that by doing so, people create problems for others who want to use the water for recreation.

4. Do not throw fish scraps into the water or leave them on shore. Even if you are not intentionally feeding alligators, the result is the same. Dispose of scraps in garbage cans near boat ramps or fish camps.

5. Do not allow pets to swim in waters known to contain large alligators or in designated swimming areas with humans. Dogs suffer more attacks than humans, probably because they more closely resemble natural prey.

6. Keep pets and livestock (especially ducks, pigs, or goats) fenced from alligator-inhabited areas.

7. Do not leave children unattended around alligators.

8. Never approach or harass large alligators (over 6 feet), because they are large enough not to fear humans.

Alligators Encountered near Human Dwellings

WHY IT HAPPENS: Due to humans moving into and developing alligator habitat, the opportunity for human-alligator interaction around homes has greatly increased in recent years. Most such encounters occur in places like garages, backyards, swimming pools, golf course water hazards, and ditches.

SUGGESTIONS:

1. If left unmolested, alligators will eventually retreat on their own to more preferred habitats away from people, so, if possible, leave the alligator alone. *Do not feed any alligator.*

2. If an alligator poses a threat to human safety, call your local wildlife agency for assistance in relocating it. Do not kill, harass, molest, or attempt to move an alligator. State laws prohibit such actions, and the potential for being bitten or injured by a thrashing alligator is great. (Relocation of alligators is quite difficult, because introducing new individuals can upset territories, spread disease, and cause conflicts. As human development continues, fewer places remain available for relocation. Alligators have strong homing instincts and can travel long distances to return to their original places. More than 3,000 "nuisance" alligators are killed annually in Florida by wildlife agencies because of direct human encroachment on alligator habitat.)

Humans Keeping Alligators as Pets

WHY IT HAPPENS: Prior to their legal protection, alligators were sold in pet stores and souvenir shops as novelty items. Such sales are now strictly prohibited in Florida and elsewhere. Only specially licensed persons may possess a live alligator.

SUGGESTIONS:

1. Do not remove any alligator from its natural habitat or accept one as a pet. Alligators do not become tame in captivity, and handling even small ones may result in bites.

2. Enjoy seeing and photographing wild alligators in their natural wetland habitats while exercising caution in approaching them closely.

[TURTLES]

Of the world's approximately 240 species of turtles, North America has 48 species. Technically, all of these can be called *turtles*, but the name *tortoise* refers to species that are entirely terrestrial (land dwelling), while species that inhabit shallow eastern coastlines are called *terrapins*.

Although variations exist among species, a general description applies to all turtles. The shell is composed of thick layers of bone and a thin layer of scales made of material much like human fingernails. The shell has two openings, one in front from which the head and front legs emerge and the other in back where the rear legs and tail are found. Turtle coloration varies, depending on species, from olive green and mud brown to bright colors. Turtles do not have teeth but, like birds, have horny beaks used to tear food apart. Their legs are stout and end in thick claws. Freshwater turtles have webbed feet, while sea turtles have evolved flattened, flipper-like feet. Tortoise feet are not webbed.

Sections on Enemies and Defenses, Conservation Notes, How to Observe, and Situations and Solutions for all turtles appear after the section on Tortoises.

Freshwater Turtles

Freshwater turtles found in North America are generally divided into four groups: bottom-walking, basking, softshell, and box turtles.

The bottom-walking group is made up of snapping turtles (*Chelydra serpentina*), alligator snapping turtles (*Macrochlemys temmincki*), mud turtles (*Kinosternon subrubrum*), and musk turtles (*Sternotherus odoratus*). These species vary in size from small (3- to 5-inch) mud turtles to large (30-inch and 250-pound) alligator snapping turtles. Snapping turtles are mud brown with no colored markings; mud turtles are the same color but have two light, irregular stripes on the head and neck. Alligator snapping turtles are distinguished by extremely large heads (this species is sometimes called the "loggerhead"), strongly hooked beaks, and three prominent ridges extending along the length of the upper shell, like those found on alligators. Musk turtles are olive green with two thin yellow stripes on each side of the head and neck.

Basking turtles include map turtles (*Graptemys geographica*), painted turtles (*Chrysemys picta*), and sliders (*C. scripta*); they are small to medium sized and green or brown with brightly colored markings on head and neck. Slider females are much larger than males, which have flat rather than arched shells; they have extremely long nails on their front feet and colorful markings on their head. Female map turtles are also much larger than males. Their shells are adorned with beautiful maplike patterns and colors, and their heads are marked with yellow stripes and whorls. The painted turtle's bottom shell is yellow or orange divided with a bright red stripe.

Turtle shells are composed of thick layers of bone and a thin layer of scales made of material much like human fingernails.

Softshells (Trionychidae family), also called "pancake turtles," have flattened, soft, leathery shells and paddlelike feet, each with three toes (most other turtles have four or five toes on each foot). Softshells range in size from 5 to 18 inches in length depending on sex (females are larger) and species.

Box turtles (*Terrapene* spp.) are terrapin species with large, high-domed shells into which the turtle can completely withdraw. Common box turtles are small, rarely growing over 6 to 8 inches long. Their young are brightly colored but change to drab olive tan as adults. The uncommon box turtle retains its bright coloring through adulthood. Box turtles are so named because their shells close up like a box using hinged portions of the lower shell at front and back. The lower shell adjusts to the upper so completely that the cavity is all but airtight when the shell is closed.

Range and Habitat

Freshwater turtles are found throughout North America in a variety of habitats, including forests, fields, streams, lakes, trees, and oceans. Bottom-walking turtles usually prefer slow-moving water found in ponds, streams, and sloughs. Basking turtles prefer more shallow water and gently sloping banks with lots of vegetation. Softshells favor river habitats. Box turtles are found in eastern forests and fields and often are seen in some urban environments. Turtles lay their eggs in nests dug on land.

Other Characteristics

Bottom-walking turtles are distinguished by their behavior of walking (they are poor swimmers) on the bottoms of lakes, streams, and rivers.

They are seldom seen on land, except for certain large snapping turtle species.

Many fishers and hunters think of snapping turtles, the most abundant and widespread of all turtles in North America, as sinister in appearance and nasty in disposition. In reality, though they may feed occasionally on game fish or water birds, they play an extremely important role in pond and lake ecology by feeding on carrion at the bottom. They are more scavenger than predator and eat both animal matter and aquatic plants. They do bite and can strike quickly, however, and should be treated with great caution. Alligator snapping turtles, found in deep rivers, sloughs, and lakes, mostly eat fish and small turtles that they lure with their "split" tongues, which resemble worms to passing prey.

Musk, or "stinkpot," turtles produce strong, unpleasant secretions from their musk glands when captured or handled. They are known for basking in trees as high as 6 feet above the water and falling on fishers or into boats; they also like to steal bait from fishhooks. They feed on shellfish, insects, worms, small fish, and aquatic plants.

Basking turtles are conspicuous, brightly colored, social turtles. Good swimmers, they tend to live near water and are frequently seen basking on rocks or logs. They are shy and will retreat into the nearest water at the slightest disturbance. They eat fish, insects, crawdads, worms, and aquatic plants. Painted turtles love to bask for hours at a time along banks of shallow lakes and ponds with abundant vegetation. They are omnivorous. Sliders get their name from their habit of sliding into the water at the least sign of danger. They bask for hours on logs, stumps, snags, and rocks. If sufficient sites are not available, they will pile on top of each other, two to three high, to share the basking space. They are primarily vegetarian.

Softshell turtles, because of their shape, are extremely strong swimmers and move surprisingly fast on land. They spend much time buried in mud or sand at the water's edge, using their long, tubelike noses to snorkel air. Oxygen is absorbed through their thin skin, allowing them to stay submerged in water for long periods but also making them susceptible to water pollution. They are shy and will retreat to the water at the first sign of disturbance. When captured or handled, they can strike quickly and strongly with their long neck and sharp beak.

Box turtles are known for their incredible regenerative capabilities and can survive serious injury such as being hit by cars, overrun by lawnmowers, and crushed by farm equipment.

Like all reptiles, turtles are cold-blooded—their body temperature is determined by environmental temperature—so they are only active when outside temperatures permit, usually from late April through September. The life span of most turtles in the wild ranges from 10 to 20 years.

Sea Turtles

Of the seven species of true sea turtles (Cheloniidae family) in the world, six are found in the coastal waters bordering the U.S. and its territories. Sea turtles range in size from the 27-inch, 110-pound Ridley (the smallest) to the 70-inch, 827-pound leatherback (the largest). They are olive green or gray and round in shape.

Range and Habitat

Sea turtles are found in both the Atlantic and Pacific oceans. They come onto coastal beaches to lay their eggs.

Other Characteristics

Sea turtles take one or more decades to reach full adult size. They are extremely long-lived; although not known for sure, their life spans in the wild are estimated to range from 40 to 75 years.

Sea turtles migrate thousands of miles annually to return to the nesting grounds where they were hatched.

Tortoises

Four tortoise species (Testudinidae family) are found in North America. They are land-dwelling turtles with hard, high-vaulted upper shells, strong scales over stout limbs, and short, unwebbed toes.

Range and Habitat

Three of the four native tortoise species are found in the western U.S. Gopher tortoises, the only species found east of the Mississippi River, live throughout the coastal plain of the southeastern states. Tortoises prefer dry habitats such as longleaf pine–scrub oak sandhills and clayhills, dry prairies, and coastal dune ecosystems. They can also live in human-made environments such as pastures, old fields, and grassy roadsides. They require well-drained sandy soils for digging burrows, low plant growth for food, and open sunny areas for nesting. They come to water only to drink or bathe. Females lay eggs in sand mounds or other sunny nesting sites near their burrows.

Other Characteristics

Because of their large shells, tortoises move slowly and feed primarily on plants. They will eat carrion, waste, and invertebrates, however. They can withdraw their heads, legs, and tail into their shell for protection.

Gopher tortoises burrow with shovellike front feet to create dens as large as 40 feet long and 10 feet wide. The width of the burrow is wide enough so the tortoise can turn around inside. These burrows are used by many other animals, such as gophers, snakes, frogs, mice, rabbits, skunks, opossums, burrowing owls, and armadillos. Tortoises can live up to 40 years in the wild.

Enemies and Defenses: Turtles

Predators such as raccoons, dogs, foxes, opossums, and skunks are serious threats to turtle and tortoise eggs and hatchlings; adult turtles have few natural predators other than alligators, raccoons, coyotes, and humans. The primary defense for most species is the ability to withdraw into the tough shell for protection. Snapping turtles further defend themselves with their aggressive nature and strong biting ability.

Conservation Notes: Turtles

Turtles and tortoises, like much other wildlife, have been commercially exploited by humans. Diamond-backed terrapins were close to extinction around 1900 because of the demand for their flesh for stew. Green sea turtles and alligator snapping turtles have also been harmed by the demand for their flesh for food. The demand for tortoiseshell jewelry has injured hawksbill and other sea turtle populations.

Sea turtles suffer from purposeful hunting, accidental capture in fishing nets, and destruction of natural habitat due to coastal development and ocean pollution. Tortoise populations are also declining, mainly because of habitat loss and damage caused by humans. Some people still hunt turtles and tortoises for food. Many turtles are killed each year by automobiles, and construction of roads isolates turtle colonies.

Tortoise racing, an activity used for years as a fund-raising event, causes serious harm to tortoises when they are removed from their natural habitat, stressed, and then not returned to their original location. Many are unable to adapt to their new location, cause disruption in the new colony's complex social structure, introduce new parasites and diseases, and mix locally adapted gene pools.

How to Observe: Turtles

Turtles are slow moving so readily observable once located in their natural habitats. Sea turtles are most available for observation when they come to land to lay their eggs. Human contact can seriously disrupt their reproductive cycle, however. Check with your local wildlife agency for the least stressful methods and locales for observing all turtle species.

Situations and Solutions: Turtles

Turtles Encountered in the Wild

WHY IT HAPPENS: Humans who enjoy outdoor activities such as swimming, fishing, hunting, and hiking may come upon turtles in their natural habitats.

SUGGESTIONS:

1. Do not attempt to capture turtles, and do not keep them as pets. They are entitled to live in their natural habitat like all other creatures.
2. Do not kill, shoot for target practice, or otherwise harass turtles.
3. Fishers using trotlines should check their lines regularly to avoid unnecessary capture of turtles, especially snapping turtles, which feed on fish bait.
4. Help protect turtle natural habitat from development by promoting wetland and coastal protection and forestry management practices that keep forests thinned (producing ground-level grasses and other food sources).
5. Avoid running over turtles on highways and roads. Urge construction of underpasses or other protection devices to create safe passageways for turtles and other wildlife.
6. Tortoise races, now legally prohibited in Florida, still occur elsewhere. Encourage the abolition of this abusive event.
7. To avoid the chance of introducing new diseases to established colonies, do not release captive turtles into the wild.
8. Be cautious in using pesticides and herbicides anywhere in natural turtle habitat because of the risk of direct or food-chain poisoning.

Sea Turtles Killed or Injured by Human Contact

WHY IT HAPPENS: Fishing practices and habitat destruction seriously threaten sea turtle populations.

1. Because sea turtles migrate over territorial boundaries, international cooperation is needed to protect them from overharvesting by hunters for food and leather, shells, and body fat. Importation of products made from sea turtles is illegal in the U.S.

2. Pollution of coastal waters kills many sea turtles through ingestion of plastics, polystyrene, and other garbage, as well as oil spill tar. Other toxic substances dumped at sea can slowly poison turtles or the animals and plants on which they feed. Support actions aimed at controlling ocean pollution.

3. Sea turtles are often accidentally captured in fishing nets and trawls, where they drown or suffer serious injury. Modification and more frequent checking of nets by commercial fishers can minimize harm.

4. Avoid human, pet, and vehicle activity on coastal beaches, which can frighten female sea turtles away from their natural nesting sites. If turtles are forced to choose other sites, eggs are less likely to hatch and young less likely to survive.

Snapping Turtle Behaving Aggressively

WHY IT HAPPENS: Unlike other turtles, which ordinarily assume defensive postures when threatened, snapping turtles squarely face their attackers, lunge, and bite. They have evolved this behavior over time, defending themselves by attacking before they are attacked because their large heads and broad necks are too big for complete retraction into their shells for defense.

SUGGESTIONS:

1. *Do not attempt to touch or feed snapping turtles.*

2. If you are bitten by a snapping turtle, clean the wound to avoid infection. Seek medical assistance for a serious bite.

[LIZARDS AND WORM LIZARDS]

Lizards are the group of reptiles with the greatest variety of shapes and forms. The general categories of lizards discussed here include night lizards, geckos, iguanas (including spiny and horned lizards and anoles), skinks, whiptails and racerunners, anguids (including the southern alligator lizard and the California legless lizard), gila monsters, and Florida worm lizards.

Generally, lizards are muscular and fast moving. Males and females differ greatly in appearance, males being larger and sometimes having elaborate crests. Coloration varies according to habitat, often to camouflage the lizard against its surroundings.

Range and habitat are included in brief descriptions.

NIGHT LIZARDS: This small family of lizards (Xantusidae) is made up of 16 species found in the western U.S., Mexico, and Central America. They measure 1½ to 5 inches, have nonmovable eyelids and long tails and legs, and are covered with granular scales. Their habitat is mainly rocky outcrops, deserts, and pebble beaches. Granite night lizards are found in southern California; the island night lizard is a rare species found only on islands off the southern California coast.

GECKOS: These brown, gray, black, yellow, orange, or green lizards (Gekkonidae family) are found in the southwestern U.S. and Florida. Their soft skin is composed of small scales, and they have large eyes with transparent, fused eyelids. Their short limbs end in five-toed feet.

IGUANAS: Members of this large family (Iguanidae) of lizards are mostly medium sized and strongly built, with well-developed hind legs specially adapted for running and leaping. They have movable eyelids and grow new teeth when old ones have worn down. Smaller iguanas tend to be insectivores, while larger species are plant eaters. Iguanas come in two main shapes: those that are flattened sideways for tree living and those that are flattened top to bottom for ground dwelling. Iguanas are distinguished by their small, bony, knoblike projections, spines, and crests.

Members of the iguana family found in North America include spiny lizards, horned lizards, and anoles. The spiny eastern and western fence lizards are known for their habit of sunning themselves on fences. The seven species of horned lizards (mistakenly referred to as horny toads) found in the U.S. inhabit primarily sandy and rocky areas. Horned lizards have squat bodies with short tails and sharp projecting scales all over their bodies; their heads are protected with 6 to 10 knifelike spines. They are generally light gray or brown with spots that provide camouflage against rocks and sand.

The green anole, known as the false chameleon, can change its body color like its African namesake (no true chameleons are native to North America). They have triangular heads with long jaws and reddish throat sacs that can be enlarged when they display for breeding or defense. They have long tails and legs that end in enlarged fingers and toes.

SKINKS: This is the largest family (Scincidae) of lizards. The many different skink species have evolved different body types depending on their habitats, but generally they have long, smooth, cylindrical bodies, narrow heads no wider than their trunks, and tapering tails. The most common skinks in North America are striped skinks such as the Great Plains skink.

WHIPTAILS AND RACERUNNERS: There are 25 to 45 species of whiptails and racerunners (*Chemidophorus* spp., Teiidae family), the New World counterparts to the true lizards, ranging from North America (except in the north and northeast) to northern Argentina. Their heads are pointed and covered with large shields, and they have a long, rough tail, small back and side scales, and larger belly scales. They either are uniformly dark colored or have patterns of spots or fine stripes on dark backgrounds. These species are commonly found in arid and semiarid hill territory covered with dry grass, low bushes, and rocks. They prefer open terrain with loose soil. Racerunners flit quickly from place to place and, when standing still, "mark time" by walking in place.

ANGUIDS: Members of this family (Anguidae) found in North America include the southern alligator lizard and the glass lizard. The alligator lizard is streamlined and short legged, with movable eyelids. It is an active lizard found in sunny, bushy places like grasslands and woodland edges, especially oak woods. Glass lizards have elongated bodies and are limbless, so they look more like snakes than like lizards.

LEGLESS LIZARDS: The California legless lizard (Anniellidae family) reaches about 6 to 10 inches long, has an elongated, snakelike body and small eyes with movable eyelids, and is silvery or tan in color with a yellow belly.

GILA MONSTERS: This family of lizards (Holodermatidae), found in southern Nevada and southeastern Utah to northwestern Mexico, is one of only two types of venomous lizards in the world. Gila monsters, sometimes called beaded lizards, have broad, slightly flattened heads; short necks; elongated, cylindrical bodies with large, bony scales on their backs; and thick, rounded tails. Their short but powerful legs end in five-toed feet. They have pink spots mixed with black brown splotches on their trunks and four or five dark bands on their tails.

WORM LIZARDS: This genus (*Amphisbaena*) is considered a group separate from true lizards; they are unusual in living exclusively underground. They have long, worm-shaped bodies with special tough, horny shields on their skulls that are used for burrowing. The only species found in the U.S. is the Florida worm lizard, native to north and central Florida. It has a flattened head, used to compress soil against the top and bottom of the tunnel while it burrows. These worm lizards prefer sandy soils and feed chiefly on earthworms, spiders, and termites. Occasionally they may be seen on the surface after a heavy rain, but if disturbed they will retreat underground immediately.

Other Characteristics

Like their close relatives the snakes, lizards are equipped with Jacobsen's organs in the roofs of their mouths, to which their tongues bring air samples for identification by smell. Although iguanas are vegetarians, most lizards feed on insects and other small invertebrates (spiders, worms) by dashing forward and grasping them in their jaws. Chameleonlike lizards (Chamaeleontidae family) use their ability to change color to stay camouflaged and grasp prey that comes within range of their long tongues.

Horned lizards are excellent burrowers. They feed on ants, although some also eat other insects and spiders. Spiny and horned lizards can change color from light to dark depending on air temperature; at cooler temperatures, they darken their bodies to absorb external heat more quickly.

Anoles can change color, an ability directly related to their visual rela-

The gila monster is native to the Southwest deserts.

tionship to sunlight. At lower temperatures, they remain darker; after having sunned themselves to reach the right body temperature, however, they turn light green to camouflage themselves while hunting insects in trees and grasses. Most skinks are insectivores, though some larger skinks also prey on small mammals and other reptiles; some are burrowers and others are tree dwellers. Whiptails and racerunners are active during the day, eat beetles and grasshoppers, and flee quickly for cover when disturbed.

Alligator lizards eat insects and other small invertebrates, including poisonous black widow spiders and scorpions. They are excellent tree climbers and can steal eggs from bird nests.

Gila monsters inject their neurotoxic venom from poison glands on the outer portion of their lower jaws through grooves on their teeth. The venom is effective on small mammals and birds but not on frogs. Gila monster venom first causes pain and numbness and then heart and lung failure in the prey, but it is seldom fatal to humans.

Enemies and Defenses

Because of their small size, most lizards are preyed upon by larger mammals, as well as by birds and other reptiles. Different species have developed individual defense methods to help them survive. Most lizards have "disposable" tails: When threatened, they can sever their tails by constricting the muscles, and the severed tail distracts the predator while the lizard escapes. The tail later regenerates, though with cartilage rather than bone. Some lizards flash brightly colored mouths and tongues to scare predators away. Horned lizards also have the unusual ability to shoot a stream (up to 3 feet or more) of blood at predators from the corners of their eyes.

How to Observe

Lizards tend to be secretive and stay out of view, making observation a challenge. Being cold-blooded, they are most active during daylight hours. Find a location of suitable natural habitat, sit quietly, and be prepared to wait for the appearance of these important creatures. Check with your local wildlife agency for specific observation locations.

Situations and Solutions

Encouraging Lizard Habitat

WHY IT HAPPENS: Encouraging lizards to share your property will create natural insect contol around your home.

SUGGESTIONS: See suggestions in the next section for encouraging amphibians on your property.

Maintaining Lizards as Pets

WHY IT HAPPENS: People are sometimes advised to keep geckos in their homes where insects are a serious problem. Others are drawn to keeping lizards as pets, generally in terrariums.

SUGGESTIONS:

1. Lizards, like all wild creatures, deserve to live in their natural habitat, not to be imprisoned for human entertainment.
2. Do not buy lizards from pet stores or capture them in the wild to keep them imprisoned. Be certain that you do not participate directly or unknowingly in the illegal importation of exotic lizard species.
3. Encourage natural habitats around your home, town, or city that allow lizards to live in the wild and fulfill their insect-control purpose in the natural food chain.

Amphibians

Amphibians (from the Greek words *amphi* and *bion,* meaning "both lives") are the oldest surviving land vertebrates. All others—reptiles, birds, and mammals—evolved directly or indirectly from amphibians. The two general types of amphibians, frogs-and-toads and newts-and-salamanders, are distinguished from other animals by their ability to live in two worlds: water and land. Amphibian life usually begins in water, with eggs that hatch to produce a larval stage of young with gills for breathing in water. As they grow into adults, the gills are reabsorbed into their bodies to become lungs so they can live on land.

Because their skin is water-permeable, amphibians secrete slimy mucus to protect themselves from moisture loss while on land and prevent excessive moisture absorption while in water. Amphibians spend much of their time on land but usually return to water to mate and lay eggs. They cannot tolerate cold or hot temperature extremes or prolonged dry spells. When conditions require, they take refuge underground, do not eat, and can remain dormant (although not truly hibernating) for many months.

Amphibians are mainly carnivorous, preying on insects and their larvae, spiders, crustaceans, worms, slugs, and snails. Most have long, sticky tongues used to catch prey. Larval frogs are vegetarians.

Amphibians are preyed upon by larger vertebrates, including other amphibians, reptiles, birds, and mammals. Depending on the species, their defensive techniques may include color camouflage, leaping away, and puffing themselves up to appear more aggressive.

Depending on species, amphibian reproductive techniques vary from internal to external fertilization of eggs laid in water. Amphibians lay large numbers of eggs to increase their odds for survival, because so many eggs and young are lost to predators. Amphibians are not generally social creatures.

Following are general descriptions and information on range and habitat for salamanders, newts and related salamanders, and toads and frogs. Information on Enemies and Defenses, How to Observe, and Situations and Solutions for all amphibians is grouped together after the section on Toads and Frogs.

[SALAMANDERS, CAUDATA ORDER]

GIANT SALAMANDERS: The North American member of the giant salamander family (Cryptobranchidae) is known as the hellbender. Found in the eastern and central U.S., it never leaves water and retains its larval characteristics, except for the gills, into adulthood. Hellbenders have broad heads, short, thickset limbs, and short, vertically flattened tails. They can reach up to 28 inches long.

MOLE SALAMANDERS: Species (Ambystomatidae family) found throughout North America, including the tiger, Jefferson, spotted, mole, and northwestern salamanders, have flattened bodies, broad heads, and smooth skin. They spend most of their lives in underground burrows created by other animals like squirrels or tortoises and are only rarely seen during breeding season, when they return to ponds to mate and lay eggs.

TIGER SALAMANDERS: This species (*Ambystoma tigrinum*), found throughout the continent, varies in color from olive green to black with bars or spots, depending on location. The California tiger salamander lives in arid environments underground near ponds. It has a blunt head, reaches 8 inches in length, and is dark with creamy spots.

SPOTTED SALAMANDERS: Found in the eastern half of North America, these salamanders (*Ambystoma maculatum*) have blue black bodies with bright yellow spots. The Jefferson salamander, found in the northeastern U.S. and Canada, reaches 8 inches long and is gray brown, often with blue spots scattered over its body. Long and slender, it has a wide snout and long toes. It lives under debris in woodlands near ponds and wetlands and returns to the breeding ponds in early spring.

NORTHWESTERN SALAMANDERS: This 9-inch salamander (*Ambystoma gracile*) found in the northwestern U.S. and southwestern Canada is brown.

PACIFIC MOLE SALAMANDERS: This family (Dicamptodontidae) includes the Pacific giant, Cope's giant, and Olympic salamanders. They are found only on the west coast of North America. The 11-inch Pacific giant, reddish brown with dark patches, inhabits the coastal forests from British Columbia to central California. The closely related Cope's giant differs in that it lives in water and retains its larval characteristics throughout life. The 4-inch Olympic salamander has large eyes and a bright yellow or orange belly; it prefers cool mountains bordering the ocean.

MUD PUPPIES: The North American members of this family (Proteidae) include water dogs and mud puppies (*Necturus maculosus*). Mud puppies range from southern Canada to the southern U.S. and measure 7½ to 12 inches long. They live in lakes, rivers, and streams, sometimes to great depths. Four different species of water dogs are found from North Carolina through Georgia and Missouri to the U.S. Gulf coast. Their preferred habitat varies according to species, from slow-moving muddy ditches to clear, spring-fed, sandy-bottomed streams, to rivers lined with leaf litter. They are all similar in appearance, with spade-shaped heads tapering to short, strongly flattened tails, and stout limbs. They are grayish brown, with dark brown to blue black spots.

SIRENS: These eellike amphibians (Sirenidae family) live in freshwater habitats such as streams, ponds, and muddy irrigation ditches; three species are found in the eastern and southern U.S. Sirens have feathery external gills, small, weak front legs, and no hind limbs. They range in size from 7 to 29 inches and in color from olive green to brown or blue black, depending on species.

Other Characteristics

Nocturnal hellbenders feed on fish, frogs, crayfish, water insects, snails, and other salamanders. Spotted salamanders are secretive, spending most of their lives completely underground feeding on worms and soft-bodied insects.

The very secretive northwestern salamander is one of several amphibian species with poison glands to deter predators. Because of their humid habitat, Pacific giant salamanders are active almost year-round and are sometimes seen during the day. Unlike most salamanders, Pacific giants have vocal cords and can produce sound.

Mud puppies and water dogs tend to be night feeders, preying on aquatic worms, insects, crustaceans, and small fish and their eggs. Sirens are also night hunters, feeding on mollusks, worms, and crayfish as well as on aquatic vegetation.

[NEWTS AND RELATED SALAMANDERS]

NEWTS: All North American newts, as well as fire salamanders, are classified in the same family (Salamandridae). Newts may spend almost half the year in water, while fire salamanders only return to water to breed.

The California newt is found in the far western U.S., and the eastern newt is widespread throughout eastern North America. Both have slender, long bodies with long tails that are vertically flattened for swimming. Newts are dark above with brightly colored underbellies. While still immature, but terrestrial, eastern newts are colored bright red to appear unappetizing to predators. After living on land for two to three years, these bright red salamanders re-enter the water and become permanently aquatic adults with dull green coloring. They prefer medium-sized ponds surrounded by woodlands or grasslands. When these ponds dry up, however, they will take refuge in leaf litter or rodent burrows.

AMPHIUMAS: Another family of salamanders (Amphiumidae) is made up of three species found only in the waters and swamps of the southeastern U.S. They are commonly known as congo eels because their tapered heads and long cylindrical bodies make them resemble eels; however, they have two pairs of tiny, weak limbs. They range in size from 12 to 46 inches and in color from gray to dark brown.

LUNGLESS SALAMANDERS: The largest family of salamanders in North America (Plethodontidae), these include the dusky, shovel-nosed, woodland, spring, red, mud, American brook, slender, climbing, and cave salamander genera. Coloration varies greatly from red-and-black to orange-and-yellow striped, to black with silvery white speckles. Lungless salamanders range from southern Canada to South America. Many species are centered in the southern Appalachian Mountains, where they have evolved in isolation over millions of years. These salamanders prefer habitat under stones near mountain streams, although some species live among trees, in caves, or in muddy bottomland.

Other Characteristics

Unlike most other salamanders, newts spend a good part of each year in the water. When they return to water each year, they actually go through a kind of reverse metamorphosis, the tail becoming wide and flat and the skin thin and permeable. Out of the water, the skin becomes much rougher, and the tail reverts to its vertical flattening. Newts shed their skin occasionally and can regenerate lost or damaged body parts. Most newts are nocturnal; they also hibernate under stones or bury themselves in mud for the winter. They are carnivorous, eating slugs and worms, and both North American species produce poison in their parotoid glands. California newt poison is very potent—just .00003 ounce of the poison is enough to kill 7,000 mice. The bright underbelly coloration of newts is a warning to predators of their poisonous skin secretions.

Congo eels spend most of their lives in the water. They are night hunters, feeding on invertebrates such as worms, crayfish, and insects as well as on vertebrates like fish, snakes, and frogs. Mucous glands make them extremely slippery and difficult to handle (for example, when removing them from fishing nets), and they can bite with very sharp teeth.

The distinguishing feature of lungless salamanders is that they breathe through their skin and throat. The floor of the mouth moves up and down, pumping air into the throat in much the same way as air is pumped into lungs in other salamanders. Lungless salamanders are generally nocturnal.

[TOADS AND FROGS]

Toads and frogs begin life as eggs that cannot survive out of water and hatch as larvae, called tadpoles, with gills and tails like fish. As they develop, tadpoles grow four legs, while their tails and gills slowly shrink.

Lungs eventually develop to replace the gills, at which time the toads and frogs are able to come onto land. Even so, they require constant moisture to keep their skin from drying out, and most return to water to breed.

Toads and frogs have short, bulbous bodies, muscular limbs, large heads with no necks, and large, forward-protruding eyes with fixed upper eyelids. Unlike other amphibians, their sense of hearing is well developed. They can produce a range of loud croaking sounds by vibrating air in the elastic tissue of their voice box; the sounds, amplified by vocal sacs under the chin, are used as mating, territorial, and distress calls.

Most toads and frogs feed on insects and other invertebrates, many using sticky tongues to capture and retract the prey into their mouths. Some also feed on rodents, birds, other amphibians, reptiles, and fish. Larger vertebrates, including reptiles, birds, and mammals, prey upon toads and frogs.

Some of the many species of toads and frogs found in North America include spadefoot toads, true toads, narrow-mouthed toads, true frogs (including bullfrogs, green frogs, and wood frogs), and tree frogs. General descriptions of each group follow, along with their range and habitat and a few details about other behavior.

Toads

SPADEFOOT TOADS: Members of the Pelobatidae family, these are not true toads but get their names from dark, fingernail-like plates on the insides of their hind feet. They prefer dry areas with sandy soil, and these "spades" allow them to dig burrows to escape dry weather. Eastern spadefoots are 1¾ to 3¼ inches long; the plains spadefoot, widespread in the central U.S. prairies, is 1½ to 2½ inches. They are smooth skinned with scattered bumps and, unlike true toads, vertical, catlike eye pupils.

TRUE TOADS: Several species of the Bufonidae family are native to North America, including the western toad, Woodhouse's toad, American toad, Gulf Coast toad, and marine, or giant, toad. True toads are identified by large, swollen parotoid glands above each eye that secrete toxins. Toads range in size from 2 to 5⅛ inches long, and coloration varies from brown, brick red, yellow, or green, to black with white-and-orange spots.

Depending on the species, true toad habitats include damp areas such as humid roadside ditches, as well as grassy lawns and forests. Some sub-species of the western toad have developed unique habitat adaptations.

For example, the salt toad has developed the unique ability to breed in pools with high salt concentrations. Another western toad subspecies has adapted to life at high altitudes and is found from sea level to 10,000 feet in the Rocky Mountains. The 9-inch marine or giant toad, the largest true toad species in North America, is found in the southern U.S.

Other Characteristics

True toads secrete toxins that irritate the mucous membranes of the mouth, throat, and eyes of any predator. The toxins can also cause nausea, irregular heartbeat, and death in small predators.

Because of its size, the marine, or giant, toad eats huge quantities of insects. This toad has well-developed poison glands that can squirt toxic secretions up to 3 feet. For this reason, its populations are not easily controlled by natural predators. In some locations where marine toads have been introduced as insect control devices (such as in the sugarcane fields of Australia), they have driven out the native frog and toad populations through competition for food and even by predation. In those areas, they are now considered pests, like the insects they were introduced to control.

Narrow-mouthed toads are fast burrowers and sometimes share burrows with lizards, moles, or tarantulas. They hunt at night and eat primarily ants.

Frogs

NARROW-MOUTHED FROGS: Species (Microhylidae family) native to North America include the eastern, Carolina, and Great Plains narrow-mouthed toads. They are found in the central and southeastern U.S. near ponds, moist marshes, and ditches, or in mountainous woods or fields. These small toads only reach ⅞ to 1⅝ inches and spend most of the day hidden in undergrowth. They have egg-shaped bodies, pointed snouts, and a fold of skin across the backs of their heads. They are reddish brown to dark gray or olive above with mottled coloring below, and, like spadefoot toads, have "spades" on their hind feet for digging burrows.

TRUE FROGS: Species of this family (Ranidae) include bullfrogs, green frogs, wood frogs, and leopard frogs. True frogs have slender bodies, narrow waists, and large, long, muscular hind legs for swimming and jumping. Their smooth skin is most often brown or green. They spend much of their time among damp vegetation along water and are found in the widest variety of habitats of all frog families.

The largest true frog in North America is the bullfrog. Bullfrogs can reach 8 inches long and leap up to 3 feet. They have thickset bodies, large, exposed eardrums and are dark green to black above (with dark spots) and whitish yellow underneath. Their native range was through the eastern U.S. to northern Mexico, but they have been introduced on the Pacific coast. Bullfrogs rarely venture out of water, living near ponds, marshes, and slow-moving streams.

Other members of the true frog family—the leopard frog of the U.S. and Canada; the green frog of the northeastern U.S.; and the pig, pickerel, and crawfish frogs of the southeastern states—resemble bullfrogs but are smaller. They range in size from 1⅜ to 5 inches long and from green to bronze to leopard spotted, depending on species. Green frogs tend to be found around water more often than the brown species.

The other true frog species—the wood frog, found in Canada, Alaska, and the northeastern U.S.—is the only North American frog found north of the Arctic Circle. Wood frogs are pink, tan, or dark brown with a prominent dark mask. They live in moist woodlands, sometimes far from water in the summer.

TREE FROGS: True tree frogs (Hylidae family) found in North America include the Pacific tree frog, canyon tree frog, cricket frog, Cope's gray tree frog, bird-voiced tree frog, green tree frog, northern spring peeper, and chorus frog. Although not all tree frogs actually dwell in trees, they share characteristics associated with climbing and life away from water, such as special toe joints adapted for climbing. Tree frogs range from ⅝ inch to 2⅜ inches long and may be greenish brown, gray, yellow, red, or black, depending on species. Habitats include sunny ponds or streams, trees and shrubs around permanent water, and swamps and wooded river bottoms.

Individual true tree frog species have uniquely adapted to available habitat. The Pacific tree frog ranges the arid plains of California and Oregon, up to 10,000 feet in the Sierra Nevada. The canyon tree frog has adapted to rocky environments and prefers deep canyons cut by streams and rivers, where its color blends in with the rocky surroundings.

Other Characteristics

Adult true frogs hunt mainly on land, tend to be nocturnal, and return to swamps and pools only to find mates and lay eggs. Male true frogs engage in territorial, ritualized fights in which two males rear on their hind legs and wrestle.

Bullfrogs, which get their name from their "booming" mating call, are

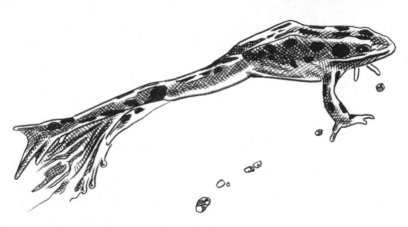

The presence of frogs indicates a healthy wetland environment.

the most voracious of all frogs, feeding on mammals, birds, fish, amphibians, and even snakes. In winter they hibernate near the water under logs and stones. Because of their large size, bullfrogs unfortunately continue to be used by humans in frog jumping contests in many parts of the U.S. They are also hunted for food in some areas.

Enemies and Defenses: Amphibians

Amphibians' natural predators include most carnivores, such as raccoons, foxes, coyotes, raptors, and snakes. Their defenses are mainly escape techniques, except that certain species—such as true toads—secrete toxins as a defense against predators. Amphibians' primary enemy, however, is humans, due to habitat destruction, especially of wetlands. Other environmental factors, such as global warming and drought, can also harm them.

How to Observe: Amphibians

Most amphibians are relatively secretive. They can most likely be observed in edge habitats near streams, ponds, marshes, and other wetland areas. During bountiful rain times, nighttime frog and toad choruses can entertain and soothe humans.

Situations and Solutions: Amphibians

Amphibians Found in Ponds, Streams, or Lakes Near Homes

WHY IT HAPPENS: Most amphibians must either live in or return to breed in ponds and other bodies of water every year.

SUGGESTIONS:

1. Do not interfere with the return of amphibians to their breeding ponds. If possible, protect their migration paths from predators and human interference such as automobiles. Amphibians are an extremely important link in the food chain because they help to control insect populations and serve as a food source for larger vertebrates such as birds, mammals, and reptiles.

2. Amphibians pose no danger to humans, although the few species that produce poison mucus should not be handled. Their secretions are not fatal to humans but can cause skin discomfort.

Encouraging Amphibians to Inhabit Your Property

WHY IT HAPPENS: By encouraging frogs, toads, and other amphibians on your property, you encourage a natural form of insect control.

SUGGESTIONS:

1. Protect timber near streams, lakes, or ponds. North-facing slopes are most productive areas for amphibians, because they tend to be cooler and moister.

2. Provide natural shelter with large flat rocks or fallen trees near or in the water and sinkholes or other depressions nearby. If these shelters do not occur naturally, use old boards or sheets of tin roofing. Also, open up nearby woodlands somewhat by felling a few trees in places to create brush piles and thick vegetative growth for shelter.

3. If there is no standing or running water on your property, consider building one or more small ponds. Ponds too small to support fish are great for frogs, toads, and salamanders. Even if they dry up in summer, they provide important spring breeding habitat.

4. It is important to let the pond "go wild" if possible. If livestock use the pond, consider fencing off a portion of the shoreline to prevent disturbance. If the pond is new or has been used by livestock, it may need more wild plants to create an appropriate habitat. Consult local wildlife agency personnel for recommendations of appropriate native plants for your area.

5. Practice good soil conservation around the pond to avoid erosion and to protect water quality. Avoid the use of pesticides and herbicides near the pond.

Large Numbers of Amphibians at One Time

WHY IT HAPPENS: When involved in their annual reproductive cycle, certain species, such as the California newt, follow their migratory paths back to their breeding grounds.

SUGGESTIONS:

1. If possible, allow the amphibians to migrate en masse. Once their breeding cycle is complete, they will disperse to individual terrain.

2. Where human development has had an impact on breeding grounds, temporary disruption of human activity may be necessary. For example, in parts of the San Francisco Bay Area, spring migration of newts requires closure of small sections of some residential streets for a day or two to allow the newts to cross to their breeding ground.

3. Rerouting amphibians that are responding to basic reproduction instinct is difficult. Humans should be willing to accept a minor and temporary interruption in their regular routine, literally, to allow nature to take its course.

Sources of Information on Wildlife Care and Control

This appendix provides addresses and phone numbers (as available) for government wildlife agencies in the United States, and selected private wildlife centers with wildlife rehabilitation permits.

The first section lists regional offices of the U.S. Fish and Wildlife Service, the states that fall within each region, and the Service's two national offices.

Then follows a state-by-state listing of state wildlife agencies (the first entry under each state) and private wildlife education and/or rehabilitation centers. The latter appear alphabetically by the name of the town where located, for example, Scottsdale, Sedona, Tucson (Arizona).

The U. S. Fish and Wildlife Service issues permits only for migratory bird rehabilitation. State agencies issue rehabilitation permits for all other animals. If you need assistance with injured or orphaned wildlife, take note of the keys that accompany each listing:

‡   Holder of U.S. Fish and Wildlife migratory bird permit
†   Holder of state wildlife rehabilitation permit
§   Permit status unknown

Other sources of such assistance are regional or unit game wardens or staff wildlife biologists employed by many states, and private individuals who hold permits to do wildlife rehabilitation. Individual rehabilitators are not included in these listings but can be contacted through state agencies, which may place an animal with a private rehabilitator if a wildlife center is not reasonably available. U.S. Fish and Wildlife Service regional offices also have information about private rehabilitators.

Also not included in these listings, but reachable through local telephone directories, are:

Humane societies
Animal shelters
SPCA branches
Veterinary hospitals and clinics
Audubon Society chapters

All of the above may provide useful information, but do not necessarily hold wildlife rehabilitation permits. Before bringing an injured or orphaned animal to any organization, make sure it has all necessary permits (or has a transfer arrangement with a nearby wildlife center, as some shelters do).

Federal and state permits must be renewed periodically, and addresses or phone numbers of government agencies may change, so all information given here should be checked against current local listings and verified in advance.

U. S. Fish and Wildlife Service

Director
U.S. Fish and Wildlife Service
1849 C Street, N.W., MIB 3012
Washington, DC 20240
(202) 208-4717

Region 1, U.S. Fish and Wildlife Service
[California, Hawaii, Idaho, Nevada, Oregon, Washington, Guam, American Samoa, CNMI]
911 N.E. 11th Avenue
Portland, OR 97232
(503) 231-6118

Region 2, U.S. Fish and Wildlife Service
[Arizona, New Mexico, Oklahoma,Texas]
500 Gold Avenue, S.W., Rm. 3018
P.O. Box 1306
Albuquerque, NM 87103
(505) 766-2321

Region 3, U.S. Fish and Wildlife Service
[Illinois, Indiana, Iowa, Michigan, Minnesota, Missouri, Ohio, Wisconsin]
Federal Building, Fort Snelling
Twin Cities, MN 55111
(612) 725-3563

Region 4, U.S. Fish and Wildlife Service
[Alabama, Arkansas, Florida, Kentucky, Louisiana, Mississippi, North Carolina, South Carolina, Tennessee]
Richard B. Russell Federal Bldg., Room 1200
75 Spring Street, S.W.
Atlanta, GA 30303
(404) 331-3588

Region 5, U.S. Fish and Wildlife Service
[Connecticut, Delaware, Maine, Maryland, Massachusetts, New Hampshire, New Jersey, New York, Pennsylvania, Virginia, Rhode Island, Vermont, West Virginia]
One Gateway Center, Suite 700
Newton Corner, MA 02158
(617) 965-5100

Region 6, U.S. Fish and Wildlife Service
[Colorado, Kansas, Montana, Nebraska, North Dakota, South Dakota, Utah, Wyoming]
P.O. Box 25486
Denver, CO 80025
(303) 236-7920

Region 7, U.S. Fish and Wildlife
Service
[Alaska]
1011 East Tudor Road
Anchorage, AK 99503
(907) 869-3542

Region 8, U.S. Fish and Wildlife
Service
[Research]
1849 C Street, N.W. ARLSQ 725
Washington, DC 20240
(202) 208-6394

State Wildlife Agencies and Local Wildlife Centers

ALABAMA

Department of Conservation and
Natural Resources
Division of Game and Fish
Wildlife Section
64 North Union Street
Montgomery, AL 36130
(205) 242-3465

‡ Solon Dixon Forestry Education
Center
Rt. 7, Box 131
Andalusia, AL 36420

‡† Southeastern Raptor Rehabilitation
Center
Auburn University Veterinary
School
Auburn, AL 36849

† Alabama Wildlife Rescue Service
2107 Marlboro Avenue
Birmingham, AL 35226

‡† Environmental Studies Center
P.O. Box 1327
Mobile, AL 36633

ALASKA

State of Alaska
Department of Fish and Game
Box 3-2000
Juneau, AK 99802-2000
(907) 465-4190

‡ Fairbanks Mini Zoo
1853 Bridgewater Drive
Fairbanks, AK 99709

‡ Juneau Raptor Rehabilitation
Association
7705 Glacier Highway
Juneau, AK 99801

‡ Swan Lake Aviaries
P.O. Box 55027
North Pole, AK 99705

ARIZONA

Arizona Game and Fish Department
2221 West Greenway Road
Phoenix, AZ 85023
(602) 942-3000

‡ Sonora Wildlife Rehabilitation
Center
1601 Placita Montuoso
Oro Valley, AZ 85704

‡† Adobe Mountain Wildlife Center
2222 West Greenway Road
Phoenix, AZ 85023

‡ Liberty Wildlife Rehabilitation
Foundation
11825 N. 70th Street
Scottsdale, AZ 85254

‡ The Icarus Facility
P.O. Box 961
Sedona, AZ 86326

‡ Arizona–Sonora Desert Museum
2021 N. Kinney Road
Tucson, AZ 85743

‡ Tucson Wildlife Rehabilitation
Council
3572 E. River Road
Tucson, AZ 85718

‡ Southern Arizona Raptor
   Rehabiliation
   3568 Saturn Drive
   Yuma, AZ 85364

ARKANSAS

Arkansas Game and Fish
   Commission
Wildlife Management Department
2 Natural Resources Drive
Little Rock, AR 72205
(501) 873-4651

‡† Little Rock Zoological Garden
   1 Jonesboro Drive
   Little Rock, AR 72205

CALIFORNIA

State of California, The Resources
   Agency
Department of Fish and Game
1416 Ninth Street
P.O. Box 944209
Sacramento, CA 94244-2090
(916) 653-7664

† Project Wildlife
   764 Glen Oaks
   Alpine, CA 92001

‡† Shasta Wildlife Rescue
   P.O. Box 1173
   Anderson, CA 96007

† Humboldt Wildlife Care Center
   P.O. Box 4141
   Arcata, CA 95521

‡† Fort Roosevelt Science Center
   P.O. Box 164
   Armona, CA 93202

‡† International Bird Rescue Center
   699 Potter Street
   Berkeley, CA 94710

‡ Red-Tail Research Foundation, Inc.
   P.O. Box 2486
   Big Bear City, CA 92314

‡ Big Bear Valley Recreation and Park
   P.O. Box 2832
   Big Bear Lake, CA 92315

‡† Burney Falls Wildlife Rescue
   P.O. Box 29
   Burney, CA 96013

‡† Bidwell Wildlife Rehabilitation
   Center
   P.O. Box 4005
   Chico, CA 95927

† Davis Wildlife Care Association
   P.O. Box 676
   Davis, CA 95616

‡† U.C. Davis Raptor Center
   University of California, Davis
   Davis, CA 95616

‡ Yolo Wildlife Rescue
   P.O. Box 676
   Davis, CA 95617

† Trinity Wildlife Center
   P.O. Box 351
   Douglas City, CA 96024

‡† Wildlife Center
   1266 Clarke Drive
   El Cajon, CA 92021

‡† Orange County Bird of Prey Center
   23352 El Perro Street
   El Toro, CA 92630

† Friends of Wildlife Rescue and
   Rehab Center
   1724 Oakhill
   Escondido, CA 92027

‡ North County Rehabilitation
   2892 Cordrey Drive
   Escondido, CA 92025

‡† Wilderness Research Institute
   (WRI)
   Wildlife Rescue Center
   9409 North Highway 3
   Fort Jones, CA 96032

† Fresno Wildlife Rescue and Rehab
   P.O. Box 9032
   Fresno, CA 93790

† Wild Bird Rehab Center
408 Daytona Drive
Goleta, CA 93117

† Sulphur Creek Nature Center
1801 D Street
Hayward, CA 94541

‡ Hayward Area Parks and Recreation
1099 E Street
Hayward, CA 94541

† Wildlife Rehabilitation Center
5285 W. Lake Boulevard
Homewood, CA 95718

‡ Amador Wildlife Care, Inc.
P.O. Box 362
Jackson, CA 95642

‡† Wildlife Center for Disease and
Toxin Investigation
P.O. Box 670
Kenwood, CA 95452

† Wildlife Fawn Rescue
2609 Bristol Road
Kenwood, CA 95452

‡ Pacific Wildlife Project
25061 Adelanto Drive
Laguna Niguel, CA 92677

‡ Kern Valley Wildlife Rescue
P.O. Box 2322
Lake Isabella, CA 93240

‡ California Wildlife Institute
3580 Garden Bar Road
Lincoln, CA 95648

† Lake County Wildlife Rehab and
Release
P.O. Box 1770
Lower Lake, CA 95457

† San Joaquin County Zoo Society
11793 Mickey Grove Road
Lodi, CA 95240

‡† Wildlife on Wheels
4575 Northridge Drive
Los Angeles, CA 90043

‡† Feather River Wildlife Care
P.O. Box 1964
Marysville, CA 95901

† Mendocino Woodlands Outdoor
Education Center
P.O. Box 267
Mendocino, CA 95460

‡† San Joaquin Raptor Rescue Center
P.O. Box 778
Merced, CA 95341

‡† Stanislaus Wildlife Care Center
P.O. Box 1201
Modesto, CA 95353

† Moorpark College
7075 Campus Park
Moorpark, CA 93201

‡† California Conservation Corps
P.O. Box 645
Montague, CA 96064

‡† Wildlife Education and
Rehabilitation Center (WERC)
P.O. Box 1105
Morgan Hill, CA 95038

‡ Placerita Canyon Nature Center
19152 Placerita Canyon Road
Newhall, CA 91321

‡† The Living Desert
47–900 Portola
Palm Desert, CA 92260

‡† Wildlife Rescue, Inc.
4000 Middlefield Road
Palo Alto, CA 94303

† South Bay Wildlife Rehab
26363 Silver Spur
Palos Verdes Estates, CA 90274

† Sierra Wildlife Rescue
P.O. Box 2127
Placerville, CA 95667

† Plumas County Wildlife Care
Center
Feather River College
Quincy, CA 95971

† Fund for Animals
18740 Highland Valley Road
Ramona, CA 92065

† Helen Woodward Animal Center
6461 El Apajo Road
Rancho Sante Fe, CA 92067

‡† Sacramento Science Center
3615 Auburn Boulevard
Sacramento, CA 95821

‡† Sacramento Wildlife Care
Association
P.O. Box 60982
Sacramento, CA 95860

‡† Project Wildlife
P.O. Box 80696
San Diego, CA 92138

‡ San Diego Zoological Society
P.O. Box 551
San Diego, CA 92112

‡ Sea World California
1720 South Shores Road
San Diego, CA 92109

‡ San Dimas Nature Center
1628 N. Sycamore Canyon Road
San Dimas, CA 91773

‡† Wild Wings of California
1837 Fernridge Drive
San Dimas, CA 91773

‡† Wildlife Waystation
14831 Little Tujunga Canyon Road
San Fernando, CA 91342

‡† Injured and Orphan Wildlife
P.O. Box 6793
San Jose, CA 95150

† Central Coast Rehabilitation Guild
P.O. Box 12437
San Luis Obispo, CA 93403

‡ Pacific Wildlife Care
P.O. Box 3257
San Luis Obispo, CA 93403

‡† California Center for Wildlife
76 Albert Park Lane
P.O. Box 150957
San Rafael, CA 94915

‡ Santa Ana Zoo
1801 East Chestnut Avenue
Santa Ana, CA 92701

‡† Santa Barbara Wildlife Care
1616 Franchesci Road
P.O. Box 6594
Santa Barbara, CA 93160

‡ Santa Barbara Zoological Gardens
500 Ninos Drive
Santa Barbara, CA 93103

† Ventura–Ojai Wildbird Care
233 W. Valerio
Santa Barbara, CA 93101

‡† Native Animal Rescue of Santa
Cruz
2200 Seventh Avenue
Santa Cruz, CA 95062

‡† Bird Rescue Center
P.O. Box 475
Santa Rosa, CA 95402

‡† Sonoma County Wildlife Rescue
P.O. Box 9360
Santa Rosa, CA 95406

‡ Marine Mammal Center
Marin Headlands
Golden Gate Nat'l. Rec. Area
Sausalito, CA 94965

† Fournier Ranch Wildlife Care
P.O. Box 242
Sierra City, CA 95125

‡ Raptor Rehab and Release Center
791 Wishard Avenue
Simi Valley, CA 93065

‡† Lake Tahoe Wildlife Care Center
1485 Cherry Hills Circle
South Lake Tahoe, CA 96158

† Scicon
P.O. Box 339
Springville, CA 93265

† Animals for Education
36760 San Creek Road
Squaw Valley, CA 93975

‡† Five Mile Creek Raptor Center
P.O. Box 99098
Stockton, CA 95209

† Wildbird Care and Rehab
P.O. Box 1336
Studio City, CA 91614

‡† Suisun Marsh Natural History
Association
1171 Kellogg Street
Suisun, CA 94585

‡† Critter Care Wildlife Rescue Team
92 Oak Knoll Road
Ukiah, CA 95482

‡ Bob Farner's Wildlife Rescue
P.O. Box 1522
Valley Center, CA 92082

† Ventura Wildlife Rescue
2009 Evans Avenue
Ventura, CA 93001

† Wildlife Rescue and Education
Center
1286 Oaknoll Drive
Vista, CA 90284

‡† The Lindsay Museum
1901 1st Avenue
Walnut Creek, CA 94596–2540

‡† Willits Wildlife Rehab Team
P.O. Box 44
Willits, CA 95490

COLORADO

State of Colorado Department of
Natural Resources
Division of Wildlife
6080 Broadway
Denver, CO 80216–1000
(303) 297-1192

‡ Aspen Center for Environmental
Studies
P.O. Box 8777, Hallam Lake
Aspen, CO 81611

‡† Denver Zoological Gardens
City Park
Denver, CO 80205

‡† Rocky Mountain Raptor Program
300 W. Drake
Fort Collins, CO 80523

‡† Raptor Center of Pueblo
5200 West 11th Street
Pueblo, CO 81003

‡ Animals Two by Two
P.O. Box 832
Silt, CO 81652

CONNECTICUT

State of Connecticut
Department of Environmental
Protection
Wildlife Division
165 Capitol Avenue
Hartford, CT 06106
(203) 566-4683

‡† Ansonia Nature and Recreation
Center
10 Deerfield Lane
Ansonia, CT 06041

‡ Beardsley Zoological Gardens
1875 Noble Avenue
Bridgeport, CT 06610

† Bristol Regional Environmental
Center
211 Goodwin Street
Bristol, CT 06011

† Roaring Brook Nature Center
70 Gracey Road
Canton, CT 06019

† The Nature Connection
5 Carter Hill Road
Clinton, CT 06413

† North American Wildlife
Association
11 Mountain View Road
East Lyme, CT 06333

‡† Hungerford Outdoor Education
Center
191 Farmington Avenue
Kensington, CT 06037

‡ Lutz Children's Museum
247 South Main Street
Manchester, CT 06040

‡† The Nature Connection, Inc.
P.O. Box 1125
Madison, CT 06443

‡ Pequotsepos Nature Center
Pequotsepos Road, P.O. Box 122
Mystic, CT 06355

‡ Oasis Wildlife Rehabilitation Unit
78 Skipper Street
New Britain, CT 06053

‡ New Canaan Nature Center
144 Oenoke Ridge
New Canaan, CT 06840

‡ West Rock Nature Center
P.O. Box 2969
New Haven, CT 06515

† Hummelhaus Rehabilitation Center
41 Ledge Road
Plainville, CT 06062

† Rehabilitation Center, Inc.
RFD 6, Box 44
Preston, CT 06365

‡ Wildlife Umbrella, Inc.
Nettleton Hollow
Washington, CT 06793

‡† The Nature Center for
Environmental Activities
P.O. Box 165, 10 Woodside Lane
Westport, CT 06881

‡ Flanders Nature Center, Inc.
Flanders Road
Woodbury, CT 06798

† Twinbrook Wildlife Rehabilitation
Center
78 Sanford Road
Woodbury, CT 06798

DISTRICT OF COLUMBIA

‡ National Zoological Park
Washington, DC 20008

DELAWARE

State of Delaware
Division of Fish and Wildlife
89 Kings Highway
P.O. Box 1401
Dover, DE 19903
(302) 739-5297

‡ Delaware Nature Education Society
P.O. Box 700
Hockessin, DE 19707

‡ Tri-State Bird Rescue and Research
Center
110 Old Possum Hollow Road
Newark, DE 19711
(listed as having Maryland permit)

FLORIDA

State of Florida
Game and Fresh Water Fish
Commission
Farris Bryant Building
Tallahassee, FL 32299–1600
(904) 488-4676

† Wildlife, Inc.
P.O. Box 1418
Anna Maria, FL 34216

† Environmental Learning Laboratory
School District of Desoto County
530 La Solona Avenue
Arcadia, FL 33821

† Wildlife Rescue and Rehabilitation
P.O. Box 13
Bell, FL 32619

† Big Bend Wildlife Sanctuary, Inc.
P.O. Box 367
Blounstown, FL 32424

† Friends of Wildlife
P.O. Box 958
Boca Grande, FL 33921

† Pelican Perch
2705 Riverview Boulevard W.
Bradenton, FL 34205

† Wildife Rescue Service of Florida,
Inc.
P.O. Box 10475
Bradenton, FL 34282

† Sparehawk Wildlife Rehabilitation
Center
15043 Eckerley Drive
Brooksville, FL 34614

‡† Cedar Key Nature Circle
P.O. Box 401
Cedar Key, FL 32625

‡ Florida Cypress Gardens, Inc.
P.O. Box 1
Cypress Gardens, FL 33884

† Amber Lake Wildlife Refuge and
Rehabilitation Center
297 Artists Avenue
Englewood, FL 34223

† Everglades Aviaries, Inc.
2201 North Dixie Highway
Ft. Lauderdale, FL 33305

† Nature Center of Lee County
Junior Museum and Planetarium
P.O. Box 06023
Fort Myers, FL 33906

† Gulfarium
1010 Miracle Strip Parkway
Fort Walton, FL 32548

† Wildlife Rehabilitation Center
1310 N. Lake Reedy Boulevard
Frostproof, FL 33843

‡† Sante Fe Community College
3000 NW 83rd Street
Gainesville, FL 32602

† University of Florida
College of Veterinary Medicine
Box J–125
Health Science Center
Gainesville, FL 32610

† Seabird Rescue League of Florida
345 Martin Avenue
Greenacres, FL 33463

† B and J's Critter Haven
2733 Quail's Nest
Green Cove Springs, FL 32043

† Big Bird Rehabilitation Center, Inc.
3730 East 5th Avenue
Hialeah, FL 33013

† Suncoast Seabird Sanctuary, Inc.
18328 Gulf Boulevard
Indian Shores, FL 34635

‡ B.E.A.K.S., Inc.
12084 Houston Avenue
Jacksonville, FL 32226

‡† Jacksonville Zoological Park
8605 Zoo Road
Jacksonville, FL 32218

† Genesis Zoological Center
P.O. Box 1992
Kissimmee, FL 34742

† Suwannee Valley Zoo
Route 1, Box 140–A
Lake City, FL 32055

† Central Florida Zoological Park
P.O. Box 309
Lake Monroe, FL 32747

† Wildwood Acres Raptor
Rehabilitation Center
240 E. Hornbeam Drive
Longwood, FL 32779

† Florida Wildlife Sanctuary and
Hospital
2600 Otter Creek Lane
Melbourne, FL 32940

† Old Cutler Wildlife Rehabilitation Center
22025 Southwest 87 Avenue
Miami, FL 33190

† Operation Wildlife Survival
13001 Southwest 63 Court
Miami, FL 33156

† Pelican Harbor Seabird Station
1275 Northeast 79th Street Causeway
Miami, FL 33138

‡† The Wildlife Rehabilitation and Environmental Education Center, Inc.
6411 Southwest 62 Terrace
P.O. Box 432763
Miami, FL 33143

‡† The Conservancy Wildlife Clinic
1450 Merrihue Drive
Naples, FL 33942

‡† Southwest Florida Native Wildlife Ark
15391 Huffmaster Road
North Fort Myers, FL 33917

† Foundation for Environmental Awareness
P.O. Box 723
Oklawaha, FL 32179

† Back to Nature Wildlife Refuge
621 Capehart Drive
Orlando, FL 32822

† Everglades Wildlife Sanctuary and Rehabilitation Center, Inc.
1121 Northwest 98th Terrace
Pembroke Pines, FL 33024

† Wildlife Rescue and Sanctuary
105 North S Street
Pensacola, FL 32505

† The Aviary at Flamingo Gardens
1260 Southwest 47 Avenue
Plantation, FL 33317

† Wildlife Care Center
2317 Southeast 14th Street
Pompano Beach, FL 33062

† Wildlife Rehabilitation Center
840 Samms Avenue
Port Orange, FL 32119

‡† Peace River Wildlife Center, Inc.
P.O. Box 512209
Punta Gorda, FL 33950

‡† Care and Rehabilitation of Wildlife
P.O. Box 150
Sanibel, FL 33957

† Pelican Man's Bird Sanctuary
1608 City Island Road
Sarasota, FL 34236

† Save the Birds Society, Inc.
3833 East 27 Parkway
Sarasota, FL 33580

† St. John's Wildlife Care, Inc.
P.O. Box 860153
St. Augustine, FL 32086

† Wild Bird Rehabilitation
4387 Porpoise Drive S.
St. Petersburg, FL 33705

† Wrede's Wildlife Rehabiliation Center, Inc.
4900 Wilderness Trail
Sebring, FL 33872

† Suwannee Rehabilitation Center
P.O. Box 365
Suwannee, FL 32692

† Goose Creek Wildlife Sanctuary, Inc.
3337 Homestead Road
Tallahassee, FL 32308

‡† St. Francis Wildlife Association
P.O. Drawer 2248
Tallahassee, FL 32316

‡† Tallahassee Museum of History
3945 Museum Drive
Tallahassee, FL 32310

† Martin's Aviaries and Rehabilitation
Center
4311 South Trask Street
Tampa, FL 33611

† Wildlife Rescue, Inc.
127 West Hiawatha Street
Tampa, FL 33604

† Florida Keys Wild Bird
Rehabilitation Center
93600 Overseas Highway
Taverniei, FL 33070

Pinellas Seabird Rehabilitation
Center
840 3rd Avenue S
Tierra Verde, FL 33715

† Woodland Hills Sanctuary
2955 Knox McCrae Road
Titusville, FL 32780

† All Creatures Wildlife Sanctuary,
Inc.
Route 2, Box 80
Trenton, FL 32693

† Bambi Bird and Wildlife Sanctuary
10948 Acme Road
West Palm Beach, FL 33414

† Dreher Park Zoo
1301 Summit Boulevard
West Palm Beach, FL 33405

† Ocean Impact Foundation
1962 South Congress Avenue
West Palm Beach, FL 33406

‡ Zoological Society of the Palm
1301 Summit Boulevard
West Palm Beach, FL 33405

GEORGIA

State of Georgia Department of
Natural Resources
Game and Fish Division
Game Management Section
Floyd Towers East, Suite 1362
205 Butler Street, SE
Atlanta, GA 30334
(404) 656-3523

‡ Bear Hollow Wildlife Trail
Gran Ellen Drive
Athens, GA 30606

‡ Wildlife Line
Route 8, Univeter Road
Canton, GA 30114

‡ Rock Eagle 4-H Center
350 Rock Eagle Road, NW
Eatonton, GA 31204

‡ Animal Disease Prevention
Building S–500
Fort Gordon, GA 30905

‡ Unicoi State Park
P.O. Box 1029
Helen, GA 30545

‡ Dauset Trails Nature Center
Route 5, Box 78, Mt. Vernon Road
Jackson, GA 30233

‡ Yellow River Wildlife Game Ranch
4525 Highway 78
Lilburn, GA 30247

‡ W. H. Reynolds Memorial Nature
Preserve
5665 Reynolds Road
Morrow, GA 30260

‡ Ida Cason Calloway Foundation
Pine Mountain, GA 31822

‡ Chattahoochee Nature Center
9135 Willeo Road
Roswell, GA 30075

‡ Wildlife Trails
P.O. Box 778
Stone Mountain, GA 30086

HAWAII

State of Hawaii
Department of Land and Natural
Resources
Division of Forestry and Wildlife
1151 Punchbowl Street
Honolulu, HI 96813
(808) 587-0166

‡ The East Maui Animal Refuge
1069 Kaupakalua Road
Haiku, HI 96708

† Waimea Falls Park
59–864 Kamehameha Highway
Haleiwa, HI 96712

‡ Panaewa Rainforest Zoo
25 Aupuni Street
Hilo, HI 96720

‡† Hilton Hawaiian Village
2005 Kalia Road
Honolulu, HI 96815

‡† Paradise Park, Inc.
3737 Manoa Road
Honolulu, HI 96822

‡ Hawaii Volcanoes National Park
P.O. Box 52
Volcanoes, HI 96718

‡ Hart and Tagami Zoological Park
47–754 Lamaula Road
Kaneohe, HI 96744

IDAHO

State of Idaho
Department of Fish and Game
600 S. Walnut Street
P.O. Box 25
Boise, ID 83707–0025
(208) 334-3700

† The Raptor Rehabilitation Center
P.O. Box 583
Glenns Ferry, ID 83623

‡† Snowdon Wildlife Sanctuary
P.O. Box 1731
McCall, ID 83638

ILLINOIS

State of Illinois
Deparment of Conservation
Wildlife Division
524 S. Second Street
Springfield, IL 62701–1787
(217) 782-6302

INDIANA

State of Indiana
Division of Fish and Wildlife
402 W. Washington, Room W–273
Indianapolis, IN 46204
(317) 232-4080

IOWA

State of Iowa
Department of Natural Resources
Wallace State Office Building
Des Moines, IA 50319–0034
(515) 281-5145

† Iowa State University
Veterinary College
Ames, IA 50011

† Morning Star Farm
RR 1
Brighton, IA 52540

† Buchanan Conservation Building
1874 125th Street
Hazelton, IA 50641

† MacBride Raptor Center
E–216 Field House
University of Iowa
Iowa City, IA 52242

† Ellsworth Community College
1100 College Avenue
Iowa Falls, IA 50126

KANSAS

State of Kansas
Department of Wildlife and Parks
Operations Office
RR 2, Box 54A
Pratt, KS 67124–9599
(316) 672-5911

† Chaplin Nature Center
RR 1, Box 216
Arkansas City, KS 67005

† Prairie Raptor Project
12660 West Armstrong Road
Brookville, KS 67425

† El Dorado Wildlife Rehabilitation
Center
640 North High
El Dorado, KS 67042

† Cimarron National Grasslands
USDA Forest Service
P.O. Box J, 242 Highway 56 East
Elkhart, KS 67950

‡ Emporia Park and Zoo
Box 928
Emporia, KS 66801

‡ Lee Richardson Zoo
P.O. Box 499
Garden City, KS 67846

‡† Brit Spaugh Park and Zoo
P.O. Box 215
Great Bend, KS 67530

‡† Dillon Nature Center
3002 East 30th
Hutchinson, KS 67502

‡† Hutchinson Zoo
P.O. Box 1567
Hutchinson, KS 67504

‡ Wildcare
University of Kansas
P.O. Box 901
Lawrence, KS 66044

† Operation Wildlife, Inc.
23375 Guthrie
Linwood, KS 66052

‡† Project Release
Kansas State University
College of Veterinary Medicine
Box 645
Manhattan, KS 66502

‡ Pittsburg State University
Biology Department
Pittsburg, KS 66762

† Salina Parks and Recreation
300 West Ash
Salina, KS 67401

‡† Deanna Rose Children's Farmstead
13800 Switzer
Stanley, KS 66221

‡† Kansas Wildlife Exhibit
455 N. Main, 11th Floor
Wichita, KS 67202

‡ Sedgwick County Zoo
5555 Zoo Boulevard
Wichita, KS 67212

KENTUCKY

State of Kentucky
Department of Fish and Wildlife
Resources
Frankfort, KY 40601
(502) 564-3400

† Oldham Civic Center and Nature
Preserve, Inc.
12501 Harmony Landing
P.O. Box 160
Goshen, KY 40026

† Louisville Zoological Garden
1100 Treveilian Way
P.O. Box 3725OK
Louisville, KY 40233

† Raptor Rehabilitators
P.O. Box 18002
Louisville, KY 40218

† Daviess County High School
Biology Department
4255 New Hartford Road
Owensboro, KY 42303

‡ Lone Oak Animal Clinic
3014 Oregon Street
Paducah, KY 42001

LOUISIANA

Department of Wildlife and
Fisheries
Louisiana Natural Heritage Program
P.O. Box 98000
Baton Rouge, LA 70898–9000
(504) 765-2800

† LSU Raptor and Wildlife
  Rehabilitation Unit
  School of Veterinary Medicine
  South Stadium Drive
  Baton Rouge, LA 70803

† Clearwater Wildlife Sanctuary
  24 Holly Drive
  Covington, LA 70433

† Wildlife In Distress
  1717 Eraste Landry Road,
  Lot A-124
  Lafayette, LA 70506

‡† Helping Hands, Inc.
  P.O. Box 7066
  Metairie, LA 70010

‡† Louisiana Purchase Gardens and
  Zoo
  P.O. Box 123
  Monroe, LA 71210

‡† Louisiana Nature and Science
  Center
  P.O. Box 870610
  New Orleans, LA 70187

† A Little Touch of Nature
  59363 Thompson Road
  Slidell, LA 70460

† Westlake Bird Sanctuary and
  Rehabilitation Center
  2110 Nichols Road
  Westlake, LA 70669

MAINE

Maine Fish and Wildlife
  Department
  284 State Street, Station 41
  Augusta, ME 04333
  (207) 289-2871

† Maine National Wildlife Refuge
  (MNWR)
  P.O. Box 1077
  Calais, ME 04694

‡† Stanwood Wildlife Sanctuary
  Box 485, Route 3
  Ellsworth, ME 04605

‡ West Quoddy Biological Research
  P.O. Box 9
  Lubec, ME 04652

† Petit Mann National Wildlife
  Refuge
  P.O. Box 279
  Millbridge, ME 04658

MARYLAND

State of Maryland
  Department of Natural Resources
  Wildlife Division
  Tawes State Office Building
  580 Taylor Avenue
  Annapolis, MD 21401
  (410) 974-3195

† Chesapeake Bird and Wildlife
  Sanctuary
  17308 Queen Anne Bridge Road
  Bowie, MD 20716

† Bay Area Rehab Center
  Centreville, MD 21617
  (410) 758-3648

‡ The Wildfowl Trust of North
  America
  Perry Corner Road, P.O. Box 519
  Grasonville, MD 21638

‡† Defenders of Animal Rights, Inc.
  14412 Old York Road
  Phoenix, MD 21131

‡ Battle Creek Cypress Swamp
  c/o Courthouse
  Prince Frederick, MD 20678

‡† Plumpton Park Zoo
  1416 Telegraph Road
  Rising Sun, MD 21911

‡ Salisbury Zoological Park
  750 S. Park Drive, P.O. Box 3163
  Salisbury, MD 21801

‡ Meadowside Nature Center
  8787 Georgia Avenue
  Silver Spring, MD 20855

MASSACHUSETTS

State of Massachusetts
Division of Fisheries and Wildlife
Leverett Saltonstall Building,
Government Center
100 Cambridge Street
Boston, MA 02202
(617) 727-3151

† Animal Rescue League of Boston
P.O. Box 265, 10 Chandler Street
Boston, MA 02117

† Museum of Science
Live Animal Center, Science Park
Boston, MA 02114

‡ Cape Cod Museum of Natural
History
Drawer R
Brewster, MA 02631

† Burlington Science Research Center
123 Cambridge Street
Burlington, MA 01803

†† Capen Hill Nature Sanctuary
P.O. Box 218, Capen Road
Charlton City, MA 01508

†† New England Wildlife Center, Inc.
19 Fort Hill Street
Hingham, MA 02043

†† New England Alive, Inc.
163 High Street, Route 1A
Ipswich, MA 01938

† Drumlin Farm Wildlife Care Center
South Great Road
Lincoln, MA 01773

† Blue Hills–Trailside Museum
1904 Canton Avenue
Milton, MA 02186

† Needham Science Center, Newman
Building
1155 Central Avenue
Needham, MA 02192

‡ Tufts University Wildlife Clinic
200 Westboro Road
North Grafton, MA 01536

‡ South Shore Natural Science Center
Jacobs Lane, P.O. Box 429
Norwell, MA 02061

† Felix Neck Wildlife Sanctuary
Box 1055
Oak Bluffs, MA 02557

MICHIGAN

State of Michigan
Department of Natural Resources
Wildlife Division
P.O. Box 30028
Lansing, MI 48909-7258
(517) 373-1263

§ Wildlife Rescue
P.O. Box 1070
Big Rapids, MI 49307

§ Cedar Wildlife Rescue
2515 Gatzke Road
P.O. Box 201
Cedar, MI 49621

§ Belle Isle Nature Center
Belle Isle Park
Detroit, MI 48207

§ Drayton Plains Nature Center, Inc.
2125 Denby Drive
Drayton Plains, MI 48287

§ Critter Alley Wildlife Care Center
4340 W. St. Joe Highway
Grand Ledge, MI 48837

§ Howell Nature Center
1005 Triangle Lake Road
Howell, MI 48843

§ Kalamazoo Nature Center
7000 North Westnedge
Kalamazoo, MI 49004

§ Ann Arbor Wildlife Relocation
8350 Willow Road
Milan, MI 48160

MINNESOTA

State of Minnesota Department of
Natural Resources
500 Lafayette Road
St. Paul, MN 55155-4001
(612) 296-6157

† Carpenter Nature Center
12805 St. Croix Trail
Hastings, MN 55033

† The Wildlife Clinic
College of Veterinary Medicine
University of Minnesota
St. Paul, MN 55108

† The Raptor Center
College of Veterinary Medicine
University of Minnesota
1920 Fitch Avenue
St. Paul, MN 55108

MISSISSIPPI

State of Mississippi
Department of Wildlife, Fisheries
and Parks
P.O. Box 451
Jackson, MS 39205-0451
(601) 362-9212

†† Jackson Zoological Park
2918 W. Capitol Street
Jackson, MS 39209

† Wild American Rehabilitation of
Mississippi
522 Robinhood Road
Jackson, MS 39206

† Wildlife Rescue and Rehabilitation,
Inc.
P.O. Box 4267
Jackson, MS 39296

† Wildlife Rehabilitation and Nature
Preservation Society
P.O. Box 209
Long Beach, MS 39560

† Wildlife Support Group
College of Veterinary Medicine
Mississippi State University
Drawer V
Mississippi State, MS 39762

† Wildlife Rehabilitation Nature
Center, Inc.
The Nature Center
141 Kaiser Lake Road
Natchez, MS 39120

MISSOURI

Missouri Department of
Conservation
P.O. Box 180
Jefferson City, MO 65102-0180
(314) 751-4115

† The Lone Wolf
1128 New Ballwin Road
Ballwin, MO 63021

† Wildlife Assistance, Inc.
P.O. Box 761
Eureka, MO 63025

† World Bird Sanctuary
P.O. Box 193
Eureka, MO 63025

† Solomon's Sanctuary
17904 Dakota Drive
Independence, MO 64056

† Lakeside Nature Center
5600 East Gregory Swope Park
Kansas City, MO 64132

† Missouri Wildlife Rescue Center
147 Grand Avenue
Kirkwood, MO 63122

† Dickerson Park Zoo
3043 North Fort
Springfield, MO 65803

MONTANA

Montana Department of Fish,
Wildlife and Parks
Wildlife Division
1420 E. Sixth Avenue
Helena, MT 59620
(406) 444-2535

‡ Copper Creek Conserve
307 W. 2nd, No. 28
Libby, MT 59923

NEBRASKA

Nebraska Game and Parks
Commission
P.O. Box 30370
Lincoln, NE 68503–0370
(402) 471-0641

† Raptor Rehabilitation Center
Route 13
Lincoln, NE 68527

‡† Wildlife Rescue Team, Inc.
P.O. Box 80127
Lincoln, NE 68501

‡ Henry Doorly Zoo
Riverview Park
Omaha, NE 68107

‡ Riverside Zoo
1600 S. Beltline Highway W.
Scottsbluff, NE 69361

NEVADA

Nevada Department of Wildlife
P.O. Box 10678
Reno, NV 89520–0022
(702) 688-1500

‡† Wild Animal Infirmary for Nevada
2920 Eagle Street
Carson City, NV 89701

NEW HAMPSHIRE

New Hampshire Fish and Game
2 Hazen Drive
Concord, NH 03301
(603) 271-3421

‡ Wings of the Dawn
P.O. Box 53
Henniker, NH 03242

‡ Science Center of New Hampshire
P.O. Box 173, Route 113
Holderness, NH 03245

NEW JERSEY

State of New Jersey
Department of Environmental
Protection
Division of Fish, Game and Wildlife
CN 400
Trenton, NJ 08625
(609) 292-8642

† Six Flags Great Adventure
P.O. Box 120
Jackson, NJ 08527

† Monmouth County Park System
Newman Springs Road
Lincroft, NJ 07738

‡ Avian Rehabilitation Center
P.O. Box 323
Marmora, NJ 08223

† Cedar Run Wildlife Refuge
Cedar Run Lake
2 Sawmill Road
Medford, NJ 08055

‡ The Raptor Trust
1390 White Bridge Road
Millington, NJ 07946

† The Morris Museum
6 Normandy Heights Road
Morristown, NJ 07960

‡† JoAnn Balliet/Wounded Knee
Wildlife Refuge
8 Eldorado Drive
Tabernacle, NJ 08088

‡ James A. McFaul Environmental
Center
Crescent Avenue
Wyckoff, NJ 07481

NEW MEXICO

New Mexico Department of Game
and Fish
Villagra Building
Sante Fe, NM 87503
(505) 827-7920

‡† Wildlife Rescue, Inc. of New
Mexico
P.O. Box 13222
Albuquerque, NM 87192

‡ Hillcrest Park Zoo
P.O. Box 760
Clovis, NM 88101

‡† Wildlife Center, Inc.
P.O. Box 246
Espanola, NM 87532

‡ Gila Wildlife Rescue
301 F Street
Silver City, NM 88061

NEW YORK

New York State
Department of Environmental
Conservation
Albany, NY 12233–4752
(518) 474-2121

† Forest Wildlife Sanctuary, Inc.
11380 Cary Road
Alden, NY 14004

† Tri-County Wildife Rehab and
Rescue
3691 Jillson Road
Attica, NY 14011

† Trailside Museum
Bear Mountain State Park
Bear Mountain, NY 10911

† Rainbow's End
RFD 6, Foggintown Road
Brewster, NY 10509

† Clearbrook Wildlife Rehabilitation
Center
HCR, Box 327
Cairo, NY 12413

† Wildlife Rehabilitation and
Educational Network
36 E. Wiggand Drive
Glenmont, NY 12077

† Volunteers for Wildlife, Inc.
Caumsett State Park
7 Lloyde Road
Huntington, NY 11743

‡ Seatuck Research Program, Cornell
University
Box 31
Islip, NY 11751

† Greencove Wildlife Rescue
RR 1, Box 1388
Lake George, NY 12845

† Kismet Wildlife Center
R.D. 1
Turin Road, Box 69
Lee Center, NY 13363

† Westchester Wildlife, Inc.
Arcady Road
Ossining, NY 10562

† Hidden Acres Wildlife
Rehabilitation Center
RD 5, Stoney Robby Road
Oswego, NY 13126

‡ Theodore Roosevelt Sanctuary, Inc.
134 Cove Road
Oyster Bay, NY 11771

† Pace University Environmental
Center
861 Bedford Road
Pleasantville, NY 10570

† Hudson Valley Raptor Center
RR 2, Box 338, Stonehouse Road
Rhinebeck, NY 12572

‡† Rye Nature Center
873 Boston Post Road
Rye, NY 10580

‡† Greenburgh Nature Center
Dromore Road
Scarsdale, NY 10583

‡ Lifeline for Wildlife
130 Blanchard Road
Stony Point, NY 10980

‡ Bide-A-Wee Home Association
118 Old Country Road
Westhampton, NY 11977

† Wildhaven Rehab Center
RD 2, Box 171, South Hill Road
Wellsville, NY 14895

NORTH CAROLINA

North Carolina Wildlife Resources
Commission
512 N. Salisbury Street
Raleigh, NC 27602–1188
(919) 733-3391

‡ North Carolina Zoological Park
Route 4, Box 83
Asheboro, NC 27203

‡ Western North Carolina Nature
Center
75 Gashes Creek Road
Asheville, NC 28805

‡ Carolina Raptor Center, Inc.
P.O. Box 16443
Charlotte, NC 28297

‡ Science Museums of Charlotte
1658 Sterling Road
Charlotte, NC 28209

‡ Piedmont Environmental Center
1228 Penny Road
High Point, NC 27260

‡ Nature Science Center
Museum Drive
Winston-Salem, NC 27105

NORTH DAKOTA

North Dakota Game and Fish
Department
100 North Bismarck Expressway
Bismarck, ND 58501–5095
(701) 221-6300

‡† Dakota Zoological Society, Inc.
Box 711
Bismarck, ND 58501

‡ North Dakota State University
Veterinary Science Department
Fargo, ND 58105

‡† Goose River Wildlife Park, Inc.
P.O. Box 111
Mayville, ND 58257

† Pembina Hills Wildlife
Rehabilitation Center
Route 1, Box 3
Milton, ND 58257

‡ Minot Park District
Box 538
Minot, ND 58702

‡ Chachinkapa Park Zoo
City Hall
Wahpeton, ND 58075

OHIO

Ohio Department of Natural
Resources
Wildlife Management Division
1840 Belcher Drive
Columbus, OH 43224–1329
(614) 265-6338

† Tri-State Wildlife Center
36 W. Charlotte Avenue
Cincinnati, OH 45215
(listed as holding a Kentucky State
permit)

OKLAHOMA

Oklahoma Department of Wildlife
Conservation
1801 N. Lincoln Boulevard
Oklahoma City, OK 73105–4998
(405) 521-3851

‡ Lake Murray State Park
Tucker Tower Nature Center
3310 South Lake Murray Drive,
No. 1
Ardmore, OK 73401

‡ Beavers Bend State Park Nature
Center
P.O. Box 10
Broken Bow, OK 74728

‡ Volunteer Animal Protection
Society
Route 1, Box 59 BBB
Cement, OK 73017

‡ Three Forks Nature Center
Sequoyah State Park
Route 1, Box 214
Hulbert, OK 74441

‡† Oklahoma City Zoo
2101 NE 50th Street
Oklahoma City, OK 73111

‡ Borin Vet/Med Teaching Hospital
Oklahoma State University
Stillwater, OK 74078

‡ Tulsa Zoological Park
5701 East 36th Street North
Tulsa, OK 74115

OREGON

Oregon Department of Fish and
Wildlife
Wildlife Division
2501 SW First Avenue
P.O. Box 59
Portland, OR 97207
(503) 229-5400

‡ Pacific Institute of Natural Sciences
512 South Mountain Avenue
Ashland, OR 97520

† Free Flight
1185 Portland Avenue
Bandon, OR 97411

† Winterwood Wildlife Refuge and
Rehab
66895 Gist Road
Bend, OR 97701

‡ Mighty River Rehabilitation
420 NW 18th
Corvallis, OR 97330

† Chintimini Wildlife Rehab Center
P.O. Box 1433
Corvallis, OR 97339

† Light Valley Tree Farm
10440 S. Fork Little Butte
Eagle Point, OR 97524

† Cascade Wildlife Rescue
980 E. 32nd Avenue
Eugene, OR 97405

† Cascades Raptor Care Center
P.O. Box 5386
Eugene, OR 97405

‡† Willamette Wildlife Rehabilitation
Center
P.O. Box 10962
Eugene, OR 97440

‡† Wildlife Images
11850 Lower River Road
Grants Pass, OR 97526

‡ Klamath Basin Raptor
5540 Valleywood Drive
Klamath Falls, OR 97603

† Fur and Feathers Wildlife Rehab
5720 S. River Loop
Lincoln City, OR 97367

† The Turtle Project
10907 NW Copeland Street
Portland, OR 97229

‡ Northwest Animal Rescue
1224 SE Walnut, Suite 194
Roseburg, OR 97470

† Umpqua Wildlife Rescue
P.O. Box 515
Roseburg, OR 97470

† Oregon Raptor Center
295 Myers Street S.
Salem, OR 97302

† Salem Wild Bird Refuge
4512 Delaney Road SE
Salem, OR 97301

† Columbia Pacific Wildlife Rescue
2416 Oregon Street
Seaside, OR 97138

† Sunriver Nature Center
P.O. Box 4248
Sun River, OR 97702

†† Northwest Wildlife Rehab Center
6265 Brickyard Road
Tillamook, OR 97141

‡ Wildlife Safari
P.O. Box 1600
Winston, OR 97496

PENNSYLVANIA

Commonwealth of Pennsylvania
Pennsylvania Game Commission
2001 Elmerton Avenue
Harrisburg, PA 17110–9797
(717) 787-6286

‡ Hawk Mountain Sanctuary
RD 2
Kempton, PA 19529

† Delaware Valley Raptor Center
Box 9335, RR 2
Milford, PA 18337

‡ Academy of Natural Sciences
19th and The Parkway
Philadelphia, PA 19103

‡ Philadelphia Zoological Garden
34th Street and Girard Avenue
Philadelphia, PA 19104

†† School of Veterinary Medicine
3800 Spruce Street
Philadelphia, PA 19104

† Schuykill Wildlife Center
300 Port Royal Avenue
Philadelphia, PA 19128

‡ University of Pennsylvania
3800 Spruce Street
Philadelphia, PA 19104

‡ Pittsburgh Aviary
Allegheny Commons West
Pittsburgh, PA 15212

‡ Scranton Zoo and Botanical Garden
Nay Aug Park
Scranton, PA 18510

† Shavers Creek Environmental
Center
203 Henderson Building S
University Park, PA 16802

RHODE ISLAND

State of Rhode Island and
Providence Plantations
Department of Environmental
Management
Division of Fish and Wildlife
Box 218
West Kingston, RI 02892
(401) 277-1267

‡ Norman Bird Sanctuary
583 Third Beach Road
Middletown, RI 02840

SOUTH CAROLINA

South Carolina Wildlife and Marine
Resources Department
P.O. Box 167
1000 Assembly Street
Columbia, SC 29202
(803) 734-3888

‡ Riverbanks Zoological Park
500 Wildlife Parkway
Columbia, SC 29210

‡ Greenville Zoo
Cleveland Park
Greenville, SC 29501

SOUTH DAKOTA

South Dakota Department of Game,
Fish and Parks
Foss Building
523 East Capitol
Pierre, SD 57501–3182
(605) 773-3485

†† Black Hills Raptor Rehabilitation
Center
P.O. Box 620
Rapid City, SD 57709

‡† Great Plains Zoo
805 S. Kiwanis Avenue
Sioux Falls, SD 57104

‡ Bramble Park Zoo
P.O. Box 910
· Watertown, SD 57201

TENNESSEE

Tennessee Wildlife Resources
Agency
Ellington Agricultural Center
P.O. Box 40747
Nashville, TN 37204–9979
(615) 781-6622

† Henry Horton State Park
Highway 31–A
Chapel Hill, TN 37074

‡† Chattanooga Nature Center
400 Garden Road
Chattanooga, TN 37409

† Tennessee Aquarium
537 Market Street, Suite 17
Chattanooga, TN 37377

† University of Tennessee at
Chattanooga
Department of Biology
615 McCallie
Chattanooga, TN 37403

‡† Clinch River Raptor Center
311 W. Broad Street
Clinton, TN 37716

† Wildlife Rehabilitation Services
Route 1, Box 301 P
Collierville, TN 38017

† Johnsonville State Park
Denver, TN 37054

† Nathan Bedford State Park
Star Route
Eva, TN 38333

† Harmony Wildlife Rehabilitation
Center
7370 Forrest Glenn Road
Fairview, TN 37062

† Aware
7616 Hall Road
Knoxville, TN 37920

‡† Knoxville Zoological Gardens
P.O. Box 6040
Knoxville, TN 37914

† University of Tennessee
College of Veterinary Medicine
P.O. Box 1071
Knoxville, TN 37091

† Exotic Friends
1004 Peter Pan Street
Madison, TN 37115

† Lichterman Nature Center
5992 Quince Road
Memphis, TN 38119

‡† Memphis Zoo and Aquarium
2000 Galloway
Memphis, TN 38112

† Wildlife Rescue and Rehabilitation
324 Belinda Parkway
Mt. Juliet, TN 37122

‡† Cumberland Museum and Science
Center
800 Ridley Boulevard
Nashville, TN 37203

‡ National Foundation to Protect
American Eagles
P.O. Box 120206
Nashville, TN 37212

† Radnor Lake State Park
1160 Otter Creek Road
Nashville, TN 37220

† Walden's Puddle
2926 Dogwood Place
Nashville, TN 37204

† National Foundation to Protect
American Eagles
700 Dollywood Lane
Pigeon Forge, TN 37863

† Grassy Creek Wildlife Foundation
Route 6, Box 616
Rogersville, TN 37857

† Wesley Woods Environmental
  Education Camp
  329 Wesley Woods Road
  Townsend, TN 37882

TEXAS

Texas Parks and Wildlife
Department
4200 Smith School Road
Austin, TX 78744
(512) 389-4725

‡ Abilene Zoological Gardens
  P.O. Box 60
  Abilene, TX 79604

‡ Austin Nature Center
  301 Nature Center Drive
  Austin, TX 78746

‡ Wildlife Rescue, Inc.
  810 Hillwood Drive
  Austin, TX 78745

† University of Texas System
  Science Park, Veterinary Resources
  Route 2, Box 151-B1
  Bastrop, TX 78602

‡ Gladys Porter Zoo
  500 Ringgold Street
  Brownsville, TX 78520

† Dallas Birds of Prey Center
  7171 Mountain Creek Parkway
  Dallas, TX 75249

‡ Dallas Zoo
  621 Clarendon Drive
  Dallas, TX 75203

‡ Dottie Smith–Dallas Birds of Prey
  Center
  7109 Winterberry
  Dallas, TX 75249

‡ Driftwood Wildlife Association
  P.O. Box 39
  Driftwood, TX 78619

‡ El Paso Zoo
  4001 East Paisano
  El Paso, TX 79905

‡ Fort Worth Museum–Science and
  History
  1501 Montgomery Street
  Fort Worth, TX 76107

‡ Wild Bird Center
  2926 Lazy Lake
  Harlingen, TX 78550

‡ Armand Bayou Nature Center
  P.O. Box 58828
  Houston, TX 77058

‡ Houston Zoological Gardens
  1513 N. MacGregor
  Houston, TX 77030

‡ Jesse H. Jones Park and Nature
  Center
  20634 Kenswick Drive
  Humble, TX 77338

‡ South Plains Wildlife Rehab Center
  3308 95th Street
  Lubbock, TX 79423

‡† Heard Natural Science Museum and
   Wildlife Sanctuary
   Route 6, Box 22
   McKinney, TX 75069

‡ Primarily Primates, Inc.
  P.O. Box 15306
  San Antonio, TX 78212

‡ San Antonio Zoological Gardens
  and Aquarium
  3903 N. St. Mary's Street
  San Antonio, TX 78212

‡ This Is For The Birds
  5701 Errol Flynn
  San Antonio, TX 78240

‡ Sea World of Texas
  10500 Sea World Drive
  San Antonio, TX 78251

‡ Wildlife Rescue and Rehabilitation,
  Inc.
  P.O. Box 34 FF
  San Antonio, TX 78201

‡ Caldwell Zoo
P.O. Box 4280
Tyler, TX 75712

‡ The Texas Zoo
Riverside Park, P.O. Box 69
Victoria, TX 77902

UTAH

State of Utah Department of
Natural Resources
Division of Wildlife Resources
1596 West North Temple
Salt Lake City, UT 84116–3195
(801) 538-4700

‡ Lagoon Corporation
P.O. Box N
Farmington, UT 84025

‡ Willow Park Zoo
255 North Main Street
Logan, UT 84321

‡ Ogden Nature Center
966 W. 12th Street
Ogden, UT 84404

‡ Hogle Zoological Garden
2600 Sunnyside Avenue
Salt Lake City, UT 84108

‡ Tracy Aviary
589 East 1300 South
Salt Lake City, UT 84105

VERMONT

Vermont Natural Resources
Department of Fish and Wildlife
103 South Main Street, 10 South
Waterbury, VT 05671-0501
(802) 241-3700

‡ The Discovery Museum (mammals
only)
51 Park Street
Essex Junction, VT 05452

‡ Fairbanks Museum and
Planetarium
Main and Prospect Streets
St. Johnsbury, VT 05819

‡ Vermont Institute of Natural
Sciences (birds only)
P.O. Box 86
Woodstock, VT 05091

VIRGINIA

Commonwealth of Virginia
Department of Game and Inland
Fisheries
P.O. Box 11104
4010 W. Broad Street
Richmond, VA 23230–1104
(804) 367-1000

† Long Branch Nature Center
625 S. Carlin Springs Road
Arlington, VA 22204

‡† Veterinary Teaching Hospital
Virginia Polytechnic Institute and
State University
Duckpond Drive
Blacksburg, VA 24060

† Wildcare
Box 1231
Matthews, VA 23109

‡ Newport News Park Interpretive
Center
13560 Jefferson Avenue
Newport News, VA 23603

‡† Virginia Living Museum
524 J. Clyde Morris Boulevard
Newport News, VA 23601

‡† Virginia Zoological Park
3500 Granby Street
Norfolk, VA 23504

† Presquile National Wildlife Refuge
U.S. Department of Interior
P.O. Box 189
Prince George, VA 23875

‡† New River Wildlife Center
1242 Poff School Road
Riner, VA 24149

† Roanoke Wildlife Rescue
8550 Martins Creek Road
Roanoke, VA 24018

† Virginia Marine Science Museum
717 General Booth Boulevard
Virginia Beach, VA 23451

‡† The Wildlife Center of Virginia
P.O. Box 98
Weyers Cave, VA 24486

WASHINGTON

State of Washington Department
of Wildlife
600 Capitol Way N
Olympia, WA 98501-1091
(206) 753-5700

‡† Wildlife Care Center
13106 148th Street, NE
Arlington, WA 98223

† Raptor Roost
297 Chuckanut Point
Bellingham, WA 98226

† Northwest Raptor Center
P.O. Box 11
Clallam Bay, WA 98326

† Sardis Wildlife Center
P.O. Box 484
Custer, WA 98240

† Myers Wild Bird Clinic
30236 Second Avenue S
Federal Way, WA 98003

† Wolf Hollow Wildlife Rehabilitation
Center
P.O. Box 391
240 Boyce Road
Friday Harbor, WA 98250

† Falconhurst Raptor Rehabilitation
Center
Route 3, Box 3488
Kennewick, WA 98337

† Raptor Rescue Center
513 Cascade Street
Leavenworth, WA 98826

† HOWL Wildlife Center
15305 44th Avenue W
Lynnwood, WA 98046

‡ Progessive Animal Welfare Society
P.O. Box 1037
Lynnwood, WA 98036

‡† Olympic Wildlife Rescue Center
54 Mox Chehalis Road
McCleary, WA 98557

‡† Wild Animal Clinic, Inc.
P.O. Box 647
Monroe, WA 98272

† Washington State University
School of Veterinary Medicine
Pullman, WA 99163

† Wildhaven Wildlife Center
P.O. Box 651
Silverdale, WA 98383

† Pilchuck Valley Wildlife Rehab
Center
12529 68th Street SE
Snohomish, WA 98290

‡ Inland NW Zoological Society
P.O. Box 14258
Spokane, WA 99214

WEST VIRGINIA

West Virgina Division of Natural
Resources
Wildlife Resources Section
P.O. Box 67
Ward Road, RTS 219/250 S
Elkins, WV 26241
(304) 637-0245

‡ West Virgina Raptor Rehabilitation
Center
P.O. Box 333
Morgantown, WV 26507

‡ Oglebay Good Children's Zoo
Oglebay Park Zoo
Wheeling, WV 26003

WISCONSIN

Wisconsin Department of Natural
Resources
Office of Endangered and Nongame
Species
Box 7921
Madison, WI 53707–7921
(608) 267-7507

† Bay Beach Wildlife Sanctuary
1660 East Shore Drive
Green Bay, WI 54302

† Great River Wildlife Center
Route 1, Box 244A
LaCrosse, WI 54601

† Wildlife Arc
5800 North Lovers Lane
Milwaukee, WI 53225

† Northwoods Wildlife Center
8683 Blumstein Road
Minocqua, WI 54548

† Aeries Treatment Center
Route 1, Box 80
Shiocton, WI 54170

† Fox Ridge Wildlife Rehabilitation
Center
Route 4, Box 358
Wautoma, WI 54982

WYOMING

Wyoming Game and Fish
Department
5400 Bishop Boulevard
Cheyenne, WY 82006
(307) 777-4534

† Ironside Bird Rescue
49 Road 2DAW
Cody, WY 82414

‡† Seedskadee National Wildlife
Refuge
P.O. Box 700
Green River, WY 82935

National Wildlife, Rehabilitation, and Environmental Organizations

Defenders of Wildlife
1228 N Street, Suite 6
Sacramento, CA 95814

Environmental Defense Fund
27 Park Avenue South
New York, NY 10010

Humane Society of the United
    States
2100 L Street, NW
Washington, DC 20037

International Wildlife
    Rehabilitation Council (IWRC)
4437 Central Place, Suite B-4
Suisun, CA 94585

National Audubon Society
P.O. Box 96005
Washington, DC 20090–6005

National Parks and Conservation
    Association
1776 Massachusetts Avenue, NW
Washington, DC 20036–1903

Natural Resources Defense Council
40 West 20th Street
New York, NY 10011

National Wildlife Federation
1400 Sixteenth Street, NW
Washington, DC 20036–2266

National Wildlife Rehabilitators
    Association
14 North 7th Avenue
St. Cloud, MN 56303

The Nature Conservancy
1815 North Lynn Street
Arlington, VA 22209

Sierra Club
P.O. Box 429005
San Francisco, CA 94142–9848

World Wildlife Fund
1250 Twenty-fourth Street, NW
Washington, DC 20037

Resources and References

This section lists books and other publications that offer useful information about coexisting with wildlife, as well as the sources used in the preparation of this book.

Habitat and Landscaping

The Backyard Naturalist, by Craig Tufts. National Wildlife Federation Backyard Wildlife Habitat Program, Washington, D.C. (Also available from this source is The Gardening with Wildlife Kit; call 1-800-432-6564.)

The Field Guide to Wildlife Habitats of the Western United States, by Janine M. Benyus. Simon & Schuster, Inc., 1989.

Garden Insect, Disease and Weed Identification Guide, by Miranda Smith and Anna Carr. Rodale Press, 1988.

Landscaping with Nature: Using Nature's Designs to Plan Your Yard, by Jeff Cox. Rodale Press, 1991.

Natural Insect and Disease Control, edited by Roger B. Yepsen, Jr. Rodale Press, 1984.

Natural Solutions for Organic Growing: Beneficial Insects and Bioselector Pest Control. Catalog of the Necessary Trading Company, New Castle, VA (703) 864-5103.

Your Backyard Wildlife Garden: How to Attract and Identify Wildlife in Your Yard, by Marcus Schneck. Rodale Press, 1992.

The following pamphlets are available from government agencies. (If contact address is not provided, see Appendix A.)

Alaska Department of Fish and Game
  Birdhouses for Alaska
  Winter Bird-Feeding in Alaska

Arkansas Game and Fish Commission, Backyard Wildlife Program, Little Rock, AR 72205, (501) 223-6353
  Backyard Wildlife Habitat
  A Home for Wildife in Your Backyard
  What Do Deer Eat?

Connecticut Department of Environmental Protection, Wildlife Bureau,
165 Capitol Ave., State Office Building, Room 254, Hartford, CT 06106,
(203) 295-9523
  Brush Piles for Wildlife
  Daylighting Roads and Trails to Create Edge Openings for Wildlife
  *Guidelines for Enhancing Connecticut's Wildlife Habitat Through Forestry
    Operations* (Wildlife Bureau Pub. No. TA-H-9)
  Mast for Wildlife
  Nesting Structures for Wildlife
  Nonpreference List of Deer Foods
  Preference List of Deer Foods
  Rejuvenating Old Apple Trees
  Snags for Wildlife
  Suggestions for Building Bat Houses and Attracting Bats

Kansas Department of Wildlife and Parks
  Wildlife in Your Backyard: A Guide to Urban Habitat Development
  Producing Fish and Wildlife from Kansas Ponds
  Wildlife Management on Croplands

Kentucky Department of Fish and Wildlife Resources
  Whitetail Deer in Kentucky

Tennessee Wildlife Resources Agency
  Bird Seed Ratings for Attracting the Greatest Varieties of Birds to Your Feeder
  Butterfly Nectar Plants
  Feeding Wild Birds
  Giving Wildlife an Edge: A Guide to Ornamental Plants for Wildlife Habitat
  Habitat Guidelines for the Bald Eagle
  The Wildlife Plant Source

U.S. Fish and Wildlife Service
  Backyard Bird Feeding
  Wildlife Diversity Through Habitat Diversity

Virginia Department of Game and Inland Fisheries
  A Planting Guide for Virginia Nectar-Seekers
  Virgina Wildlife Habitat Program
  Wildlife Plantings, Boxes and Platforms

Birds

The Audubon Society Field Guide to North American Birds, Western Region, by Miklos D. F. Udvardy. Alfred A. Knopf, Inc., 1980.

The Audubon Society Field Guide to North American Birds, Eastern Region, by John Bull and John Ferrand, Jr. Alfred A. Knopf, Inc., 1977.

Peterson Field Guide to Western Birds, Third Edition, by Roger Tory Peterson. Houghton Mifflin Co., 1990.

Peterson Field Guide to Eastern Birds, Third Edition, by Roger Tory Peterson. Houghton Mifflin Co., 1980.

The Birder's Handbook: A Field Guide to the Natural History of North American Birds, by Paul R. Ehrlich, David S. Dobkin, and Darryl Wheye. Simon & Schuster, Inc., 1988.

Bird Watching Basics, Florida Game and Fresh Water Fish Commission.

Rescue and Rehabilitation of Oiled Birds (Fish and Wildlife Leaflet 13.2.8), U.S. Fish and Wildlife Service.

Tricks to Control Birds (including falcon cut-out to prevent birds from striking windows), U.S. Fish and Wildlife Service.

Periodicals

American Birds, National Audubon Society, NY
Birding, American Birding Association, Austin, TX
Ecology, Ecological Society of America, Duke University Press, Durham, NC
The Elapaio, Hawaii Audubon Society, Honolulu, HI
The Florida Naturalist, Florida Audubon Society, Maitland, FL
Iowa Bird Life, Iowa Ornithologists' Union, Davenport, IA
The Jack Pine Warbler, Michigan Audubon Society, Kalamazoo, MI
The Journal of Wildlife Management, Wildlife Society, Washington, DC
Kentucky Warbler, Kentucky Ornitholigical Society, Louisville, KY
Maine Quarterly Audubon, Maine Audubon Society, Falmouth, ME
Maryland Birdlife, Maryland Ornithological Society, Baltimore, MD
Massachusetts Audubon, Massachusetts Audubon Society, Lincoln, MA
The Migrant, Tennessee Ornithological Society, Cookeville, TN
Natural History, American Museum of Natural History, New York, NY
Nebraska Bird Review, Nebraska Ornithologists' Union, Lincoln, NE
New Jersey Audubon, New Jersey Audubon Society, Franklin Lakes, NJ
The Oriole, Georgia Ornithological Society, Atlanta, GA
Pacific Discovery, California Academy of Sciences, San Francisco, CA
The Passenger Pigeon, Wisconsin Society for Ornithology, Hartland, WI

The Raven, Virgina Society of Ornithology, Williamsburg, VA
South Dakota Bird Notes, South Dakota Ornithologists' Union, Brookings, SD
Western Birds, Western Field Ornitholgists, Tiburon, CA
Wildlife Review, U.S. Fish and Wildlife Service, Colorado State University, Fort
Collins, CO

Mammals

The Audubon Society Field Guide to North American Mammals, by John O. Whitaker,
Jr. Alfred A. Knopf, Inc., 1980.
Encyclopedia of Mammals, by Dr. David MacDonald. Facts on File, Inc., 1987.

Reptiles and Amphibians

The Audubon Society Field Guide to North American Reptiles and Amphibians, by John
L. Behler and F. Wayne King. Alfred A. Knopf, Inc., 1979.
Peterson Field Guide to Reptiles and Amphibians, Second Edition, by Robert C.
Stebbins. Houghton Mifflin Co., 1985.
*A Field Guide to the Reptiles and Amphibians of Eastern and Central North America,
Third Edition*, by Roger Conant and Joseph T. Collins. Houghton Mifflin Co.,
1991.

Wildlife Observation

Watchable Wildlife: A New Initiative, by Sara Vickerman. Defenders of Wildlife,
1989.
A Guide to Animal Tracks. Connecticut Department of Environmental Protection.
The following states have Watchable Wildlife programs, which provide written
information on good locations for wildlife observation. Contact state agencies
listed in Appendix A for further information on programs in: Alaska,
Colorado, Idaho, Montana, Oklahoma, Oregon, Tennessee, and Wyoming.

Bibliography

Benson, Delwin E., et al. *In Celebration of America's Wildlife: Teacher's Guide to Learning.* U.S. Fish and Wildlife Service in cooperation with Colorado State University.

Buettner, Gudrun, ed. *The Audubon Society Encyclopedia of Animal Life.* New York: Clarkson N. Potter, Inc., 1982.

Cerulean, Susan, and Patricia Millsap. *What Have You Done for Wildlife Lately? A Citizen's Guide to Helping Florida's Wildlife.* Florida Game and Fresh Water Fish Commission, Nongame Wildlife Program, 1991.

Goetz, Philip W., ed., and faculties of the University of Chicago. *Encyclopedia Britannica.* Chicago: University of Chicago Press, 1991.

Grzimek, Dr. Bernhard, ed. *Grizmek's Animal Life Encyclopedia.* New York: Van Nostrand Reinhold Co., 1972.

Heintzelman, Donald. *Wildlife Protectors Handbook: How You Can Help Stop the Destruction of Wild Animals.* Santa Barbara, California: Capra Press, 1992.

Hodge, Guy, ed. *The Humane Control of Wildlife in Cities and Towns.* Helena, Montana: The Humane Society of the United States and Falcon Press, 1991.

MacDonald, Dr. David, ed. *Encyclopedia of Mammals.* New York: Facts on File, Inc., 1987.

Mertens, John M. *Living Snakes of the World.* New York: Sterling Publishing Co., Inc., 1987.

Pearl, Mary Corliss. *The Illustrated Encyclopedia of Wildlife.* Lakeville, Connecticut: Grey Castle Press, 1991.

Salmon, Terrell P., and Robert E. Lickliter. *Wildlife Pest Control Around Gardens and Homes* (Publication 21385). Davis, California: Cooperative Extension, University of California, Division of Agriculture and Natural Resources, Dept. of Agricultural Information and Publications, 1984.

Terres, John K. *The Audubon Society Encyclopedia of North American Birds.* New York: Alfred A. Knopf, 1980.

Index